DISCIPLINE AND DEMOCRACY

Teachers on Trial

ALLEN KOSHEWA

Foreword by Jerome C. Harste

7/05

p 110 MLK
p. 111
p. 117 lang. of civility
p 147 freedom of speech
p 149
p. 210-211 T'er R'er
p. 216 detention
p 218-219 caring
p 220-221 discipline

Heinemann
Portsmouth, NH

Heinemann
A division of Reed Elsevier Inc.
361 Hanover Street
Portsmouth, NH 03801–3912
www.heinemann.com

Offices and agents throughout the world

Library of Congress Cataloging-in-Publication Data
Koshewa, Allen.
Discipline and democracy : teachers on trial / Allen Koshewa : foreword by Jerome C. Harste.
p. cm.
Includes bibliographical references and index.
ISBN 0-325-00181-2 (acid-free paper)
1. School discipline. 2. Classroom management. I. Title.
LB3011.K66 1999
371.102′4—dc21 99-27806
CIP

Editor: Lois Bridges
Production: Vicki Kasabian
Cover design: Jenny Jensen Greenleaf
Cover illustration: Macie Leanne Nunn, age 11
Author photo: Ahmed Alberto Kelso
Manufacturing: Louise Richardson

Printed in the United States of America on acid-free paper
03 02 01 00 99 DA 1 2 3 4 5

To Roberta and her students

Contents

Foreword

JEROME C. HARSTE

Discipline and Democracy: Teachers on Trial poses curriculum as a democratic social practice. In the day-to-day management of classrooms, children should have a voice, participate in decision making, and experience democratic living firsthand.

One's initial response is "Hold it. If adults can't agree on what kids should be learning, how can kids?" Living democratically in classrooms invites a slew of problems because, after all, democracy is not without problems. In practice, it has never been particularly good at handling dissension, or even tension. Too often democracy becomes a banner that hides individualistic and corporate greed rather than a force for promoting communal good.

In education, democracy often gets translated into public policy as consensus and conformity. That is what standardized tests, cultural literacy (à la Hirsch), and standards are all about. The end result is a one-size-fits-all curriculum.

Despite such problems with "democracy," there are exceptions. Many educators, like those in this book, are exploring what learning based on difference might look like. They believe that such a model better fits a multilingual and multicultural society claiming to be democratic than a model based on uniform goals.

Discipline is one of the most abused and most misunderstood concepts in education. Like democracy, discipline can't be taken for granted, handed out as fiat, or established through the adoption of some behavioral management scheme. It ought to be an ongoing discussion as well as a lived-through, yearlong experience in every classroom.

In this book, classroom community and democracy are explored as a relationship rather than as singular and discrete entities. The fundamental question underlying the book is: In a society claiming to be democratic, what kind of classroom community should be fostered?

This question needs to be explored with children. Allen Koshewa and Roberta Taylor, the teacher with whom he worked, provide an excellent demonstration of how to do this. The opportunities that arise for exploring this relationship with children may seem mundane, but they're not. Can we or can we not have drinks and snacks at our desks throughout the day? How do we stop put-downs in this class, and between this class and others in the school? Who has the right to speak when in this classroom? Regardless of the surface structure, the deep structure underlying such questions is curriculum at its most critical.

Classroom discipline is often treated as an afterthought. The core of curriculum is seen as teaching the 3Rs, the hard sciences plus a little social studies, health, and more recently computer science. Art and music are thrown in for fun—to lighten the academic load. Discipline, like starting with clean dishes when cooking, is seen as context—a bothersome little detail that should have been attended to. Good teachers have discipline, bad ones don't.

How many generations of new teachers have been given this advice from seasoned colleagues? "Start out tough. You can always lighten up after Christmas." One of my undergraduates recently told me that her supervising teacher's advice was "Don't smile until after Christmas!" In lieu of the perpetuation of such simplistic teaching tips, there is a lot of sage advice given in this book. Most of it is implicit, like the fact that the first issue teachers need to address is space. Have I allocated sufficient time in my classroom for discussions on community?

Discipline and Democracy blueprints how one teacher created such a space for "a class from hell." Oh, she had writers workshops, literature discussion groups, multiple-ways-of-knowing curricular invitations, inquiry projects, and math investigations, but that is only one part of the story. The main story line involves the surrounding curriculum within which all of these "best practices" were embedded.

How students behave surrounds all the practices described here. That is why *Discipline and Democracy: Teachers on Trial* is unusual; it's the only book I know that fully explores classroom management as the heart of curriculum.

The initial assumption Allen and Roberta made was that their classroom would be somehow better if it were a cohesive community; one in which everyone worked together to maintain a common set of moral and ethical values. Nice, cohesive classroom communities, after all, seem to be the basis of the current party line.

What they learned is that classroom communities are rarely cohesive and often not nice. Fifth grade group-think can be neither democratic nor pretty.

But their story is an important one. Just as we learned that children need to be reading literature that allows them to see themselves in the book, so teachers need to read professional literature that allows them to see the real classrooms they face, including the less than idyllic gangs and cliques that inhabit them.

Classroom discipline should be an educator's prime concern, if it isn't already. That said, teachers should not expend the bulk of their energy maintaining law and order. Few of us entered teaching to test our resolve against the will of the children we teach or to see how quietly we could march kids down the hall. Yet a working democracy relies upon a certain degree of order.

This book is essential reading for new teachers, but I also recommend it highly as stimulating material for teacher study groups. From reading this book, new and veteran teachers can learn how to face difficult students without abandoning their most fundamental democratic beliefs and values.

If curriculum is a metaphor for the democratic lives we want to live and the democratic people we want to be, then classroom management is a topic of long neglect and much-needed conversation. This book will help us gain as well as maintain perspective on the relationship between democracy and order.

JEROME HARSTE *is the Martha Lea and Bill Armstrong Chair in Teacher Education and Distinguished Professor in Language Education at Indiana University.*

Acknowledgments

I want to express my heartfelt thanks to many people: Laurie Hanawa for her inspiration, her insight, and her ability to coin the perfect phrase; my father, Paul Koshewa, for his self-discipline, compassion, patience (as both a teacher and parent), and his ability to "be philosophical"; Jerome Harste for his commitment to collaboration and his constant attempts to integrate theory and practice; Ahmed Alberto Kelso for his continual support and encouragement; Bobbi Jentes Mason for her ability to convey her passion for learning; Peggy Albers for her friendship, her collegiality, and her scholarship; Michael Jackson for his keen understanding of human relationships as the crux of teaching and learning; Carolyn Burke for her extraordinary ability to examine the underlying assumptions of an argument; Bob Arnove for his dependability, integrity, and dedication; Dorothy Menosky for her generosity, her humor, and her hardware; Karen Grady for her wit and wisdom; Virginia Harvin for her belief in my potential; and Lois Bridges for her perfect balance of editorial support and challenge.

I would also like to acknowledge the memory of my mother, Nancy Koshewa, who hated school and helped me understand the difference between education and schooling.

Last but far from least, I extend a very special thank-you to "Roberta Taylor" for her gifted ability to inspire people by seeing the best in them.

Introduction

Questioning Our Beliefs: Teaching and Research

Encountering the Unexpected

Most teachers eventually encounter a class that throws them off guard and defies their previous assumptions about teaching. Suddenly, everything that always "worked" in the classroom no longer works, and the teacher's beliefs about education are called into question. In elementary schools, a group like this gathers a reputation, no matter how the students are divided into separate classes, and their teachers warn those at the next grade level to prepare for the "kids from hell."

Such a group of students is the subject of this book. Originally, I did not intend to write about discipline approaches in teaching. Instead I had chosen to examine how Roberta Taylor,* a fifth-grade teacher with whom I had conducted research for three previous years, helped her students construct a positive, productive learning community. During the three years I had worked with her, Roberta had allowed her students a wide latitude of choice and successfully solved the problems that arose. As her 1996–97 school year began, I wondered how the new group of students would construct this year's community. How would the students view community building, I wondered? How would they collaborate? And how would Roberta implement her democratic practices on a day-to-day basis? I wanted to better understand the factors that can facilitate or hinder the democratic ideals of equality and justice that, due to Roberta's own aspirations toward those ideals, her classroom community emulates.

The 1996–97 class turned out to be the biggest challenge of Roberta's career. Initially, the students reacted positively to her democratic approach, and many inquiries flourished. But as the year progressed, her students became increasingly hostile and combative. Eventually, they began to subvert, and even destroy, the democratic ideals she strived to convey and enact. She faced many problems, including insolence, bullying, and rebellion. As a

*Names of people and places in the book, with the exception of my own name, have been changed.

result, my inquiry became concerned not only with how a democratic classroom community can be enacted, but how a democratic environment can be maintained in the face of discipline problems. My questions about democratic community building became subsumed by a larger question: What practices can facilitate a democratic learning community that maintains discipline by regulating its own conduct?

I confess that I began my year in Roberta's class with a somewhat naïve view of community. I assumed that, as Roberta nurtured a sense of community in her classroom, her students would become more sensitive and collaborative. There is a widespread complacency among educators that if we, as teachers, build community, the community members will respond to each other more positively and become more socially responsible. This is a dangerous view of community; a chapter of the Ku Klux Klan is a community but hardly leads to more socially responsible outcomes. When I began the school year in Roberta's class, I knew that not all communities are idyllic, and that building a democratic classroom is not a seamless process, yet I expected to see a steady growth in her students like I had in previous years. Like Roberta, I had great faith in the power of curriculum to provide democratic options and to build a responsible community. But as I observed and analyzed Roberta's 1996–97 class, I saw that strong communities did not automatically and immediately form simply as a result of good curriculum. As I gathered detailed examples of the day-to-day manifestation of democratic practices in the classroom, I began to question my assumptions about the relationship between community building and discipline.

Roberta's 1996–97 students found it difficult to share power and support each other's learning throughout the year. The school year was fraught with social conflicts. The students were able to balance individual and group goals only after a significant breakdown in classroom discipline in late April and early May. After the school year ended, I reflected upon what had happened and began to read widely about some of the issues that emerged. Finally, I began to write the story and to analyze the students' descent into anarchy.

This book focuses on interpreting how Roberta managed to preserve a democratic approach to teaching when challenged by significant discipline concerns. Although it deals specifically with a fifth-grade classroom, what I learned from Roberta's class has wide application to students in other grade levels, particularly middle school students, who frequently test the limits of authority as they grapple with issues of autonomy and identity. It is not easy to nurture the autonomy and self-esteem of resistant students, as Roberta and I learned.

Becoming a Teacher-Researcher

I did not arrive at my perspective on the book's issues overnight. Twenty-one years ago, I taught in an urban school and followed the textbook guides, resolutely believing that learning could be doled out with the help of textbooks and measured by test scores. A thirteen-year-old student challenged my shallow view in 1978, shortly after I began teaching English and science to seventh-grade students in a low-income area of Atlanta, Georgia.

Throughout the school in Atlanta, discipline was a daily buzzword for most of the teachers. The team leader of each grade had tracked the students into four separate groups, each containing about thirty students. The first group comprised high achievers; the second, motivated but somewhat unruly students; the third, relatively unsuccessful students; and the fourth, students with severe learning and/or behavior problems. Many teachers had trouble with the second and third groups, and most of us dreaded the fourth. Some of the older teachers had developed a militaristic style that frightened the students into submission. The frequent use of paddling as a punishment was a mainstay of these authoritarian teachers, and the overbearing Joan, with her steely blue eyes and jutting chin, was the worst tyrant of all. Never hesitant to wield the paddle, Joan was upheld by both teachers and administrators as a model disciplinarian.

I, on the other hand, was considered a weak disciplinarian, as my students' talking and movement around the classroom sometimes disrupted effective learning. Although I fared slightly better than the teacher I had replaced—a teacher who had cowered by the desk while the students fought and destroyed each other's property—only students from my "best" class regularly turned in their work and studied for tests. Although I planned occasional experiments and field trips to make the science curriculum meaningful, my classes consisted mostly of the familiar textbook work: Students read the chapters, answered the comprehension questions, and studied for tests. Students expected this routine, it caused less disorder and confusion than more open-ended activities, and I could easily mark the papers and "evaluate" the students.

A student from the best class stopped me dead in my tracks one morning. Judy, a good-humored and somewhat rebellious student, slyly began asking me some questions about conifers from the worksheet they were expected to complete. I was shocked to realize I could not answer my own questions, and tried to cover up my hypocrisy by mumbling something along the lines of "Oh, now how could I have forgotten that?"

"You don't even know the answers!" cried Judy derisively.

At that point, I began to realize that I needed to critically question and examine my own teaching practice. Throughout twenty subsequent years of teaching, I have experienced much success as I attempt to base classroom activities upon student interests and questions. Yet I have continued to make terrible mistakes as well, from stubbornly refusing to modify a spelling program for a child with a learning disability in 1982 to inflicting group punishment in 1996. During these years, I have reflected on these successes and failures. Because of this ongoing reflection, I continue to articulate my beliefs, while at the same time changing my teaching approaches to better align them with those beliefs. I have attempted to listen to students, to document their conversations, actions, and written communication, to share ideas with colleagues, and to pursue professional development in order to effect positive change. I eventually realized that a teacher-researcher does all these things, and that these endeavors constitute action research. As a teacher-researcher, I believe that teaching is learning, and that what I am learning—about the students, about the subject matter, about the process of learning—is central to the teaching enterprise.

When I first met Roberta, I immediately sensed in her a kindred spirit. Roberta rejects formulaic approaches to teaching. She conveys a passion for life and learning that inevitably results in surprising and memorable classroom experiences. She always feels that there is more to learn, and her systematic attempts to document and analyze what happens in her classroom facilitate that learning. The fact that the students in this book failed to internalize Roberta's philosophy in ways that her previous students had done led us to new understandings of discipline and democracy. The problems we faced also helped us become better teacher-researchers.

Roberta's Classroom

Roberta has been teaching fifth grade at Robinson Elementary School, a public school in Riverdale, Indiana, since 1989. Riverdale is a town of approximately sixty-five thousand people, located within an hour's drive from a large city. It contains several large industries and is dominated by a large university. The average income of families not associated with the university is below the national average. Minorities constitute approximately 10 percent of the population.

During the 1996–97 school year, when the major events of this book took place, Robinson Elementary served 491 students, grades 3–6. Of those students, roughly 10 percent were deemed low income and qualified for free lunches. At each grade level, there were four homeroom classes. The school had a special-education program that served children with physical and developmental disabilities, some of whom were included in regular classes. Roberta had twenty-six students in her class, twelve boys and fourteen girls. Her class was self-contained, so students remained with her all day, except for a daily fifty-minute period for "specials" (PE, art, music, or library).

When I first walked into Roberta's class in January 1994, I immediately felt welcome. The classroom was implementing an inquiry-based curriculum, in which classroom learning is centered around student questions and interests. A small group of students was observing the classroom pet, and several individuals were adding descriptions of historical events to a time line that encircled the room. Four students were talking about books in a bean bag area, and others were working on a science project. Some of these students had physical and developmental disabilities, and several were relying on partners for help. All seemed very excited about what they were doing. Obviously accustomed to guests in the room, the students engaged me in animated conversation concerning their various learning endeavors, and new alliances were formed as we began to explore ideas together. The classroom was a warm, vibrant oasis that brimmed with energy and enthusiasm.

That day marked the beginning of my collaboration with Roberta. I became a regular participant-observer—and frequently a team-teacher—in Roberta's class, and conducted several research projects in her classroom during the next two-and-a-half years. In 1996, I asked Roberta if I could spend a year in her classroom to study community building. She eagerly agreed. Adding to the spirit of collaboration was the enthusiasm of Karen, who would be Roberta's student teacher in the fall, and Ivy, who was scheduled to student teach in January. The four of us planned to spend the entire first week of class teaching as a team, frequently allowing students to choose among small-group activities. Throughout the year, Karen, Ivy, and I continued to help Roberta plan the curriculum from an inquiry perspective, in which the curriculum is developed in an ongoing manner in accordance with student questions, concerns, and decisions.

Research as Reflection

A key component of being a researcher is documenting events as thoroughly as possible and then spending sufficient time reflecting on the implications of those events. The trouble is, I thoroughly documented Roberta's 1996–97 school year, pondered the implications for two years, and *still* can't figure it all out. But I don't worry about that—at least not all the time. That's because I know that examining the issues that emerge in a classroom and thinking through which strategies addressed them (or didn't address them) are more valuable than pinpointing causes and effects and coming up with formulas for "the next time." There never is a next time, because every crop of students differs, and the judgment call of every teacher relies upon the complex input of the moment.

Social science research operates in much the same way as reflective teaching. Despite widespread beliefs to the contrary, we cannot disentangle the complex web of daily events into separate factors, feed them into a computer, and then statistically predict what students will do. No matter how often we are able to predict a person's behavior, agency ensures that the unexpected can always happen, and what works in one classroom may not work in another. Ethnography, the written observation and interpretation of humans in their everyday environments, illuminates human behavior; it doesn't offer formulas for modifying it. Ethnography "reveals the general through the particular, the abstract through the concrete" (Peacock 1986, 83). By relying upon the lived experience so central to ethnography, this book tells the story of Roberta's school year as it unfolded. Indeed, conversations in the book are verbatim, and I have attempted to corroborate my interpretations of events with Roberta and her students.

Now that I have criticized research as a tool for prediction, I shall nevertheless, within the course of this book, try to draw conclusions about what may facilitate democratic classrooms that maintain a healthy modicum of discipline. An important role of the teacher-researcher is to understand and explain teaching and learning. Though my conclusions about democratic teaching are far from final, they may help us understand what teachers need to do in order to promote democratic learning within some framework of group regulation. I do not intend to take a soothsayer role and claim that a certain set of strategies will "work." As Ronald Butchart (1998) writes, "The question is never 'What works?'—all manner of barbarity works, if the end is orderliness alone" (3). Discipline is positive only if the strategies that facilitate discipline also facilitate wholesome interpersonal relations and fair, equitable practices within a constructive learning context. Discipline strategies, then, should emphasize problem solving and help realize human potential.

When making decisions about discipline and democracy, teachers must prioritize issues in the heat of the moment. When I make poor decisions as a teacher, it is usually because I haven't identified the most salient issues at hand, not because I don't have appropriate strategies at my disposal. Only by focusing on issues of discipline and democracy can teachers make good decisions that balance individual and group rights, teacher rights and student rights. Strategies help, of course, but just because you have a strategy doesn't mean that you can immediately pinpoint the source of a crisis and thus choose the best strategy. This is why I highlight both strategies and open-ended issue questions throughout the book.

Having an abundance of taped conversations and field notes helped me identify the issues and strategies that seem most important in light of the turmoil of Roberta's 1996–97 school year. Running the tape recorder during the normal course of a school day allowed me to participate in classroom events and collect data at the same time. Transcribing the classroom conversations and my interviews with students allowed me to "put participant language under a microscope" (McCarthy 1998, 130). Comparing my notes with Roberta's notes provided additional data and allowed shared interpretations to inform our teaching practices. Unlike Roberta, I had the luxury of being able to simply observe and take notes whenever I wanted to, but I constantly marvelled at the way that Roberta actively documented student comments and actions on Post-It notes as she taught. Since then, I have aspired to do the same thing in my own fifth-grade classroom, but am far less adept at this than Roberta.

Although the breakdown in discipline and democracy that occurred in Roberta's class was alarming, the blame cannot easily be placed on any particular occurrence or person. Even Roberta, who ultimately was in charge of the classroom, might have failed just as often had she made different decisions about how to run her classroom. The difficulty in isolating causal factors is why, in educational research, distinguishing what happens "because of" rather than "in spite of" a given factor is a complex, ongoing concern that must continually be a subject of inquiry.

But uncertainty does not relegate teachers to inaction. After all, ideas need not be fixed or determinate in order to be relevant and practical. I am still speculating on specific factors which gave rise to events in Roberta's classroom, but I do so with the confidence of having effectively applied some of my conclusions in my own teaching and with the reassurance that teachers will explore these ideas in the contexts of their own classrooms and share the results with others.

Clifford Geertz (1988) claims that ethnographies "enabl[e] conversation across societal lines—of ethnicity, religion, class, gender, language, [and] race" (147). I have written this ethnographic tale of a fifth-grade classroom with this end in mind. Issues concerning topics as diverse as violence, academic assessment, and the performing arts permeate the narrative that constitutes the bulk of Chapters 1 through 6. At the end of each of these chapters, a section called "Stepping Back" analyzes the events in the story in terms of current theory and research. A subsequent section titled "Listening to Students" uses the students' own words to highlight their perspectives of the book's events. "Lingering Questions," the next section in these chapters, poses questions intended to facilitate your own conversations about vital issues that emerged. A final section, "Further Reading," recommends books that elaborate upon ideas that have been examined so far. Chapter 7 looks back on the entire school year and emphasizes approaches that may best facilitate a compassionate approach to discipline and an effective approach to democratic teaching. It, too, ends with "Lingering Questions."

Intersecting conversations about issues in this book may illuminate new ways to erode traditional, authoritarian approaches to discipline. Discussions of the book's contents may also help teachers foster democratic classroom communities that compassionately protect the rights of its members. Ultimately, such conversations can improve the quality of life, both inside and outside of schools, for "reflective thought is a way of enrichment. . . . It urges that we replace our craving to know how to know with a desire to know how to live" (Jackson 1995, 163). How, then, should we try to live with each other in classrooms? This book attempts to answer that question.

1

Crafting Community

Initial Encounters

Innocent vulnerability emanated from the faces of the ten-year-old children who entered Roberta's classroom for the first time in late August. Only a few children stepped into the room with confidence; others either hesitated by the doorway, looking insecure, or stuck close to their parents until Roberta, Karen (Roberta's student teacher), or I approached to welcome them. One by one, Roberta asked the students if she could photograph them with a Polaroid camera; the photos would accompany the biography sheets (titled "Getting to Know You and Your Family") that the children would soon complete. As the arrivals became more frequent, Karen and I kept up the conversation, trying to make the students and parents feel comfortable until Roberta had a chance to talk to them personally. At the time, we had no idea that the comfort zone we were creating would later become a battleground, and that it was the teachers, rather than the students, who would feel uncomfortable.

This orientation session, a prelude to the first day of class the next week, was characterized by a friendly hum of conversation despite some of the uncertainty and discomfort. Most conversation was extremely positive and pleasant, and the aura of anticipation was almost tangible. Several parents told Karen and me that they had requested Roberta as a teacher for their children, citing sensitivity, the research-oriented curriculum, and previous siblings' academic growth in her class as reasons for their request. A few parents made some negative comments. Fortunately, I was well-acquainted with Roberta's teaching, having already spent nearly three years conducting research in her class, and my stalwart faith in her ability to bring out the best in her students, along with my understanding of her approach, helped deflect the barbs. When Ms. Durham, Susan's mother, stated authoritatively that Roberta's "unstructured" classroom "would not serve all children well," I was able to show the ways in which Roberta's class was actually quite organized. When Ms. Bianco, Patrick's mother, said she wasn't sure if Roberta could challenge Patrick, since he was "gifted, although he didn't qualify for the gifted program," I was able to provide specific examples of how Roberta had both supported and challenged exceptional children in the past.

Later in the day, as Roberta, Karen, and I reflected upon our observations and the conversations we'd had during the orientation session, we all projected a sense of hopeful excitement about the new school year. The negative comments had been mostly from parents who had a history of being adversarial. Ms. Katz, for example, had accosted Karen with her misgivings concerning whether Roberta could address her son's ADHD (Attention Deficit Hyperactivity Disorder). The previous spring, Ms. Katz had called Roberta at home and interrogated her. Since parents could request (but weren't guaranteed) specific teachers, she wanted to determine if Roberta would be a suitable teacher for her son. Roberta had confronted her directly, saying that she knew of her history of criticizing teachers and that, if she taught Gerald in the fall, she would expect Ms. Katz to support her educational decisions. Judging from the remarks she made to Karen during the orientation session, Ms. Katz still had major reservations about Roberta's ability to meet her son's needs. Karen simply reassured Ms. Katz that the three of us would do our best to ensure that Gerald had a good year.

Roberta, Karen, and I agreed that all but a few interactions had been friendly and positive during the orientation. We noted that many parents had enthusiastically helped their children complete the biography sheets. Each of us had also observed that some parents had explored the room, looking at the book racks, the thematically arranged resources, the reading corner, the display case, the computer tables, the rabbit, and other features of the classroom. We all had noticed that laughter had contributed to the congenial atmosphere of the orientation session.

Conference Planning: "You Could Cut Off Their Heads"

After "debriefing" the session together, Roberta, Karen, and I delved into our plans for the beginning-of-the-year "orientation conference." Roberta had conducted a similar orientation, modeled after conferences run by professional organizations, the previous year. It was the first time, however, that other adults would participate. Ivy, the student teacher who would work with Roberta during the spring semester, was planning to help us conduct the conference.

Since all four teachers would be workshop presenters, students were able to choose among simultaneous sessions at the beginning of the first school day. Most sessions pertained to academic planning—some to generate interest in topics, some to solicit student ideas concerning curriculum, and others to plan activities. We expected the conference to allow us more individual contact with the students. We also thought it would give students a sense of ownership of the class, since they would be offered choices and invited to participate in educational planning. Interspersed between the sessions were all-group presentations meant to provide information or to initiate projects.

During the first session, Roberta first focused on the students, asking them to introduce themselves. Their personalities began to emerge more clearly, even though most students' comments were brief and perfunctory. Only two students spoke at length: Patrick, who wanted to present himself as an authority on "different subjects, such as math," and André, who used a stream-of-consciousness patter as a bid to become the class clown.

After the students introduced themselves, Roberta addressed classroom expectations. First she solicited questions about behavior. After Roberta mentioned that students would be able to retrieve things from their lockers without obtaining permission, the straw-haired, elfinlike Gerald asked, in an awed tone of voice, "Do we actually get our *own* locker?" A few students asked facetious questions, including André, whose ethereal blue eyes twinkled when he asked, "Can we go in the closets during silent reading?" When discussing behavioral expectations, Roberta mentioned a few general rules such as being orderly in the hall and treating each other with respect. She then asked if students felt they "knew the school rules" by now. They answered affirmatively, and Roberta then said that if these were called into question, they could be discussed at that time. Roberta emphasized health and safety, along with how we would like to be treated, as baselines of conduct.

Roberta's subsequent comments about curriculum surprised many students. She announced that she was viewing the first four weeks of class as an "orientation" that would determine many of the academic options for the rest of the year. During that time, she explained, students would have a chance to choose topics, plan a variety of learning engagements, and think about ways to conduct research. During the first month, she continued, she would likely say "Try it" when students asked her if they could do something. Roberta also explained "Focus Study," in which students choose their own social studies research topics from the required textbook, and "Explorers Club," in which students choose research topics from any field of study. She showed them the text sets—collections of picture books, novels, nonfiction books, magazines, articles, photographs, and other materials organized by topic or theme and stored in plastic crates around the room. She then held up a copy of the social studies textbook on U.S. history, asking, "Could we learn everything there is to know about U.S. history in one year?"

Maureen spoke up. "You couldn't learn about the lives of all the people in the U.S., and all of that is part of U.S. history."

"It sure is," said Roberta, "and how could you learn more about people?" This question sparked many interesting answers, and the discussion about social studies research continued for some time. During the discussion, Roberta added to student suggestions, mentioning community resources that hadn't occurred to them. She also pointed to the text sets, and said, "Think of the whole world, as these crates are just a small part." She paraphrased Maureen's earlier comment concerning the value of human resources, and said, "I couldn't fold up a person and put them in one of those crates."

"No, but you could cut off their heads," a voice rang out. Patrick's sarcastic response was indicative of the tone he would often take during classroom discussions. His comment spurred the intended laughter. Roberta chose to ignore the comment and continued, explaining that the students would soon have time to go through the social studies books and mark topics that could serve as springboards for their Focus Study.

After the discussion, the students were given a chance to explore the social studies textbooks, but many pursued their own agendas. Several were organizing their supplies, looking at other items in the room, or talking. Gerald was playing with the computer keyboard, and Sally and Jessica were primping in front of the mirror in the reading corner. We redirected their attention by reminding them that this was the time to look at the books as a prelude to deciding on research topics.

Procedural information (concerning the management of attendance, seating arrangements, storage crates, backpacks, lockers, snacks, etc.) was discussed last. Roberta asked students to determine class jobs and write the job descriptions. Most of the student questions about procedures sought "legal" definitions of terms such as "healthy snacks" and "appropriate time." There was a vigorous debate about the various jobs that would be rotated among the children on a weekly basis.

After discussing the job descriptions, students raised many questions concerning the procedures for drinking water. Unlike most teachers, Roberta allowed students to get water at will from a large dispenser in the classroom. Students were asked to bring in coffee mugs—later known as "water mugs"—and the "water monitor" job would involve getting ice from the freezer, filling the dispenser, refilling it when necessary, and emptying it at the end of the day. Some students were very surprised that they wouldn't need permission to get up and fill their water mugs. Billy, who had recently moved to Indiana, said, "Last year my teacher drank pop but wouldn't let us have water." There were more questions and comments about the water "rules" than there were about the week-long trip to the woods in the spring or about "Conjunctions," a more elaborate conference planned for November that would involve presentations and workshops given by parents and community members.

Before beginning small-group sessions, the students were grouped according to choices they had made earlier in the day. During my own sessions ("Math Ideas" and "Talking About Books"), I intended to learn about the students' background experiences and attitudes and to engender enthusiasm for curricular possibilities in math and reading.

The Math Ideas group included only five students, and none had listed the topic as a first choice. During the math session, I discovered that the students' feelings about math were overwhelmingly negative. My opening question, "What do you think about math?" unleashed a Pandora's box of complaints. I said little, merely asking a few questions here and there to clarify issues or to request more information. A common criticism was that math wasn't "useful." After students had had their say, I began explaining some important everyday uses of math, such as being able to ascertain unit prices of groceries in order to buy the cheapest brands. When asked to imagine other useful ways to explore math, everyone contributed ideas. These included understanding sports statistics and using math to learn how to "build things."

My next session, Talking About Books, started off with a bang, because the eight students who had signed up for it all enjoyed reading and wanted to talk about a variety of genres and authors. I was struck by the students' insights into the reading process. Doug, for example, talked about the importance of "sticking with a book, even if the beginning is boring." Maureen's comment that many novels had been made into movies spurred an animated discussion about films and the novels upon which they were based. A comparison of the book and film of Roald Dahl's (1988) *Matilda* was particularly lively. Three students criticized the movie for making the protagonist's magical powers too sweeping: "Magic shouldn't be too easy," noted Elizabeth. A critical but glowing appreciation of books predominated the discussion. When we moved on to ideas for using books in class, the suggestions included conducting research about settings in novels, making posters and projects to share completed books, drawing pictures based on scenes in books, and turning literature into performances. The latter suggestion was unanimously heralded by the group, and related ideas blossomed: Kirsten suggested the students write a play using characters from a novel, and others wanted to read folk tales aloud, write a musical based on a novel, and act out book scenes in mime. Some of these suggestions later materialized as important classroom experiences.

The teachers—as I shall refer to Roberta, the student teachers, and myself when I write of us collectively—all felt that the conference had yielded the seeds of a supportive learning environment. We felt that the conference had allowed the students to reflect on past learning experiences, and had provided a window into some topics that we could develop as inquiry cycles. The students' math ideas, for example, fit well with Karen and Roberta's plan to introduce two "Math Clubs," in which students would choose to embark upon one of two practical projects entailing the use of math. We all agreed, however, that allocating more time for both small-group and whole-group sessions would have increased the breadth and the depth of the conference.

The Writing Process: Family Stories

During the first week, the students embarked upon a writing cycle that was to culminate in a published anthology of "family stories." We wanted to elicit these stories, which could be autobiographical pieces or stories handed down through the family about another family member, through intensive reflection, discussion, and prewriting sessions. Although Roberta had introduced "family stories" in previous years, new input from Karen and me resulted in variations on how they would be written, including extra prewriting activities, more focus upon effective response groups, and a new way to illustrate the stories.

Roberta had planned to begin the writing cycle by reading Bill Martin's (1987) *Knots on a Counting Rope* to the students aloud, but when Elizabeth and Maureen discovered the book, they asked Roberta if they could practice a Readers Theater version of the text and then read it aloud to the class themselves. As the first performance of the year, it was an auspicious beginning. We were all sitting in a circle, completely silent, when the girls began their dramatic enactment. Elizabeth's voice sounded quiet, hoarse, and contemplative, befitting the way the grandfather's character is portrayed in the book. Maureen, playing the little boy, imbued her character's voice with childlike wonder. During the reading, only three students showed signs of not listening. Gerald, in spite of my whispered directives to do otherwise, made slurping noises, lay down and sat up several times, interrupted the reading with irrelevant questions, and slapped his neighbors, first with the knotted rope that was being passed around, and then with his hands. His neighbors responded with self-restraint, simply saying, "Stop it!" I immediately sat next to Gerald, and he settled down. Meanwhile, Patrick and André were drawing attention to themselves in other ways, mostly by interjecting free-association commentary intended to mock the story content. Their comments were extinguished by silent reprimands from Roberta, Karen, and me. The other students seemed transfixed by the performance; their applause revealed their delight, and the subsequent discussion revealed many nuances in the story.

I then conducted a guided imagery session, which we hoped would help students (and teachers, since we were writing along with the students) remember peak events in their lives. I slowly generated a chronological reflection, making general statements such as, "Try to remember your first adventures. Perhaps brothers and sisters were there, or friends, or playmates from a preschool. Perhaps you wandered off and got lost, or took an exciting trip with your family . . ." After the guided imagery session, we all created "clusters" or "webs" in order to remember the many events that, later, could serve as the basis for a family story.

We then all began to draft, or "freewrite," a story about a salient event from our clusters. After fifteen minutes or so, even though none of us had finished a draft, Roberta, Karen, Ivy, and I publicly responded to each other's unfinished pieces as a demonstration of how to effectively utilize a response group. Student reactions were mixed; later, informal interviews revealed that many of them had been bored or impatient with the demonstration, and several had felt left out because student responses to our work had not been elicited.

The students' response groups were marked by several successes and failures. At least six students, according to teacher observations and self-reporting from the students, focused on story content in a relevant way, both citing strengths and providing critique of others' stories. At least four responders noted sections of stories in which authors could "show, not tell" what happened. Some authors either took the initiative to get specific feedback or later complained there wasn't enough of it. "I don't know if it's greediness," said Maureen, "but sometimes you just want people to say more about your piece." Some of the authors had taken notes for future reference, and Billy claimed that he was "going to start over and write everything over and add some things too." Other groups, however, reported that they hadn't learned much from their sessions.

Susan, Patrick, and Maureen had volunteered to be videotaped, and their response session was an unmitigated failure. Susan and Patrick were making faces at the camera during part of the session and all three students spent most of the time explaining their own story rather than offering questions, asking for clarification, or making suggestions. Patrick's comments in particular drew attention to himself rather than to story revisions.

Later, after obtaining the participants' consent, we showed the video of the poorly conducted response group. This turned out to be a valuable way to inspire better response groups in later sessions. To help students reflect upon the merits and problems of the videotaped session, Roberta had provided them a form on which to write responses they would have offered, along with effective and ineffective strategies they observed. During the discussion of these notes, students mentioned the excessive explanations, the camera-conscious antics, the interruptions, and the absence of true listening. Susan, Maureen, and Patrick took the criticisms well, and even talked about how their next response session could be better.

Within two weeks, the family stories had been completed and compiled, and an anthology was given to each student. From inception to completion, the stories had undergone less change than expected. Although it appeared that at least half of the students had constructively critiqued their own and others' work, few had pursued extensive revision. In fact, only four students had substantially altered or expanded their final drafts according to the suggestions of their peers. Furthermore, more than half of the students included fewer than seventeen sentences in their final draft. Yet this class had been given far more time and assistance during their first Writers Guild piece than any of Roberta's previous classes. It was clear to us that many students in this class lacked the investment in their work that we had expected to see.

Watching the Clock

The clock incident that occurred during the first week of school provided another look at the students' periodic lack of follow-through. On the third day of class, the bell that normally signaled the start and end of the day began ringing every few minutes, and the clock began exhibiting very unusual movements. Early in the morning, the hands kept jumping ahead for five or ten minutes, and by mid-morning the hands would periodically spin around. Later in the day, the clock actually began moving backwards.

Not surprisingly, the clock's malfunctioning and the constant ringing of the bell distracted the students and elicited many comments and questions. Gerald found the noise particularly distracting, but his questions about the problem revealed an intense interest in and understanding of machinery. As the frequency of the loud ringing increased, the students became louder and more unsettled. The tension generated by the jolting interruptions mounted until the bells became the topic of several student conversations. Roberta overheard several questions about the cause of the bell problem, and asked the class if they wanted to learn more about the clocks from the electricians themselves. Student response was immediate and enthusiastic, so she invited the electricians to come to the class to answer questions. The question-and-answer session initially generated keen interest in the electricians' story. The electricians explained that the "timing wires" of the bells had not been marked, and while going through the walls to investigate and remedy the problem, the electricians had found decades-old newspapers, antique Coke bottles, and

The most significant category revealed by my analysis was that of "image." Although I did not use this exact word in each description, I found that four students seemed obsessed with the image they projected. Patrick wanted to be viewed as smart, André as the class clown, and Veronica and Sally as belonging to the "cool" group. Later in the year, these same students, along with Ben, Billy, and Brian, became so preoccupied with how others perceived them that they would go to extravagant lengths to win approval.

Many of my summaries of individual students focused on how and when they were listening—or not listening, indicating that undercurrents of inattention may already have been an issue early in the year. André was one of several who tuned out others when they were talking. Bert, Hope, and Henrietta were the only students who maintained a high level of engagement all week. At least half of the other students seemed to be engaged most of the time.

My summary of Katherine singled her out as the most enigmatic student in the group. Roberta and Karen also felt uncertain about Katherine's strengths and weaknesses. As we got to know her better, Katherine surprised us. Early in the year she demonstrated an emotional flatness, low achievement, poor social strategies, and an almost complete absence of motivation and inquiry. By the end of the year, however, she not only had made great strides both socially and academically but revealed an exceptionally mature understanding of the sociological forces at work in the classroom.

The Generative Nature of Story

From the first day of the school year, Roberta had clearly set the tone of the class in several ways. First of all, she had visibly shared power with Karen, Ivy, and me and, to a large extent, with the students, presenting educational decisions as open to challenge and welcoming curricular suggestions. Second, she had established several rituals that provided opportunities for equal participation and debate. "What's on My Mind?," for example, was a type of class meeting in which students chose the topics to be discussed. What's on My Mind? became a twice-weekly ritual that students rarely wanted to forfeit, even if an enticing alternative was offered. Third, Roberta had articulated her educational philosophy to both students and parents both in a packet (sent home during the first week of school) and at Open House. The first part of the packet was a letter in which she highlighted the following six whole language principles as the foundation of her educational beliefs:

Oral and written language develop whole to part.

Language and literacy are socially constructed.

Literate behavior is learned through real functional use.

Demonstrations are critical to learning.

All learning involves risk taking and approximation.

Learners must take responsibility for their own learning.

The latter belief that "learners must take responsibility for their own learning" bothered several parents who, throughout the year, expressed negative reactions to Roberta's teaching. At Open House, Roberta had explained to resistant parents that, by emphasizing student responsibility, she did not abdicate the role of the teacher in structuring learning. Yet she had a feeling, soon to be confirmed, that some parents were suspicious of her learner-centered approach and were waiting for her to motivate their children according to *their* view of what motivation meant.

Roberta's letter also detailed educational approaches and procedures in her classroom. The remainder of the document included two journal articles, one about a previous class she had taught, and the other about the importance of direct experience in learning.

In September, Roberta had conferences with four sets of parents; of the four, only André's parents had expressed overall dissatisfaction. Mr. and Ms. Katz, Gerald's parents, had indicated a willingness to give Roberta's approaches a chance, and the other parents brought up concerns that all of us shared. In addition to these conferences, Roberta had many informal conversations with parents, either by telephone or at school. As the Conjunctions conference drew nearer, her communication with a large number of parents became more frequent.

In class, the Explorers Club, an inquiry cycle in which students chose topics to research both at school and at home, was under way. Though given an option to work in pairs, most students chose to work alone, and class time devoted to research was usually characterized by concerted involvement in gathering and sorting information. School days were busy and full, occupied by the Math Clubs, math "tile teasers" and "stumpers," the Explorers Club research, silent reading, read-aloud sessions, literature groups, Focus Study research, group meetings, Writers Guild, What's on My Mind? discussions, and Invitations sessions, as well as weekly library, music, and art classes, and twice-weekly physical education classes taught by specialists.

Read-aloud sessions captured the students' interest for extended periods of time. In mid-September Roberta was reading Jerry Spinelli's (1991) *Fourth Grade Rats* as a "read aloud." This children's novel concerns fourth-grade peer pressure to bully younger students, and the story generated considerable debate about what constituted age-appropriate behavior. During one discussion that followed a read-aloud session, the students who participated seemed far more interested in the question of when one should outgrow childish lunch boxes and teddy bears than in the dominant theme of bullying as a false indicator of strength and power. Kirsten initiated a poll, and three boys and three girls unabashedly admitted that they still owned teddy bears. Others who confessed to ownership tried to argue that their teddy bears were not really teddy bears because they bore university emblems, Coca-Cola logos, or sports mascots. Roberta told a story about former fifth-grade students hiding blankets and teddy bears during the weeklong outdoor education program at Bartlett Camp, and this fueled further debate concerning the legitimacy of teddy bear ownership. Kirsten presided as a self-appointed judge of the comments, publicly weighing the logic of each argument. The discussion ended with a general student dismissal of teddy bears as unsuitable for fifth graders.

On the day that Roberta read the next-to-last chapter and announced that there was only one chapter left, the children began loudly chanting, "Read! Read! Read!"

"Oh I will," was Roberta's immediate response. "I couldn't stop there."

After she finished the novel, a new debate centered around what toys fifth graders should or should not own. The discussion essentially addressed the degree to which a group should accept individual deviations from group norms. A classroom commitment to debate was in evidence, as at least eighteen students participated and many of them weighed the logic of competing arguments. The students' commitment to a public forum was becoming evident. At the same time, the discussion showed the power of peer norms to regulate individual behavior.

By the end of September, the teachers felt that most students had made great strides in terms of engagement in classroom tasks and discussions, but we also perceived an imbalance of power, particularly during class meetings. Positive student reflections on classroom learning events, enthusiastic parent feedback, and a general sense of social cohesion in the classroom were all signs of growing support for the inquiry approach. Roberta, Karen, and I were concerned, however, that discussions were not always characterized by full participation. The three of us frequently shared our observations and interpretations of the way that several class members attempted to suppress the voice of others. We wanted dominant students such as Patrick and Brian to monitor and control their dominance during both small-group and whole-group discussions and activities, and we wanted silent students such as Julie, Katherine, and Mei-Ling to offer their opinions and make visible contributions. We were convinced that encouraging quieter students to publicly share their experiences whenever appropriate would improve listening, include these students in group decisions, and enhance empathy.

The results of a questionnaire I gave to Roberta's students inspired our hope that their understanding of stories would make them more actively seek and listen to each other's narratives. The questionnaire, part of a university research project, was intended to detect patterns of belief concerning the concept of "story." In response to the question "What significance does the concept of 'story' have for me as a learner?" many of Roberta's students had thought deeply about the learning potential of story. Some wrote about the entertainment value and the communicative role of stories. Several either implicitly or explicitly stated that stories can further the understanding of others. Katherine, who had spoken and written very little since the school year began, wrote that "story means . . . the right to imagine things other people would never think of. It can be sad, funny, and sometimes heartwarming, and heartbreaking." Bert wrote that "people can express themselves with stories, stories can be passed down for generations." Ben wrote that, because of stories, "we don't all see the same thing, we all have a different perspective." Other students indicated that story helps people learn, and Patrick wrote that it helps people listen better. Most of Roberta's students saw story as something revelatory, something all-encompassing and vital. This seemed to be a good omen, pointing toward the potential of the students to revel in reading and writing.

Transformations and Revelations

By October, many student capabilities had emerged. The four most significant were Kirsten's ability to spark debate during class meetings, Hope's strategies for instantly garnering the attention and interest of the whole class, Gerald's increasing engagement in class activities and his efforts to overcome antisocial behavior, and Anne's success in school. Anne had a history of academic failure, but now, despite her previous difficulties, she was reading independently, discussing her work with classmates, and using a variety of outside resources for her research projects. Unfortunately, less desirable traits were also emerging. Brian was using his leadership to control class discussion topics. Patrick's frequent attempts to dominate discussions had been less successful, but he continued his constant interruptions, his self-flattery, and his put-downs in spite of the visible, and sometimes verbal, disapproval of others. Susan had become an irritating source of interruption for the teachers, constantly wanting adult direction, supervision, or approval. Billy's transformation was one of the most disturbing manifestations; he was becoming more and more aggressive, insulting, and distractingly silly. André's actions were also disturbing; he constantly avoided work as he rationalized nonproductive tasks, talked aimlessly, or stared blankly into space.

Selfish preoccupations did not overshadow the sensitive side of individual students. An autumn leaf hunt in early October prompted students to voluntarily fill their learning logs with poetry, drawings, and notes. A number of social interactions elicited compassion, the most notable being Gerald's disclosure of his Attention Deficit Hyperactivity Disorder. When Gerald revealed his disability to Hope in front of some other students, Hope demonstrated understanding and caring.

"I have ADHD," Gerald quietly told Hope after she mentioned that he was getting distracted from their group's project.

"What's that?" she asked. When the other three students heard her question, their ears perked up. Gerald explained his condition and described how difficult it was for him to concentrate and stay still, despite medication. A brief silence fell upon the group before Hope responded.

"I had no idea," she said. "Why didn't you tell us sooner? If you had, we could have helped you more."

Gerald, during an interview with me later in the year, discussed his decision to share his condition. I asked him whom he had told about having ADHD, and he said, "Well, people I can trust, you know, like the people who are nice to me." Apparently, Hope was one of the few students in Roberta's class who fit that bill.

Ominous Rumblings

Rumors about boyfriend/girlfriend pairings had also begun by early October. In late September, I overheard four separate remarks concerning who was "going with" whom. Like many teacher observations, these overheard remarks didn't reveal their significance until later in the year; at the time we were unaware that peer pressure to associate with "popular people" was so extensive. By the end of the school year, this pressure had become an overriding concern for a large majority of students in all four fifth-grade classes.

A field trip to the courthouse, which took place in early October, also signaled the peer pressure problems to come. Roberta had asked several parents to lead small groups during the all-day trip, and several of these parents experienced shouting matches in which students interrupted parent leaders and tried to dictate group behavior. Roberta observed some of this rude behavior and intervened by talking privately with the offending individuals. In other cases, the incidents were reported to Roberta later. Roberta was surprised that one father was not bothered by, and did nothing to discourage, the rude behavior that Roberta had observed in his group.

The field trip sent up a red flag for Roberta. Never before had she had behavior problems on field trips. The main problem seemed to be an abuse of leadership, as students who were disrespectful had overpowered those who normally acted responsibly. When she talked with me about the field trip, Roberta expressed concern that the class wasn't "acting like a community," and that she would think twice about how she might conduct future field trips.

Several outbreaks of rudeness occurred in the classroom as well. Sally and Jessica had a major dispute and tried to involve others in their shouting match. On two separate occasions, Billy pushed several students. I was the sole witness to perhaps the most explosive display of anger, which occurred when Charles was asked to clean up the mess around his storage crate at the end of the day. The other students had just left the room, and Charles stormed back in, muttering many expletives, shouting about the "fucking crate." Continuing to swear, he violently flung a chair out of his way and began crumpling and throwing papers in a fit of rage. I slowly approached, realizing that I would best help him by remaining as calm as possible. I told Charles to be careful about what he was saying, and then asked if I could help him clean up. He didn't answer.

"Would you like me to help you?" I repeated.

"I don't care," Charles answered in an antagonistic voice.

"Well, it seems you do care," I said. "Otherwise, you wouldn't be so mad." I started picking up some of his papers and books and organizing them into piles. Charles then began doing the same. His actions were no longer conveying fury, but he refused to make eye contact with me. When everything was in the crate, he put it away and silently left the room, not looking back.

The same week, Roberta planned a day of archaeology workshops as a prelude to several related workshops that would be held during Conjunctions week in November. A local archaeologist and several graduate students presented several basic archaeology concepts to small groups of students. During their first session, the children had the opportunity to examine artifacts and other materials at three different stations in the room. Later, the group was divided into three groups for separate sessions that would probe the subtopics in more depth. Although enthusiastic, the small groups seemed somewhat on edge. Small disputes flared into arguments, some of which temporarily disrupted the sessions. The presenters were not getting their due attention.

At first, I discounted these incidents, thinking they were exceptions to the rule, since throughout September the classroom had ordinarily been a positive and productive place. But as I considered the harmonious atmosphere of Roberta's previous classes, in which this kind of behavior was a rarity, perpetrated by only one or two students, I began to worry that some of her present students were unusually aggressive and volatile. I had my first inkling that trouble was brewing.

Stepping Back: The Teacher-Researcher

In many ways, every teacher is a researcher. Teachers use the information they elicit to systematically explain what they observe and to determine what conditions might facilitate learning. Not every teacher, however, takes extensive notes, pursues professional development, invites researchers into the classroom, discusses learning theories with students, parents, and colleagues, and sees curriculum in terms of authentic questions about subject matter and learning. Practices such as these help bridge the gap that sometimes exists between what is theorized about the classroom and what actually happens there. As a teacher-researcher, Roberta continually attempted to examine her beliefs about teaching and learning. For her, the relationship she had with each of her students helped gauge her success in aligning belief and practice.

1. Roberta prioritized her relationships with students. She agrees with McEwan (1998), who feels that an ultimate goal of a democratic classroom is "the security and self-esteem of every student" (153). For Roberta, the teacher-researcher not only needs to learn about effective teaching, but needs to learn about the thoughts and lives of students as the essential basis of instruction. Her visions of what students can achieve are based on concrete knowledge about student interests and potential. She is convinced that only when students value their own questions and abilities do they see classroom learning as worthwhile.

Roberta's attempts to know students well were demonstrated by her frequent conferences with individual students, her elicitation of personal narratives and family stories, and her attempts to document student thoughts and actions. She dealt with student problems in a highly personal manner, trying to privately ascertain facts and to collaboratively brainstorm solutions.

2. Roberta sought to further her understanding of students by documenting classroom conversations and events. Since she actively took notes every day, I was able to compare my own extensive notes with hers. Our attempts to base our analyses of events on concrete observation helped us sort out facts. Furthermore, our attempts to compare observations gave our interpretations a critical edge.

Roberta's documentation also helped her track progress. She videotaped all student presentations throughout the year, for example, and both she and her students reviewed some of these videotapes to pinpoint strengths and weaknesses. Roberta's narrative progress reports were particularly rich in examples, largely because of the records she kept of student comments, actions, written work, and presentations.

3. Roberta attempted to collaborate with students, parents, and colleagues. She was willing to share power with students by seeking student input on schedules and curriculum on a regular basis. She also demonstrated collaboration by actively scouting resources for the students' Focus Study and

Explorers Club research projects. In Writers Guild, Roberta sometimes wrote her own pieces and invited response groups to critique her rough drafts.

When preparing for Open House, Roberta involved the students in the planning and presentation because she was interested in what they felt was important about the classroom and the way it was run. Open House, for Roberta, was also an opportunity for her to share her philosophy of learning with parents and to hear their perspectives. Instead of dismissing the accountability concerns of Dr. Lingle and Dr. Martine, she allowed them to criticize her views openly. In so doing, she attempted to establish respect through dialogue. Later collaborations with parents led to classroom visits and Conjunctions sessions.

Roberta's collaboration with colleagues extended beyond the confines of Robinson Elementary School. By organizing study groups, presenting at conferences, taking courses, and becoming politically involved in education issues, she built networks of support and exchanged ideas. Her open invitation for me to study her classroom also exemplified her commitment to professional collaboration.

4. Roberta frequently provided choices. To better determine what learning ventures would best serve students, she provided more than one option during most of the school day. During presentation sessions and class meetings, everyone was expected to focus on the same thing at the same time, but at other times students usually pursued different activities simultaneously. For Explorers Club projects, students chose any topic or theme to research. For Focus Study, they selected a research topic related to the mandated social studies curriculum. When pursuing Literature Study, students chose one of several books to read. Math also involved choice; students joined the Math Club that interested them the most. Invitations sessions, in which students were invited to freely explore a variety of thematically chosen objects and materials, were predicated upon choice. Even details such as how to respond to literature were infused with choice. When asking students to respond to books she had read aloud, for example, Roberta let the students choose from a menu of strategies (such as describing characters, writing questions, and sketching scenes) that they collaboratively devised during the first week of school.

As Roberta's principal, Beth Waters, pointed out during an interview, Roberta's choices necessarily entail parameters. At the end of the school year, Beth said:

> Roberta very carefully plans and sort of, guides I guess is the word, or facilitates; it's not just a wide open "do whatever you want," which I think people misunderstand sometimes. And [she] monitors, constantly, what's going on and gives a lot of feedback—written, verbal. . . . So I think kids are always academically growing because they get that on a continuing and constant

> basis. . . . They're more excited about learning when they have choices and feel empowered and that's probably what keeps them going and interested in what they're studying.

In the realm of discipline, choice also prevailed in Roberta's room. When students' conduct fell outside of expected parameters, they were likewise given outcome choices. When discipline problems occurred, Roberta, as a teacher-researcher, was more interested in understanding and solving the problem than she was in controlling the students. She didn't assume that unpunished misdeeds would lead to greater transgressions, but assumed that reflecting on behavior problems with the students would provide a better basis for wiser choices in the future.

5. Roberta strived to articulate and enact her philosophy of learning. Her beliefs are founded upon a whole language philosophy, in which learning is viewed as a natural process that is nourished by stimulating and nurturing environments. By October, many approaches indebted to whole language philosophy were in place in Roberta's classroom. Literature Circles, in which student discussions of books focused on authentic responses and personal connections, emphasized the entire reading process. Writers Guild was designed to take students through different written genres for a variety of purposes, yet at the same time granted students a wide latitude of choice in their writing. The students were constantly accumulating writing pieces; pieces in the prewriting and drafting stage provided fodder for future writing, while other pieces went through response, revision, editing, and publication stages.

The project orientation in Roberta's classroom also was consistent with whole language and process approaches to learning. Roberta tried to synthesize mandated curriculum with a process orientation through Focus Studies. Rather than regurgitate textbook facts, students skimmed and scanned required textbooks to choose topics for further research. During Explorers Club time, research projects were not restricted to required topics. Math Clubs allowed students to utilize mathematical operations within the context of entire projects as well, and the first two Math Clubs—writing a grant for a bird feeding station and creating games based on baseball statistics—put math in a functional context as students revised their projects in order to have a precise, polished product. Science projects—somewhat underemphasized during the first four months of school—also began with approximate understandings and developed into more refined, accurate forms.

Roberta's use of text sets also can be traced to her familiarity with whole language theories (Short, Harste, and Burke 1996). Some of her text sets are related to the social studies and science topics that she is supposed to cover, while others reflect student and teacher interests. In addition to serving as research data for Focus Study research, the text sets are constantly being explored for other purposes as well. Students often followed Roberta's lead by saying, "Let's look in the text sets!" and they emulated her excitement about books by sharing their discoveries.

6. Roberta tried to take a problem-solving approach to discipline problems rather than rely upon rewards or punishments to control behavior. Whether using class meetings to address misuse of class time, using a videotaped response group to discuss responsible critique, or reflecting on inattention during a presentation, she presented problems as opportunities to think through possible solutions. When encountering resistance, Roberta did not set up reward systems or punish students through "time out" or exclusion from favorite learning activities. Instead, she tried to deal with problems, such as the rudeness during the field trip, as opportunities to expand problem-solving strategies. When student strategies weren't successful, she provided guidance but emphasized the important role that failure plays in learning.

Roberta's approach to discipline departs significantly from common, traditional approaches. For more than two hundred years, teachers in the United States have relied on threats and intimidation to command compliance (Finkelstein 1989). Although corporal punishment has become more uncommon, nonphysical forms of intimidation still proliferate, and are even recommended in discipline guides for teachers. Chernow and Chernow (1989), for example, endorse the "scare technique," recommending that the teacher deal with noncompliance by saying "something outrageous to the student, for example, 'I'm going to fail you' [or] 'I wouldn't do that if I were you.' You do this calmly, indicating you are in complete control. It is helpful if you learn to say these things through slightly clenched teeth" (156). Others, such as Seeman (1994), recommend intimidation through rules, by advising teachers to "forbid any bathroom going mid-class, which is my preference (they must learn to go before or after)" (195). Canter and Canter (1992), widely known for their "assertive discipline" approach, compare classroom discipline to law. They present such a tidy procedural package for maintaining discipline that, according to their claims, teachers will no longer be "forced to constantly make choices about how to react to student behavior" (46). Roberta eschews such approaches, relying on neither personal threats nor strict rules to exert her power. She understands that discipline involves constant judgment calls.

Roberta avoids reward systems, believing like Kohn (1993) that rewards "[displace] other possible motivations. And they change the *attitude* we take toward the activity" (35, emphasis in original). During the first few weeks of the school year, students sought rewards for good behavior as well as academic achievement and, in interviews, several students told me they were disappointed that Roberta didn't have a "point system." These students had had a fourth-grade teacher who implemented a point system to reward completed work and good behavior; this teacher spent her own money to buy prizes that became more and more expensive and elaborate as the year progressed. Some of Roberta's students from this class, accustomed to rewards, told me at the beginning of the year that there was "no use" doing work if no reward awaited its completion.

Rewards for behavior risk similar pitfalls. Many students will ask what they will get if they comply with certain rules or requests. Kohn (1998) provides a good example of the shortsightedness of rewards when he tells of students in a Connecticut school who turned in their own lunch money as "found" money in order to obtain rewards for honesty. Roberta celebrated achievement through compliments, discussions, or displays, but she refused to dangle carrots in front of children in order to get them to work or behave.

Teacher-researchers are likely to view behavior problems as "a need to learn about better ways of teaching" (Stanley 1998, 256–257) rather than view them in terms of compliance alone. Roberta tried to garner authority and respect as a result of her day-to-day decisions about what to attend to and what to ignore. In her opinion, formulas that construe behavior as completely predictable squelch not only student autonomy, but teacher autonomy as well.

7. Roberta presented herself as a learner. During the "family story" writing cycle, she took on a participant role, brainstorming, writing, revising, and editing her work along with the students. When she allowed Elizabeth and Maureen to take over the prewriting presentation of *Knots on a Counting Rope,* she encouraged student leadership and emphasized her role as a participant. Roberta's questions about the videotaped response groups were not merely didactic; they were genuine inquiries concerning what could spur an effective combination of support and critique. And when the students had finished their final drafts, she included students in the planning, photocopying, assembly, and distribution of the anthologies. When the clock malfunctioned, her teacher-researcher stance made her receptive to the learning potential of the problem, and she actively mobilized the resources that could help answer the student questions that arose. In every way, Roberta positioned herself as an inquirer who took on facilitator and participant roles.

Students in Roberta's class also pondered the relationship between learning and teaching. Guest presentations in Roberta's room positioned the presenters as teacher-researchers. When either Roberta or her students gave a presentation, the presentation ended with a question-and-answer session. This session in turn led to another presentation, based on follow-up research intended to answer audience questions. Roberta is what Fried (1995) would call a passionate teacher, someone who conveys a passion for learning by creating partnerships with students. By presenting this model of learning, Roberta demonstrated the power of conceptualizing oneself as a lifelong learner.

8. Roberta asked authentic questions. She rarely asked questions to which she knew the answers. Display questions—questions intended to elicit a specific answer—put the asker in a testing mode, whereas authentic questions help teachers better understand student thoughts and experiences, the subject matter, and the learning process. Roberta regarded curriculum as ongoing inquiry rather than as merely the material or activities that are taught. Of course, some learning ventures such as math problems may involve right answers, but an inquiring teacher will want to learn more about how students find—or fail to find—the right answers, the thinking and reasoning processes that led to the answers.

The prevalence of traditional schooling practices that privilege "right answers" has led to dangerous assumptions about intelligence, even prompting teachers to equate intelligence with school success (De Bernardi 1996). Roberta assumed that her students were intelligent and capable and she effectively elicited their ideas. This is one reason, I believe, that she has had tremendous success with students who had records of academic failure.

Perhaps the most authentic question that good teachers regularly ask is "What can I learn about the students?" It is no coincidence that Roberta, Karen, and I all began discussing individual students and their learning potential when we met after school to discuss our impressions of the first two weeks. Both the questions we asked and the way that we tried to confirm and disconfirm our impressions were indicators of learning.

Listening to Students: The Role of the Teacher

At the beginning of the school year, several students wanted Roberta to take a more authoritarian approach. In math, for example, several students requested that she implement competitive math skill programs that included rewards for achievement. Although Roberta didn't outright refuse to consider these (and indeed did introduce some timed math practice as a response to student requests later in the year), she explained her rationale for wanting students to focus on math problem solving as well as accuracy and her desire for students to work for the satisfaction of learning rather than for tokens that represented teacher approval.

Several students also clamored for punishment, although the following interview with Crystal reveals the ambivalence that accompanied such requests:

C: In my brother's classroom, I think it was last year, you had a little card for each day. And it said, like, kicking or yelling in the classroom. And the teacher put down a sticker for every time they did it. And then if you got, like, four, then you'd have to talk to the teacher. I thought that was pretty neat.

AK: But then it becomes the teacher's responsibility to be the policeman.

C: I just liked that because it was cool.

AK: So you'd rather the teacher keep track of your behavior.

C: I guess. I don't know. . . . One week, Ben could watch Patrick and see if he's being bad, and Patrick could watch Veronica and so on. And I'd watch Katherine and Doug would watch Ben. . . . But when Sally got mad she could just put down a lot of stickers. So I don't think that'd work.

AK: Earlier you mentioned trust. I think that's an important term. How much should a teacher trust the students? Should we just assume that when we're not looking you're all working, you're all being polite to each other, you're being responsible? Or should we be on the lookout for infractions, for misbehavior?

C: I think you should be on the lookout.

AK: So we shouldn't just trust that you do the right thing?

C: I think there are a few people you guys can trust: Maureen, Kirsten, and Elizabeth, I guess. . . .

AK: So we should only trust certain people and not the others?

C: [You could trust a different person] every week—say this week it would be Ben. . . . The whole week you could watch him and see if you could trust him. And then you'd just go through the whole gang until you could trust everybody.

AK: Don't you think, in general, we trust people until the trust is broken?

C: Yeah.

AK: And then how could we teach, really focus on teaching, if we're spending so much time watching people's behavior?

C: I don't know.

AK: Well how much do you personally feel you should be trusted? Do you really want us to be looking at your behavior all the time to try to find out when you're not doing something right?

C: I wouldn't like that.

AK: Then why do you want to impose that on everybody?

C: I don't know.

Students like Crystal wanted to be trusted, yet didn't realize the extent to which a reward/punishment system can inhibit trust. Furthermore, she was ill equipped to come up with intrinsic reasons for being responsible.

Most students, however, liked the collaborative aspect of Roberta's teacher-researcher stance. When I conducted informal interviews with students, many stressed Roberta's collaborative role in helping them "figure out" how to conduct their own research. During the first month, student descriptions of Roberta frequently included words such as "supportive" and "helpful." The fact that she "didn't yell at them" was mentioned by several students, suggesting that their former teachers had often raised their voices in anger. Student interviews confirmed that Roberta had not presented herself as an authority, but as a learner whose mission was to support the learning of her students.

Student interviews also revealed the great value they placed upon the many choices that Roberta offered, even when they were difficult choices. During the Conjunctions sessions in November, for example, students had to choose between recess and presentations. Students liked being able to decide whether or not to miss recess, as Doug's interview shows:

AK: Are there times when people have had to give up what they want personally for the sake of the whole group?

D: Yeah, like during Conjunctions. . . . We didn't go out to recess because of all the stuff we were doing. We missed recess for other stuff a few times. If we're doing something that wasn't in the schedule, then we have to give up something that isn't quite as important.

The students' understanding of a teacher-researcher orientation emerged when I asked them, later in the year, what "made a big difference" in their learning. Many students answered the question by mentioning the Explorers Club presentations, during which students presented their research to the rest of their class. Students also talked about the opportunity to teach other students something they didn't know during math and Focus Study presentations. Katherine, for example, implied that Explorers Club research spurred learning through teaching:

> Well, if you want to learn about something you don't know, you should just think of an idea you want to learn about and that could be [what you study]. Like, I wanted to do bears. . . . I love bears. And I love dogs, and I'm going to study dogs for my next [Explorers Club research]. As you can tell, I love animals. For other people, if they want to learn about something else, they can teach about it because they're presenting what they learned.

Kirsten, during an interview, similarly posited questions and reflection as indicators of learning:

AK: What really makes you feel convinced that you've learned something, or learned something well? What are the indicators of learning to you?

K: Well, this sounds really weird, but when I can contemplate something and not understand it. Like if I'm thinking about King Arthur and I keep thinking about him a lot but I don't fully understand what I'm thinking about, that tells me that I've learned something, because I've learned something new that makes me want to go on to this stuff that I don't know anything about.

Kirsten's statement attests to the importance of learning experiences that are within one's reach but slightly beyond one's current level of knowledge or functioning. Her description also points to the value of "lingering questions," which Roberta frequently brings up as an important aspect of learning. When we are left with many questions about something we have studied, we know that we have learned enough to formulate new questions, and we are aware that there is much more to learn. Thus, questions may be as important as answers in assessing learning outcomes.

Lingering Questions

What might characterize a learner-centered classroom environment, in contrast to a teacher-centered or student-centered one?

What strategies might help a teacher take notes while at the same time being fully engaged in teaching?

What kind of leadership does a teacher need to exert in order to facilitate student, parent, and colleague collaboration?

How can professional development be better geared toward supporting teacher research?

What kind of research should teachers conduct?

How might the role of a teacher-researcher be reconceptualized?

Further Reading

History of Discipline in the United States

Butchart, Ronald E., and Barbara McEwan, eds. 1998. *Classroom Discipline in American Schools: Problems and Possibilities for Democratic Education.* Albany: State University of New York Press.

Finkelstein, Barbara. 1989. *Governing the Young: Teacher Behavior in Popular Primary Schools in 19th Century United States.* New York: Falmer Press.

Kohn, Alfie. 1993. *Punished by Rewards: The Trouble with Gold Stars, Incentive Plans, A's, Praise, and Other Bribes.* Boston: Houghton Mifflin.

Teacher as Researcher

Applebee, Arthur N. 1996. *Curriculum as Conversation: Transforming Traditions of Teaching and Learning.* Chicago: University of Chicago Press.

Beane, James A. 1997. *Curriculum Integration: Designing the Core of Democratic Education.* New York: Teachers College Press.

Fox, Mem. 1993. *Radical Reflections: Passionate Opinions on Teaching, Learning, and Living.* New York: Harcourt, Brace & Company.

Fried, Robert L. 1995. *The Passionate Teacher: A Practical Guide.* Boston: Beacon Press.

Goswami, Dixie, and Peter R. Stillman, eds. 1986. *Reclaiming the Classroom: Teacher Research as an Agency for Change.* Portsmouth, NH: Heinemann.

Graves, Donald. 1991. *Build a Literate Classroom.* Portsmouth, NH: Heinemann.

Hubbard, Ruth S., and Brenda M. Power, eds. 1993. *The Art of Classroom Inquiry: A Handbook for Teacher-Researchers.* Portsmouth, NH: Heinemann.

Paley, Vivian. 1995. *Kwanzaa and Me: A Teacher's Story.* Cambridge, MA: Harvard University Press.

Short, Kathy G., and Carolyn Burke. 1991. *Creating Curriculum: Teaching and Students as a Community of Learners.* Portsmouth, NH: Heinemann.

Reading/Writing Process

Atwell, Nancie. 1987. *In the Middle: Writing, Reading and Learning with Adolescents.* Portsmouth, NH: Heinemann.

Bridges, Lois. 1997. *Writing as a Way of Knowing.* York, ME: Stenhouse Publishers.

Calkins, Lucy M. 1994. *The Art of Teaching Writing.* 2d ed. Portsmouth, NH: Heinemann.

Daniels, Harvey. 1996. *Literature Circles: Voice and Choice in the Student-Centered Classroom.* York, ME: Stenhouse Publishers.

Goodman, Ken. 1996. *On Reading: A Common-Sense Look at the Nature of Language and the Science of Reading.* Portsmouth, NH: Heinemann.

Graves, Donald H. 1994. *A Fresh Look at Writing.* Portsmouth, NH: Heinemann.

Hindley, Joanne. 1996. *In the Company of Children.* York, ME: Stenhouse Publishers.

Lensmire, Timothy J. 1994. *When Children Write: Critical Revisions of the Writing Workshop.* New York: Teachers College Press.

Mayher, John S., Nancy Lester, and Gordon M. Pradl. 1983. *Learning to Write, Writing to Learn.* Portsmouth, NH: Heinemann.

Samway, Katharine Davies, and Gail Whang. 1996. *Literature Study Circles in a Multicultural Classroom.* York, ME: Stenhouse Publishers.

Short, Kathy G., Jerome Harste, and Carolyn Burke. 1996. *Creating Classrooms for Authors and Inquirers.* 2d ed. Portsmouth, NH: Heinemann.

Smith, Frank. 1994. *Understanding Reading: A Psycholinguistic Analysis of Reading and Learning to Read.* 5th ed. Hillsdale, NJ: Lawrence Erlbaum Associates.

Weaver, Constance. 1994. *Reading Process and Practice: From Socio-Psycholinguistics to Whole Language.* 2d ed. Portsmouth, NH: Heinemann.

Whole Language Philosophy

Church, Susan. 1996. *The Future of Whole Language: Reconstruction or Self-Destruction?* Portsmouth, NH: Heinemann.

Crafton, Linda K. 1991. *Whole Language: Getting Started . . . Moving Forward.* Katonah, NY: Richard C. Owen Publishers, Inc.

Edelsky, Carole, Bess Altwerger, and Barbara Flores. 1991. *Whole Language: What's the Difference?* Portsmouth, NH: Heinemann.

Goodman, Ken. 1986. *What's Whole in Whole Language?* Portsmouth, NH: Heinemann.

Krashen, Stephen D. 1999. *Three Arguments Against Whole Language and Why They Are Wrong.* Portsmouth, NH: Heinemann.

Pace, Glennellen. 1995. *Whole Learning in the Middle School: Evolution and Transition.* Norwood, MA: Christopher-Gordon Publishers.

Watson, Dorothy, Carolyn Burke, and Jerome Harste. 1989. *Whole Language: Inquiring Voices.* New York: Scholastic.

2

Law and Order

The Trial

In early October, a small incident, in which Brian was accused of false copyright, evolved into a major inquiry on legal issues that lasted for nearly two months. When doing a journal activity during a field trip, Charles and Brian had drawn some advertisement designs ("business advertisements," as Brian called them) and logos for health products, gels, and hairsprays in their learning logs. Doug saw the designs and started talking about how someone could copy them. Consequently, Brian drew the copyright sign next to his design. Doug immediately declared Brian had violated copyright laws. After Doug joked about Brian's "violation of the law" with other students, the topic became a conversation piece among class members. Within a day, several students had planned to hold a mock trial in an attempt to determine whether or not Brian was innocent of breaking copyright laws.

By morning, "the trial" had become a buzzword, and I overheard students saying that it would be held outside during the after-lunch recess period. Roberta and Karen learned that Doug had been designated the prosecutor and Kirsten the defense attorney. Andrew would be the judge, and the jury would be selected randomly. Speculations about the trial permeated the first morning activities.

Later in the morning, Roberta granted a student request for a class meeting to plan how the trial would be conducted. During the meeting, heads swiveled as one student after another contributed questions and suggestions. Doug, his tousled hair and freckles a perky setting for the excited sparkle in his eyes, presided over the discussion, describing his vision of a "realistic" trial that would include, in addition to the players already mentioned, a "court recorder" (Elizabeth) and someone (yet to be chosen) to select the jury. Students raised questions not only about the roles of those in the trial but also about how the jury would make a decision. Questions also concerned what provisions might be made for excessive jury deliberation and whether or not there would be a retrial if the loser found the outcome unfair. Fascinated, all three teachers wanted to witness this event, and we asked the class if we could attend and videotape it. There were no objections.

On the playground, during after-lunch recess, the students convened for the trial. By the time Roberta, Karen, and I arrived, Patrick had somehow usurped Andrew's place as judge. Jessica had taken on the task of jury selection. She and a panel of jurors had gathered near the shelter and the rest of the cast of characters were either seated on or standing around the picnic tables under the shelter. As Roberta operated the video camera, Doug began the proceedings by proclaiming that Brian had been accused of false copyright. André's question, "What does that mean?" was ignored by the rising tide of chatter, and even screaming, in the "court."

"I wasn't writing a book," said Brian, in an attempt to defend himself. "It's a business."

"Order in the court!" shouted Patrick, adding a few decibels to the rising noise level.

"If you start a riot, you will be taken from the court!" shouted Doug.

"Is there no evidence?" asked Bert, but before any could be produced, people began shouting and screaming.

"Copyright laws—maybe we'll have to find out about that," said Ted, barely audible over the simultaneous directions being yelled out by the crowd.

"Order in the court!" bellowed Patrick. He shouted this several times, but the noise level remained high and disorder prevailed.

During a pause in the pandemonium, Doug initiated a debate concerning whether Brian's design could be legitimately copyrighted.

"Does anyone here think people should be allowed to write the exact same thing, the exact same title and everything that Brian has done?" he asked the crowd.

Two students loudly asked, "Is there no evidence?" but attempts to show the design documents were disrupted by loud talking and shouting, interspersed with more calls for "Order in the court!"

At this point, Susan screamed very loudly, for no apparent reason. Since this was the students' recess time, Roberta, Karen, and I chose to ignore her scream and see what evolved. The eagerly anticipated trial soon began to deteriorate as many students began to shout over each other. Some of the leaders, including Kirsten, Brian, and Ted, tried unsuccessfully to control the group so that the event could continue as planned. Students from the other classes who had drifted over to the shelters disrupted the proceedings further, some of them denouncing the whole affair as stupid and stomping away to play elsewhere.

Jessica, watching the participants disperse, began yelling "Shut up!" at Susan and other screamers. Then she summoned the jurors to the area just outside the shelter by yelling "Jury members over here!" The jurors complied, while other students continued to run around and shout. Gerald began clowning in front of the video camera, as Roberta panned the camera to capture the dispersed action.

After barely a huddle, the jurors were headed toward Brian, shouting "Guilty! Guilty! Guilty!" with rapacious fervor.

In what seemed a very short time, only a small group of children remained, and they began to verbally process what had happened. These students agreed that the trial had not been conducted properly, and several individuals, especially Ted and Kirsten, were quite concerned about it not being a fair trial. Kirsten felt that she, as defense attorney, did not have a chance to present her case.

After the recess bell signalled the end of the recess period, the class members who had drifted off rejoined the rest of us under the shelter. The debriefing then took a wonderfully analytical turn. Doug began talking about the lack of jury deliberation and the infiltration of the jury by members of other fifth-grade classes. Topics such as subpoenas, juror bias, and hung juries were brought up. After a while, Roberta suggested we all return indoors so that we could take notes while continuing the discussion.

In the classroom, students analyzed the anarchy that had disrupted the trial. Some wanted an immediate retrial, but Roberta requested that it be deferred and proposed that the next hour be allocated to planning the retrial. The students enthusiastically agreed. Roberta suggested they discuss issues in small groups. She, Karen, and I then circulated and took notes on what issues emerged. By the time a whole-class meeting was called, the students' research questions had filled three overhead transparencies. The questions included the following: How is the judge appointed? What needs to be done in order to make sure the jury is fairly selected? How does the case need to be researched? How will order be maintained? How will evidence be presented and analyzed? What if the jury decision is not unanimous? Can a judge's sentence be challenged? How can reporters cover the trial?

As the students scrambled to answer these questions, they began to talk about the issues, write ideas, or look for appropriate resource books. Many students circulated to elicit opinions and check out the information others discovered. Some students appointed roles as they all tried to clarify who would do what during the retrial.

As the planning for the retrial continued over the next few days, Kirsten emerged as a strong class leader. She repeatedly called small-group and whole-class meetings to clarify roles and procedures. She conducted her own research about legal proceedings and encouraged Ted, Doug, and several others to do so. She insisted on refining the jury selection procedures by calling into question the way the jury had been selected. Doug also emerged as a new leader. He scouted classroom texts as resources and organized a library expedition to find more print resources to use. That night, as Roberta later learned, Doug convinced his parents that researching trial procedures was "homework," thus gaining permission to work on trial plans late into the night.

The new jury selection was complicated by the fact that a number of students, randomly selected to be interviewed and then actually chosen for jury duty, did not want to be on the jury. I pointed out that reluctance or unwillingness to be on a jury is the reason that it's considered a legal obligation. This led to a heated discussion of whether or not there should be any exemptions from jury duty.

"Can't we just make *kids*' rules?" asked Mei-Ling, her question at odds with her earlier stance that the procedures ought to be authentic.

It was finally decided that those selected for jury duty could be exempted only if they offered a convincing case of conflicting interest, such as the demands of their other roles in the retrial. New role categories emerged from the research, including physical planners, examiners of evidence, press representatives, secretaries, schedule planners, and security officers. As the students met in small groups to allocate these roles, consensus and equal participation became very important. In the press group, for example, Elizabeth wanted to decide how the retrial would be recorded and also wanted to assign roles. Mei-Ling, previously willing to follow the decisions of others, took a firm stance about how decisions about reporting should be made.

"*We* should decide who should do it and how the stuff will be put down," she emphatically exclaimed. "We're all reporters."

Mei-Ling also challenged another student's presumption that André, being a boy, would be best qualified to serve as "cameraman" for the video. This led to a discussion concerning what sort of background would qualify someone for this role.

"If André does it," said Elizabeth, "we'll have to call him 'camera girl.'" This was not the first time that this sort of taunting had emerged in a small-group setting, and I was concerned that perhaps it was becoming a pattern.

André, uncharacteristically, chose to ignore the baiting and continued the conversation concerning roles.

"Who's the lawyer? I want to interview him."

"What about jury members?" asked Mei-Ling. "Can we interview them?"

Such questions continued to be discussed, and the teachers encouraged the students to investigate the answers in the context of real trials, and suggested where to look for more information.

Throughout the retrial, important legal issues were brought to light, such as what can and cannot be copyrighted and how to determine the impartiality of jurors. During group meetings on these subjects, the teachers answered questions, posed new ones, and tried to supply guiding resources. Eventually a group of law students from the university helped everyone understand and address important issues raised by the trial. They visited the classroom and conducted a number of activities. Weeks later, the retrial was held at the law school. The students eventually learned that copyright laws are more inclusive than they had realized, actually protecting the kind of designs that had been created. Meanwhile, United States law had become a major inquiry topic that would captivate the class for several months.

The students' interest in the trial and retrial was a major example of their fascination with rules and the regulation of conduct. The cohesion of the group as they prepared for the retrial bridged some of the gaps between the "popular" and "unpopular" members of the community. Although there were instances of exclusion, particularly during the negotiation of jury selection procedures, eventually all students participated in the retrial and, for several months, there was a strong sense of community and absorbed engagement whenever trial-related activities took place.

Before the trial, Roberta and I had been lamenting that there hadn't been a stronger sense of community in the classroom compared to previous fifth-grade groups. In former years, students had supported each other's learning fairly consistently by October, and group meetings had quickly evolved into discussions relatively free of interruption or the domination of a few. This year's group, however, still seemed unsettled, and the many successes they were achieving were occasionally offset by the pushy behavior of Billy, Patrick, Maureen, Hope, and other students who tended to wrest control over group situations. The trial, however, gave us hope that social and academic concerns would come together. Each student seemed keenly interested in the trial, and group meetings concerning the proceedings were characterized by a unity of purpose, more in-depth response to peer questions and comments, and civil turn-taking. Furthermore, research on legal issues was involving all class members in productive reading and discussion. We felt confident that the improvements we were seeing would result in a more positive classroom community, and that parents would respond well to the fact that their children were so engaged in classroom pursuits.

Parent Conferences

Parent conferences were held during the first week of November, and Roberta was looking forward to them. Roberta had talked with many parents about their volunteer participation in the upcoming Conjunctions workshops, but had had little time to discuss the children. Several parents had been difficult to reach. The conferences would provide opportunity for face-to-face communication with all the parents.

In addition to looking forward to dialogue with parents, Roberta was hoping to finalize the plans for those who would participate in the Conjunctions conference, scheduled for the third week of November. Conjunctions would entail a solid week of simultaneous presentations and workshops, given by teachers, parents, and community members. This year, eleven parents had already agreed to offer workshops, some involving more than one session, on such diverse topics as the Vietnam War, Native American dancing, and quilting. Community members who were scheduled to present included archaeologists, a museum curator, a political refugee from El Salvador, a geologist, American Sign Language teachers, a city councilman, and law students. In addition, Roberta, Karen, Beth (the principal), and I were planning workshops in playwriting, cooking, travel planning, and songwriting, respectively. Roberta felt sure that the many extra hours of planning for Conjunctions would increase parent participation in their children's education and help bring the community into the classroom. The parent conferences were well timed, as Roberta could make one last pitch for parent involvement in Conjunctions.

Knowing that my schedule would prevent me from attending all the conferences, Roberta suggested that I try to attend those involving either difficult children or difficult parents. The first conference I attended was with Gerald's parents. Because of Ms. Katz's history of complaints concerning her child's teachers, we had expected this conference to be the most difficult, but it turned out to be surprisingly pleasant. Both parents were thrilled by Gerald's enthusiasm about school, his increased social integration, and his overall progress. Other parents who might have been difficult, given their history in former years, turned out to be positive, with three exceptions: Ms. Bianco, who made excuses for Patrick's social problems; Brian's parents, who were furious that the conferences were running overtime; and André's parents, whose comments conveyed several mixed messages.

Roberta began the conference with Dr. Lingle and Dr. Martine by soliciting their views of André's progress so far. Their responses consisted mostly of unflattering generalizations about André's behavior and character: academically, he "spaces out at home," "struggles with homework," and "doesn't see the purpose of many practical tasks." Socially, they claimed, he was "very judgmental about his peers," "slow to warm up to teachers," and "never does well with large groups." Roberta then offered her own perspective, focusing more on André's achievements and needs rather than on generalizations about his personality.

"André needs to figure out what he needs to do," said Roberta, explaining that he rarely took the initiative to clarify directions and get started on class tasks, even when everyone else had begun. She acknowledged that he might have had a history of doing poorly in large groups, but added, "I love it when he's really part of a group and we're seeing more of that." Roberta went on to emphasize his successes, including a recent composition from Writers Guild, and his willingness to display a painting he'd created. Then she clearly stated that he needed to listen to others, control his talking, and take more responsibility for completing assignments.

As they listened to Roberta's analysis of André's progress, André's parents exhibited negative body language and made negative comments. Dr. Lingle leaned back in his chair, and Dr. Martine pushed her chair away from the table. The way that Dr. Martine's arms were tightly folded across her chest was an odd contrast to her limp torso, which was submitting to gravitational forces as she slumped in her chair. Dr. Lingle began asking about André's painting, but Dr. Martine interrupted him, declaring that André "doesn't like to be praised" and that she did not want Roberta to publicly discuss his artwork or writing. Although Roberta, Karen, and I had all seen André respond positively to public affirmation of his work, we were not able to say so before Dr. Lingle changed the subject. He expressed concern that André didn't "get his work done," but then said "we don't want to hear about any more problems," a statement we should have immediately clarified, but didn't. Dr. Martine mumbled something about "organizational structures," and then Dr. Lingle used the phrase again, saying that he wanted to "spend a few hours in the classroom to better understand the organizational structure." Roberta assured him that he was welcome to visit the class. She ended the conference by stating that, if they wished, she would stay in touch by e-mail, and that Dr. Lingle could let her know when he was planning to visit. Both parents responded cordially.

Karen and Roberta felt that the conference hadn't gone well. Trying to be encouraging, I mentioned several positive statements André's parents had made. But as I looked over my notes, I realized that the couple's unwillingness to take an active role in addressing André's problems seemed to override their few agreeable comments. In addition, there had been a tangible tension throughout the conference.

Later in the week, Roberta tried to put the adversarial nature of the meeting into a larger perspective by thinking of the other conferences, which had gone remarkably well. Even Brian's parents, who had exploded with rage at having to wait for over thirty minutes when Roberta fell behind schedule, ended up being quite positive once they calmed down. By scheduling conferences at the convenience of parents and working long after the school hours set aside for conferences, Roberta had been able to conduct relatively in-depth conferences with at least one parent of all but two children. The students not discussed in conferences were Mei-Ling, whose parents did not speak English fluently and had a history of not attending conferences, and Billy, whose parents had not responded to several previous communication attempts.

Several conferences could be described as glowing. During Bert's conference, which Bert had chosen to attend, his mother's role in fostering his love of learning was evident. All of us shared perspectives, raised questions, made lighthearted comments, and laughed. According to Roberta, most of the other conferences were congenial, and all but a few parents expressed satisfaction with their children's progress. The few who expressed concerns, with the exception of André's parents, had some positive reactions that overshadowed their reservations. Some of the reservations of these parents, Roberta felt, were largely justified. Julie's mother was concerned about Julie's apathy and lack of follow-through in completing work, and Charles' mother was concerned about his headaches, his difficulties in making friends, and his periods of despondency. All of us thought that these were legitimate problems.

Other problems cited by parents, Roberta felt, were exaggerated. Ms. Katz bemoaned Gerald's "slow" progress in math. Ms. Durham claimed that Susan "needed structure," but the teachers actually felt that Susan needed to be more independent and less reliant on routine and teacher instructions. Ms. Bianco dramatically insisted that Patrick's "brilliance" was not being "thoroughly challenged." Although Roberta had a different perspective, she was glad that these concerns had been brought to light so that they could be scrutinized and, if necessary, addressed further.

The issues in André's case were less clear-cut, and nagged at Roberta. André's parents wanted Roberta to take more responsibility for André's behavior yet to withhold praise that might nurture his self-esteem and sense of responsibility. Roberta hoped that Dr. Lingle's visit to the classroom would help him understand André's problems in the school setting. Since neither parent had volunteered to give a Conjunctions presentation, she was glad he was planning to visit during Conjunctions week and would witness the active parent involvement in the conference. She also felt that experiencing a Conjunctions workshop might foster his appreciation of the curriculum. As it turned out, Dr. Lingle didn't visit the classroom or attend any Conjunctions sessions. Instead, his wife wagered a full-scale attack on Roberta just a few days before Conjunctions took place.

E-mail: Resistance and Support

After the meeting, Dr. Lingle sent frequent messages, and he and Roberta were keeping track of André's work via a friendly, ongoing e-mail dialogue. In mid-November, however, Roberta received an e-mail message from André's mother that constituted the first in a series of hostile notes. It began by citing facts: André had not brought his math "stumper" home and had told his mother that he had to reread his entire novel because he hadn't done his journal responses and couldn't remember what happened in the book. She then wrote that the math assignments had no purpose and that André was beginning to dislike school. Her e-mail seethed with accusations as she claimed that Roberta was constantly on André's back, that she wasn't challenging him, that her curriculum was unstructured, and that her methods were totally inflexible. She ended the note by implying that Roberta's curriculum was boring and that her rigid methods were harming André and setting him up for failure.

After Roberta shared the e-mail with me the next day, I was at first incredulous that Dr. Martine saw Roberta as inflexible, as she had already tried several different approaches to help André complete assignments—verbal and written encouragement, a record-keeping system for assignments, daily checks with him, and other special provisions. Roberta showed me a rough draft of her response, in which she assured Dr. Martine that she "want[ed] him to enjoy coming to school and to love learning" and that there had to be a solution to the problem. Her note also detailed the purposes and procedures of the math stumper and literature responses. She finished by stating that the e-mail message had upset her, but she would continue searching for ways to help André.

Dr. Martine responded with another nasty e-mail, this time accusing Roberta of having low expectations of André, not reasoning logically with him, and embarrassing him by praising him publicly. Ironically, her long message ended with a disclaimer that she did not intend to question Roberta's teaching and that she hoped they could work together. Awash in a sea of responsibilities pertaining to the Conjunctions workshops and feeling very vulnerable, Roberta did not respond immediately to this new e-mail. Although Dr. Martine had, ostensibly at least, expressed the desire to work together with Roberta, her message did not invite collaboration, and seemed designed more to defend her position than to amend the situation.

An e-mail message from Anne's mother, Ms. Ward, provided a stark contrast to that of André's mother. The message, which was sent shortly after Dr. Martine's messages, was the product of a month of close communication. Anne's mother had been quite concerned about her daughter, because for years Anne had hated school and had tried to avoid schoolwork. Ms. Ward's message was an affirmation of Roberta's belief in the recursive nature of success and confidence.

> Just a quick note to tell you how Anne has been so excited about coming and participating in school. We had already [restricted fats] at home, so Anne was excited [about the healthy snacks]. She was afraid that others would be bringing candy/chips, etc. and she would feel out of place. So you helped in a way you didn't even know. She has just been so excited about successfully doing the [math tiles], even though we have struggled getting started. . . .
>
> You are such an inspiring teacher, an accepting teacher, an encouraging teacher. . . . I have learned from you too. . . . I just want you to know what a treasure you are.

Conjunctions: Collaborations and Conspiracies

The week before Conjunctions began, the students studied the carefully crafted brochure, which contained brief abstracts of every presentation along with designated hours and attendance limitations. A few days before the conference, the students signed up for workshops, based on preferred selections and availability. In most cases, students obtained their first choices, and, given that there were attractive alternatives for the few workshops that were full, we heard few complaints when first choices weren't obtained.

During the swirl of events that surrounded Conjunctions, all students, at one time or another, participated actively. Several students who had rarely shown much enthusiasm in class, including Julie and André, responded excitedly to some of the presentations. After the week ended, written student evaluations of the sessions were glowing. In spite of the tremendous success of Conjunctions week, however, there were several occasions of power struggles, disruptions, and peer acceptance of rude behavior.

The first session that I attended was a smashing success. The law students had performed short plays based on two children's stories, *Goldilocks* and *Cat in the Hat,* then led follow-up discussions of the legal issues involved and how they would really be addressed in a courtroom. After this, a "Parts of a Trial" workshop was offered for those who were interested.

During the discussion that followed the performances, the children became very excited about the legal issues raised by the plays. Never had I seen Anne and Ben so animated during a class discussion. Anne astutely speculated on why certain events in the plays had been ambiguous and articulated what might and might not constitute evidence for criminal activity. She balked at the law students' suggestion that evidence of previous crimes might be appropriate.

"If you commit a crime once," Anne protested passionately, "it doesn't mean you're going to do it again!"

Julie, in a gesture I found surprising not only because Anne was becoming her best friend in the class but also because she almost never took a stand publicly, was the only student to disagree. Her lips made a determined straight line in her chubby face as she firmly declared that previous criminal activity should be admissible evidence.

As opinions were offered, there was universal participation in the small-group discussion. Ben, whose designer haircut and sporty clothes gave him a clean-cut look, was particularly eloquent when he tendered multiple explanations of the two crimes, and when he explained to the others why it was the prosecutor's job to prove guilt.

The issue of unanimity became an important one for this group. A number of students felt that juries should not be required to make unanimous decisions, and even the law students' explanation of reasonable doubt did not sway them. Although there were questions about what can happen if someone is wrongly convicted of a crime, relying on majority rule rather than unanimous rule seemed worth the risk to at least six students.

A few situations from the students' lives were then brought into the discussion, including one student's concern for pets in her neighborhood that, in her opinion, were being neglected or even abused. The concept of injunctions was then introduced and their ramifications discussed.

By the time the discussion ended, students were able to recap many of the important points. Kirsten, for example, told me she had learned that defendants were protected by "presumed innocence and a defense lawyer," and Maureen added that "proof beyond a reasonable doubt and a jury that agrees" provided additional protection. Later in the day, I overheard several conversations about the two plays and the subsequent discussions.

The "presumed innocent until guilty" concept came up during a five-minute break in the afternoon during which the whole class was playing the popular game of "Seven Up." In this game, seven students come to the front of the room while others put their heads down on their desks and raise up their thumbs. After seven thumbs have been touched, the other students are allowed to look up and the seven "victims" guess who touched them. I had seen this game played several times earlier in the school year, but this was the first time I had witnessed vociferous accusations of "peeking," precipitated in this case by three correct guesses. The accusations had a rather nasty tone, and only abated when the "innocent until proven guilty" maxim was mentioned.

The intense concentration that characterized the law sessions seemed to permeate the other Conjunctions sessions held on Monday. On Tuesday, however, I heard reports of unruliness during one workshop. That afternoon, I experienced it directly when I conducted the first of two songwriting sessions with eight students.

I began my songwriting workshop by playing several songs on the piano and discussing their components: rhythm, melody, and chords. Since the eight students all said they played musical instruments, I discussed some of their knowledge in light of these components and the songwriting endeavor. André and Ben did not contribute anything to this discussion, perhaps because they were the only students in the group who couldn't read music at all.

The students themselves decided which other students they would work with, and I was pleased that each group included someone who had a fairly substantial musical background. Anne and Katherine, both violinists, began planning their song immediately. I began working at the piano with Ted and Brian, since they were the first to request its use. The other four students (Patrick, Veronica, André, and Ben) went to the somewhat secluded reading corner. The reading corner, closed off by a tall bookcase and strewn with large bean bag cushions, was normally a quiet area where students read silently, pursued partner reading, or discussed books.

Ted and Brian were full of enthusiasm but uncertain about the ins and outs of melody and chords, since Ted was a drummer and Brian a fledgling musician. Both boys were ablaze with questions, and I was happy to answer them. They wanted to produce a dark, "thundery" tune, and an ominous composition was indeed materializing. As soon as I felt they could continue independently, I went to the other side of the room where Anne and Katherine were already writing a melody on their music papers.

I was helping Anne and Katherine with their notation when I heard angry voices coming from the reading corner. Before peering around the bookcase, I paused to listen for a short while and quickly realized that the conversation consisted of ugly insults being hurled back and forth between André, Patrick, and Ben. Veronica didn't seem to be saying anything, but was laughing loudly after each verbal assault.

I walked around the bookcase and asked for their attention, but my request was ignored. By this time Veronica had joined Ben and André as they spewed insults at Patrick. Patrick was defending himself by calling the others "idiots," "liars," and "stupid." I raised my voice and demanded they stop. The insults stopped, but the complaints began.

"Patrick wasn't doing what he was supposed to," accused Veronica, and the others followed with "he said, she said" charges.

I told them I didn't want to hear the insults, but instead wanted to hear how they could work together to produce a song. Patrick claimed that he had made some suggestions that had been categorically dismissed. I tried to mediate by asking if there was a way that the group could alter or expand any of the ideas suggested so far. The only idea that all could agree to work on was one that Ben had proposed earlier, that they write about someone who hated his boss and wanted to quit work. With at least the germ of an idea to work with, I insisted that the students work on this theme individually until each had some possible lyrics written.

Sulking, the four went to separate tables. Patrick, Ben, and Veronica got out paper, and André just sat there doing nothing. I went over to Anne and Katherine, who had reached an impasse in their progress. As I helped the two girls, Ted and Brian continued to work out a theme on the piano. The others, however, sat sullenly, refusing to write.

By the end of the two-hour session, the two hard-working pairs had finished a rough draft of their melody, and simply needed to revise it and work on chords. The other four, however, had produced nothing in writing. I delivered an ultimatum that they should bring some potential lyrics to the next session as a condition for continuing the songwriting workshop.

At the start of the next two-hour session, two days later, I asked each student to share what they'd done and what they still needed to do. I consulted with the two pairs who were ready to continue. After I'd given them brief directions, I then met with the other four as a group. Only Patrick had written any lyrics. I said that I was disappointed that the others had not followed through, and asked them if they wanted to discontinue the songwriting altogether. Acting surprised, they were adamant to continue; Ben had brought in his electric guitar and Patrick had brought in some lyrics, they pointed out, so they were ready to start. I reminded them that I had specified that ideas on paper were a prerequisite to working on the song. Ben said they all liked Patrick's ideas and wanted to work together on revising them. I relented, seeing this as an opportunity for them to rectify the previous day's infractions.

I stayed on as a facilitator until I felt that all four were collaborating. As ideas began to fly, I found myself getting caught up in their excitement. Their idea of writing about a disgruntled gas station attendant was turning into poetry, and as soon as Ben suggested they write a chorus about the attendant's wish for another job, he started improvising: "I want to be, I want to be, I want to be . . ." and paused.

"An archaeologist!" shouted André, and we all laughed. The suggestion was immediately embraced. Satisfied that all four students were working as a team, I left the group to help Anne and Katherine write some chords to accompany their melody.

By the end of the two-hour session, the students were ready to record all three songs on audiotape. Ted and Brian played their "Monster" song, an instrumental, as a duet. Then Anne and Katherine played the melody of their instrumental, "Garden of Roses," on violin as I accompanied them on the piano. The fractious four had managed to complete both lyrics and a blues-inflected melody, although they had not gotten around to writing chords. Despite discordant harmonies, they successfully sang "I Want to Be an Archaeologist." Their rendition was a cappella because of technical problems with the electric guitar and, more significantly, because of a general inability on the part of any of the group members to actually *play* the guitar. All eight students were tremendously happy about their compositions. When the rest of the class heard them, the composers were visibly thrilled by the hearty laughter and spontaneous compliments.

Ms. Bianco did not have the opportunity of a second session to help her resolve the conflict that arose during her own Conjunctions workshop. Although I did not observe the workshop, I pieced together the facts afterward from several informal interviews. Patrick, who happened to be her son, was again in the center of the fracas. In this case, however, all twelve participants were involved in the shouting match. The disruptions prevented Ms. Bianco from completing her presentation, but she did manage to quiet down every student except for Patrick. Aware that she was running out of time, she sent him into the hallway. Soon he was making faces at the window, which resulted in more riotous disruption. Ms. Bianco, visibly furious, marched to the hallway and ordered him to report to the principal. Beth was understandably amused to learn that Patrick's own mother had sent him to her office. Ms. Bianco's angel had fallen from grace, although her version of the event, as relayed to Roberta, was not couched in those terms.

Breaking the Law

Two more of Roberta's students fell from grace the week after Conjunctions: Sally and Julie were suspended for having conducted a conspiracy to consume alcohol at school—yet another in a series of bathroom incidents that had been affecting students from two of the other classrooms. Ms. Fox and Ms. Worthington, in early October, had learned that their fifth graders had held secret meetings in the bathrooms. This was the first time, to our knowledge, that the bathroom conspiracies had resulted in a major violation of school rules. At first, the bathroom meeting, discovered by Ms. Worthington, may have looked like another gossip session. Upon closer inspection, however, the teacher realized that the girls had been drinking alcohol. Further investigation revealed perfume bottles filled with rum that the girls had been drinking.

Sally, implicated by the others as the chief engineer of the plan, initially denied any involvement. According to the others, the day before, on the bus, she had been talking about the plan to drink alcohol at school. As the allegations against her continued, Sally was called to the principal's office to discuss the matter with Beth and Roberta. After Sally again pleaded innocence, Beth indicated that she had sufficient reason to believe that she was not telling the truth. Sally's composure seemed challenged by this statement, and soon, after a few more questions, she broke down and confessed that it was she who had convinced Julie to steal the rum from her parents and carry it to school in perfume bottles. The girls were immediately suspended, in compliance with district policies concerning alcohol on school premises.

Good-byes and Reflections

Karen finished her student teaching in November, and her departure was marked by a genuine show of appreciation from the students. In addition to the "What I Will Always Remember" booklets that had become a tradition in Roberta's class over the years, the students wrote extra notes and cards. Karen's own reflections were paradoxical; while she felt that some students had demonstrated independence and responsibility, she felt that others remained excessively dependent on peers and teachers.

The innovations Karen had introduced to the math program had generated positive attitudes toward math, even though she had encountered some resistance to her later Math Club lessons. Karen's first Math Club group had invented an elaborate baseball statistics game, and their computation skills in such areas as figuring averages had strengthened considerably. Roberta's group had actually obtained a $200 grant to build a bird-feeding station on the school grounds. A Conjunctions workshop offered by Sally's father had yielded birdhouses for the project, and students continued to compare prices of other materials and equipment, this time with the concrete goal of setting up the station before the end of the year. Math "checkpoints" were helping students stay accountable for computation. The ongoing tile teaser and math stumper work had gained more force as students more actively shared their problem-solving strategies, and students who hadn't volunteered to present in front of the group were beginning to do so.

By the time she left, Karen had been orchestrating the class for over two weeks with little intervention on Roberta's part. During the two weeks when she had led the class, she and Roberta stayed at school until suppertime or later, working to ensure that instructions, materials, and expectations for activities were clear and organized. Karen's chief discipline challenges had cropped up when small groups of students (Patrick, André, and Ben were frequent offenders) deliberately chose to ignore her directions, choosing instead to socialize in a disruptive manner. Karen and I had several conversations about possible consequences. These conversations often included Roberta, who, in addition to written feedback, suggested ways in which Karen could regroup students and modify activities to prevent the disruption problems.

In addition to working hard, Karen had contributed tremendously to the classroom through her astute observations and plentiful ideas. She often observed alliances, arguments, and inquiries that Roberta and I had failed to notice, and her knack for trying new approaches impressed Roberta and me. We were sorry to see her go.

By the winter break, a sense of harmony predominated. Routines had become more firmly established, and the students settled into an even rhythm. Most students were regularly turning in their homework, class work time was consistently productive, negative attitudes about math had dissipated, and only a few students seemed unwilling to participate in all-group discussions. Even shy and insecure students such as Julie, Katherine, and Crystal were volunteering to speak. Despite occasional resistance and rudeness, the children were, on the whole, working well together, and Patrick, Gerald, and other socially alienated students were becoming more accepted. Relieved that the students were at last becoming more supportive of each other, Roberta and I felt hopeful about the rest of the year as we parted for the holidays.

❖

Stepping Back: The Social Construction of Curriculum

The students' spontaneous creation of a trial and the inquiry cycle that it precipitated were shining examples of an inquiry curriculum, one in which student questions shape what is studied and how. Within such a curriculum, inquiries stemming from social interactions have the same learning potential as do inquiries that stem from preplanned topics. What began as play and social interaction—Charles' and Brian's creative "business advertisements," Doug's accusation of copyright violation, and subsequent disagreements—evolved into collaborative research concerning civil litigation. All this was possible because of several strategies Roberta used to enhance the social aspect of curriculum.

1. Roberta implemented an inquiry curriculum that stressed collaboration and research projects on student-chosen topics. The students' trial, precipitated by their own inquiry, provided a more in-depth exploration of civil law than the social studies textbook would have offered. It provided an experience beyond the scope of mere assimilation of information, and was exactly what the students and Roberta wanted to do in order to explore the implications of copyright law. As Dewey (1938) reminds us, learning depends on the quality of the learning experience. Roberta agrees that enriching experience is basic to learning, and supports Harste's (1994) contention that curriculum should reflect how we want to live.

The current educational climate in which Roberta and other teachers operate is beginning to threaten inquiry classrooms. Although Roberta's principal granted her a great deal of latitude in interpreting state mandates, many teachers are not so fortunate. A project-oriented curriculum that focuses on student questions and interests is not compatible with one that is bent upon covering content in the race to score well on standardized tests. Wolk (1998) contrasts "covering" with "learning" when he writes that people wrongly assume that "what is taught in school is learned, and that for someone to learn something it must be taught" (34). In the mad rush to cover mandated content, teachers rarely have time to find out what students know and what they might want or need to know. As Roberta well knew, a research-oriented classroom that values social sharing of what is being studied often sacrifices breadth for depth.

Roberta's willingness to have two student teachers in her classroom during one academic year was another manifestation of her belief in collaboration. She gave these teachers the latitude to try new approaches, which resulted in Karen's successful Math Clubs and Ivy's upcoming science explorations. Throughout the year, Roberta noted that their ideas transformed the curriculum in positive ways. Roberta has worked with graduate students and university professors for many years, and my collaboration with her has also fueled her ongoing reconceptualization of curriculum.

2. Roberta understood that a social orientation to learning needs to be supported by parents. The parent conferences revealed that most of the parents understood and supported, to varying degrees, Roberta's approach to curriculum. The fact that the students, on the whole, were happy in Roberta's class probably was a major factor of these parents' support. Student attitudes toward school often act as a barometer that corresponds closely to parent dispositions toward the teacher.

Both students and parents understood that the "homey" atmosphere of Roberta's classroom stressed comfort and communication, but not all parents condoned such a classroom climate. André's parents viewed her classroom as lax, rather than as relaxed. The resistance of André's parents, and in particular their opinion that Roberta's class was unstructured, may have sprung from the widespread myth that whole language classrooms are disorganized environments in which "anything goes." Roberta had positioned herself as a whole language teacher early in the year, which left her vulnerable to the prejudice that such a stance can unleash.

Roberta wondered if her willingness to confront parent beliefs that differed from her own left her more vulnerable to opposition. Dr. Martine's second e-mail message conveyed more than just theoretical or philosophical differences, however; it constituted a personal attack. Although some of her concerns may have been legitimate, like her son she used the guise of speaker intentions to justify unkind words.

Ms. Ward's e-mail message was typical of the kind of parental support Roberta usually received. Anne and her mother felt positive about Roberta, Roberta felt positive about Anne and her mother, and Anne, as a result, was feeling positive about herself. Anne was producing good work and this turnaround was probably boosted by Roberta's emphasis upon the social context of learning. She felt accepted by Roberta, was making friends, and for the first time felt confident about her ability to learn. Fortunately, Ms. Ward understood the basic importance of successful social integration, and her note in itself was a reminder that social relationships are part and parcel to learning.

3. Roberta tried to promote autonomy in the classroom. Autonomy issues came to the fore during the law inquiry. The pandemonium of the first trial showed that students could initiate group research projects but did not have good strategies for sustaining inquiry and regulating group behavior, perhaps because of little previous experience. There was also evidence that some students disregarded minority rights: Students wanted to control who would do what during the retrial; the students discussing law did not see the value of a unanimous jury decision; and dominant students sometimes kept others from contributing to discussions. Peer status lurked beneath many conflict situations, and the letter from Anne's mother, Ms. Ward, alluded to her daughter's fear of not belonging, of "feeling out of place." At this point in the year, students were not universally accepting all members of the class as equal participants, and the students still needed a great deal of guidance in establishing a social climate that respected individual autonomy.

Dr. Martine's critique of public praise forced Roberta to examine the relationship between praise and autonomy. External praise as an incentive for achievement can be a double-edged sword, since praise can be a form of evaluation in which the person who praises positions himself as the bearer of correct knowledge or good taste. This kind of praise could actually discourage autonomy. André's autonomy, in fact, did seem to be inhibited by praise, but it was peer rather than adult approval that guided much of his action. Encouraged by his classmates, André often took on the role of class clown, making silly and rude remarks. Although desire for adult approval might have made him more responsible, it might have merely shifted the locus of responsibility from peers to adults.

In retrospect, Roberta, Karen, and I realized that pointing out André's achievements may have unconsciously highlighted his preponderant lack of achievement. Gordon (1989) writes that "when a teacher says to a student, 'Today you understood the lesson because you were attentive,' the message that most likely comes through to the student is 'Mostly you're *inattentive*, and that's unacceptable to me' " (48, emphasis in original). To avoid such messages, Roberta often asked students questions about their achievements, a practice that Kohn (1999) recommends. She also tried to focus on reflective feedback and appreciation rather than evaluative praise. She tried to describe how she felt about specific achievements rather than use evaluative adjectives such as "good" or "nice." She retained the social conventions of compliments but avoided lavish or manipulative praise, such as extolling a student for being in his seat. She supported attempts to meet high expectations by validating approximations along the way.

Roberta trusted that students would make good independent decisions, but of course they didn't always live up to such expectations. The alcohol incident showed that trust may allow for autonomy, but doesn't guarantee responsible social decisions. A widespread quest for popularity was fueling subversive behavior and making students more dependent on each other, as they replaced teacher authority with peer authority. Roberta realized, however, that she could only regain authority through respect. She knew that true autonomy involves moral decision making that, in the democratic tradition, weighs both individual and group gain.

4. Roberta avoided reward and punishment systems, solving behavior problems through negotiation rather than through procedural authority. Patrick's expulsion from his mother's Conjunctions session and Sally and Julie's suspension from school are two examples of the ineffectiveness of a traditional approach that emphasizes procedural authority. In both cases, punishing the undesirable behavior did not solve the underlying problems that each incident represented. Patrick's "punishment" of being sent to the principal was seen as closure on the incident, even though no plan for change had been formulated. Since Sally and Julie's case involved the consumption of alcohol, districtwide policy dictated they be suspended, which, in essence, amounted to the withdrawal of learning opportunities for several days. Ironically, school district policies that categorically dismissed social and interpersonal curriculum (but emphasized the same academic standards for all) denied the students academic opportunity as a punishment for a perceived social transgression. The alcohol incident could have evolved into an inquiry on alcohol or a public scrutiny of fifth-grade peer relations. Instead, the procedural consequences of suspension bypassed the learning potential of openly addressing the social dimensions of the problem.

Routine procedures and tasks can be used as a preventative discipline tool as well as a punitive one (Doyle 1985). Students accustomed to silent, independent seatwork often see this as a behavioral norm, and some students even clamor for the order and predictability of worksheets (Kucer 1998). So a paradox emerges: If students are not familiar with an inquiry approach to learning, they may become disruptive; yet quelling disruption with worksheets never allows students to get beyond the initial "play" stage of independent inquiry. Roberta gave students many behavioral choices as they worked together, but tried to prevent discipline problems by planning learning endeavors that would actively engage the students. When this didn't work, she dealt with behavior problems case by case rather than imposing isolation or doling out rewards or punishment according to a prearranged plan.

Classrooms in which a great degree of social latitude is allowed are not likely to have the orderly, conformist cast that pervades an authoritarian classroom. Reward and punishment systems, however, restrict social latitude. Such systems may promote order, but "when a teacher runs her classrom by a system of punishments and rewards, the student is encouraged to become a passive recipient of her control" (Ohanian 1999, 55). Students like Patrick, who may act disruptive in a democratic environment, may be more orderly in a classroom that rewards speedy, correct responses and obedience. Yet in a highly controlled setting, students do not have the freedom that underlies responsible decision making and critical scholarship. In a democratic classroom, discipline is not a problem that is taken care of so that teachers can get on with the curriculum. Instead, discipline—in terms of learning how to respect others, sustain engagement, and take on responsibility within a community—is an essential part of curriculum.

Conversations about respect and self-discipline were constantly occurring in Roberta's classroom, whether in the context of literature study, class meetings, or private problem-solving interventions. Roberta expected civil conduct and negotiated its terms individually if it wasn't immediately forthcoming.

5. Roberta's students were allowed to converse responsibly, drink water, and eat snacks throughout the day. When Judy Best (1995) described the social environment of her elementary classroom to me, she critiqued the common notion that students should always be "on task." If she visited her principal's office and found him on the phone, she told me, she would not assume that he wasn't getting his work done. Roberta took a very similar approach in her own classroom, allowing social interactions to permeate most learning projects. When conversation diverted from the topic being studied, she expected it to veer back, and it usually did. When it didn't, she asked herself if the conversation constituted a brief interruption or a disruption, redirecting the conversation if she thought it was interfering with learning.

To Roberta's students, no aspect of the classroom symbolized the social nature of curriculum more than their water mugs. The fact that students made their own decisions about drinking water and eating snacks enhanced the social aspect of the classroom. Knowing they could make decisions about drinks and snacks may have helped students realize that they were expected to make responsible decisions about their learning and conduct as well.

6. Roberta consciously shared power by allowing students to make many decisions about the curriculum. She believed that students could create curriculum, and therefore they did. Roberta's vision of a shared curriculum reinforced the students' sense of autonomy, as did their social latitude. From the contents of the display case to the scheduling of daily lessons, student input affected most aspects of the classroom. Students made decisions about discussion topics, classroom supplies, curricular choices, and the physical arrangement of the room, all exemplars of an environment in which the teacher has consciously chosen to share authority and power (Oyler 1996). Roberta's students were allowed to define and redefine what counts as classroom knowledge and, as Manke (1997) maintains, this alters power relations in the classroom.

Students gained a great deal of power over their own learning when Roberta pushed them to conduct research in preparation for a retrial. The way in which the retrial became an important part of the curriculum is an example of integrated curriculum in action. As Beane (1997) points out, integrated curriculum does not merely blur knowledge domain boundaries (by, for example, integrating math and science) but, more importantly, organizes learning in terms of problems and issues, collaboratively identified by teachers and students. Roberta had to exert her power, however, in order to share it. She helped sustain the momentum of interest in the legal issues that emerged by responding to student questions and interests, planning a wide variety of engagements to address those questions, and negotiating how related topics could best be investigated. By allowing students to actually plan the retrial, she highlighted the social aspect of an inquiry curriculum and enhanced the collaboration that was naturally occurring.

7. Roberta utilized many forms of ongoing assessments to provide a social context for evaluation. Although there is overlap between the terms *evaluation* and *assessment,* Roberta distinguished between them. Evaluation implies the measurement of learning according to fixed standards or the achievements of others, while assessment implies a look at the personal significance of the learning, not merely its allegedly objective measurement. Roberta tried to assess students in an authentic manner, within the context of classroom communication. To assess learning, she relied upon students' comments and actions, as well as artifacts such as journals, learning logs, projects, portfolios, artwork, and videotapes of student presentations.

Roberta's progress reports contained narrative descriptions of the students' progress, but school regulations required that these be accompanied by checklists and grades. To ensure that those grades were as fair as could be expected, given the limitations of grades, her final grades were heavily influenced by conferences with the students and by documentation of both work-in-progress and final products. When Roberta held conferences with students about grades, she usually found that student perceptions of their learning and progress were highly consistent with her own.

Roberta's view of assessment as ongoing, reflective decision making that furthers learning is a stark contrast to a view of assessment as measurement-oriented evaluation, yet the latter serves as the basis of most curricular guidelines. Unless evaluation is recast as an ongoing process of assessment that values different learning outcomes and autonomy, mandated standards and grading systems, in which students often learn that schooling means failure, will continue to prevail.

8. Roberta assigned projects that stressed sustained curricular engagement. She tried to make learning fun, but she also saw learning as more than just fun. Curricular engagement is a term that implies ongoing involvement with curriculum, and differs from the commonly used phrase "on-task behavior," a concept Erickson (1982) denounces as an "asocial view of learning" (170). Although Roberta believes that learning is fun, and has a broad view of engagement that includes breaks and interruptions, she does not believe that engagement alone will guarantee sustained, high-quality work. In all learning environments, but particularly in ones that allow wide social latitude, students must have the self-discipline to persevere if learning is to become more than just a superficial experience.

Just as conditions such as happiness and sadness are not static states, neither is fun. Children become excited about learning not only because it is fun, but also "because it meets an abiding human need" (Haberman 1995, 33). Sizer (1984) feels that learning may involve stress, and that teachers may fail to push their students in order to avoid the chaos and behavior problems that inducing stress may entail. Learning cannot always be fun; it is a transaction between play and work, between inspiration and frustration, between fun and struggle. Learning is, indeed, innately satisfying, but this satisfaction is unlikely to be perceived unless the learner has consistently experienced not merely engagement, but sustained engagement.

One example of sustained engagement could be seen in Roberta's reading curriculum. Unlike many elementary reading programs in which students read stories from basal readers or anthologies and piece together bits of texts to answer comprehension questions, Roberta's reading approach focused on reading and writing for authentic purposes. Her students pondered human experience through literature, conducted research, and sent letters to newspaper editors to effect social awareness or change. Students in her class discussed literature regularly and integrated reading and writing into all their content area work.

As valuable as it is, planning "fun" curriculum is not enough to ensure sustained engagement. If curriculum is merely a grab bag of fun activities that don't promote deep, sustained engagement, it may not lead to a high level of accomplishment. Fun activities need to be accompanied by an acknowledgment that sustained engagement may entail struggle, frustration, and hard work and the assurance that, as a community of learners, others are there to help make that hard work ultimately satisfying.

Listening to Students: Learning to Feel Good About Learning

When curriculum is socially constructed, choice pervades the everyday interactions of the classroom. The theme of choice arose again and again when I asked students to comment upon Roberta's classroom. Every student, during interviews throughout the year, mentioned choice as a principal reason they became interested in a certain topic or project. Many students, for example, told me that choosing among a wide variety of literature choices made them more interested in reading.

Students frequently mentioned Conjunctions, a paragon of the curricular enactment of choice, as being a highlight of the year. When I watched the students signing up for Conjunctions sessions, I was struck not only by their excitement but also by the quality of conversations the students had as they attempted to learn more about the sessions and to decide which ones to attend. For the sign-up session, the topics seemed to be the basis of their decisions far more than who was signing up for them, and I was impressed that the constant social pressure to associate with popular peers and avoid unpopular ones was not a driving force behind the sign-up decisions.

Throughout the course of the year, every single student, without exception, mentioned that being able to fill their water mugs at will contributed, in one way or another, to a positive classroom learning environment. An excerpt of an interview with John is a case in point; interestingly, he casts the "privilege" of getting water as a "responsibility" that affects classroom climate in a positive manner:

AK: What's been the best thing about this class for you this year?

J: Nobody hates each other this time. Like last year, I had people that didn't like me very much in my class. I don't have anybody that don't like me that much in this class.

AK: Why is it different this year?

J: Because we got more responsibilities and stuff.

AK: For example, what kinds of responsibilities?

J: Like getting water in the classroom. We did have water last year, but we couldn't get out of our seat anytime we wanted to get a drink.

When discussing what prompted them to pursue in-depth research despite the distractions that socializing in the classroom could cause, they frequently mentioned that the research was fun. They claimed the classroom research was fun for two primary reasons: because the work was oriented toward activities and projects and because they were able to socialize as they worked. Ted's reflection on the class provides an example:

T: [In this classroom] we get to do fun hands-on things . . . [which] makes me more interested, which makes me want to learn more. I get to see parts of me that I never have seen before. . . . Say there are people who haven't been considered a good student. This year they might find out that they are a good student by doing all these fun things.

AK: How do you know when you've learned something, or learned something well?

T: You feel good. You feel good inside. You feel like you've learned something fun and you've achieved something . . . if you reflect on it, you'll know that feeling.

While Ted stressed fun as a primary motivation for learning, he found the satisfaction of outcomes, of having achieved something, as important, alluding to the importance of sustained engagement.

Lingering Questions

What aspects of curriculum can enhance its social nature?

What kinds of classroom procedures and rules need to be in place at the beginning of the year?

When does socializing inhibit, rather than enhance, learning?

How much responsibility should a teacher assume in terms of making learning fun and entertaining?

How can teachers ensure that praise is authentic and doesn't become too evaluative or manipulative?

What approaches best facilitate sustained engagement?

Further Reading

Inquiry Learning/Curricular Engagement/ Socially Constructed Curriculum

Allen, JoBeth, Barbara Michalove, and Betty Shockley. 1993. *Engaging Children: Community and Chaos in the Lives of Young Literacy Learners.* Portsmouth, NH: Heinemann.

Apple, Michael W. 1995. *Education and Power.* 2d ed. New York: Routledge.

Applebee, Arthur N. 1996. *Curriculum as Conversation: Transforming Traditions of Teaching and Learning.* Chicago: University of Chicago Press.

Beane, James A. 1997. *Curriculum Integration: Designing the Core of Democratic Education.* New York: Teachers College Press.

Dewey, John. [1902] 1971. *The Child and the Curriculum.* Chicago: University of Chicago Press.

Five, Cora Lee, and Marie Dionisio. 1996. *Bridging the Gap: Integrating Curriculum in Upper Elementary and Middle Schools.* Portsmouth, NH: Heinemann.

Girard, Suzanne, and Kathlene R. Willing. 1996. *Partnerships for Classroom Learning.* Portsmouth, NH: Heinemann.

Green, Anne. 1995. *Let Them Show Us the Way: Fostering Independent Learning in the Elementary Classroom.* Winnipeg, Canada: Peguis Publishers.

Levy, Steven. 1996. *Starting from Scratch: One Classroom Builds Its Own Curriculum.* Portsmouth, NH: Heinemann.

Pinar, William F., William M. Reynolds, Patrick Slattery, and Peter M. Taubman. 1995. *Understanding Curriculum: An Introduction to the Study of Historical and Contemporary Curriculum Discourses.* New York: Peter Lang Publishing.

Postman, Neil, and Charles Weingartner. 1969. *Teaching as a Subversive Activity.* New York: Dell Publishing Company.

Short, Kathy G., Jean Schroeder, Julie Laird, Gloria Kauffman, Margaret J. Ferguson, and Kathleen M. Crawford. 1996. *Learning Together Through*

Inquiry: From Columbus to Integrated Curriculum. York, ME: Stenhouse Publishers.

Whitin, Phyllis, and David J. Whitin. 1997. *Inquiry at the Window.* Portsmouth, NH: Heinemann.

Social Approaches to Discipline

Ginott, Haim G. 1972. *Teacher and Child: A Book for Parents and Teachers.* New York: Macmillan Publishing Company.

Gordon, Thomas. 1989. *Discipline that Works: Promoting Self-Discipline in Children.* New York: Plume.

Assessment

Anthony, Robert J., Terry D. Johnson, Norma I. Mickleson, and Alison Preece. 1991. *Evaluating Literacy: A Perspective for Change.* Portsmouth, NH: Heinemann.

Azwell, Tara, and Elizabeth Schmar, eds. 1995. *Report Card on Report Cards: Alternatives to Consider.* Portsmouth, NH: Heinemann.

Bridges, Lois. 1995. *Assessment: Continuous Learning.* York, ME: Stenhouse Publishers.

Graves, Donald, and Bonnie Sunstein, eds. 1992. *Portfolio Portraits.* Portsmouth, NH: Heinemann.

Hansen, Jane. 1998. *When Learners Evaluate.* Portsmouth, NH: Heinemann.

Johnston, Peter H. 1992. *Constructive Evaluation of Literate Activity.* White Plains, NY: Longman.

Martin-Kniep, Giselle O. 1998. *Why Am I Doing This? Purposeful Teaching Through Portfolio Assessment.* Portsmouth, NH: Heinemann.

Roderick, Jessie A., ed. 1991. *Context-Responsive Approaches to Assessing Children's Language.* Urbana, IL: National Council of Teachers of English.

3

Tranquility and Turbulence

The New Year

The first two weeks of January constituted a period of calm adjustment, as students settled into old routines and Ivy, beginning her ten weeks of student teaching, introduced new ones. Ivy had visited the class periodically throughout the first term and had established a good rapport with the students. Pleased with Karen's exceptional student teaching, Roberta and I hoped that Ivy would be similarly successful. We were especially looking forward to her science units, since she had a strong background in science. Right away, Ivy began teaching science lessons and took responsibility for one of the two math groups.

Science had mostly been on the back burner during the first semester, but Roberta and I felt that other subject areas had been effectively probed, particularly math and social studies. Many student projects and presentations provided evidence of growth. Although the students' intense interest in legal matters passed its zenith once their own retrial had been conducted and analyzed at the law school in December, legal perspectives still emerged during classroom discussions. Brian even organized another mock trial, this time involving the comic strip characters Calvin and Hobbes. Explorers Club research on social studies topics was in full swing, and class time devoted to the research was usually focused and productive. New Math Clubs started, and the students continued to be interested in each other's daily presentations on math problem-solving strategies.

Literacy engagements were likewise flourishing. Literature Circles were becoming lengthier and more issue oriented, over half the students were exceeding expectations concerning independent reading, and most students' writing folders and journals provided a record of a wide variety of written work. The students responded enthusiastically to a poetry unit, and poetry—discovering it, writing it, reading it aloud during group meetings, and performing it as Readers Theater—had caught on as a popular pursuit. It became so "cool" to share poetry, either discovered or self-created, that students voted to establish poetry-sharing sessions as regular, twice-weekly slots on the schedule. Students occasionally created songs, and the easels were constantly in use. An interest in playwriting was emerging as well, with students frequently writing short plays or turning literature passages into plays.

The "cool" social pursuits were not, in the eyes of the teachers, as commendable. Across the fifth grade, "going steady" (even though, for the fifth graders, this might connote merely having ongoing conversations with a member of the opposite sex for several days) had become extremely important, and the rumor mill was active. In other fifth-grade classes, rumors circulated that students, frequently with the cooperation of parents, were going on dates at the mall, and boys had reportedly sent bouquets of flowers to their girlfriends. Disputes and fights—often witnessed or perhaps even instigated by Roberta's students—were erupting on the playground as a result of alleged associations with unpopular students. In Roberta's class, Jessica, Sally, and Veronica were frequent initiators of conversations concerning who was going with whom, and more than once the accusations produced tears.

Although boy-girl intrigues had led to some hurt feelings and occupied a lot of the students' time, a strong class solidarity was slowly forming. Part of the solidarity involved complicity in secret schemes, and bathroom conspiracies with students from other fifth-grade classes had resumed. Students left out of such plans—most notably, Gerald, Andrew, Anne, Katherine, and Charles—went about their own business and, on the whole, were left alone rather than criticized or teased. Despite the students' preoccupation with social concerns, their interest in academic projects and their ability to sustain those projects were expanding.

Group meetings had gathered new force, and students were more frequently presenting their written compositions or art during this time. For the first time, students were asking others to share their work with the entire group. André surprised us by volunteering to share a poem he had written. The poem, which bleakly described a lifeless earth, disclosed an introspective, sensitive side of André. The warm reception of his poetry reading was indicative of the more active support class members were giving each other.

Students were also more able and willing to tie in learning content to personal stories. In late January, I unexpectedly found the opportunity to do the same, and the story I told spurred a spate of research. The students, while researching social studies topics selected from an earlier textbook exploration, were investigating print resources when I began conversing with Jessica and Elizabeth, who were studying slavery.

"My ancestors!" I cried, when I saw a printed reproduction of a 1769 slave auction notice from Charleston, South Carolina, that Jessica and Elizabeth were examining. Because of my grandfather's genealogical work, I recognized my ancestors' names. Although I had known they were slave owners, I was shocked to learn that they had auctioned off newly arrived "cargo" as well. As I further investigated the matter, I continued to compare notes with Jessica and Elizabeth. They were fascinated by my story and not only told others, but excitedly shared their research discoveries with me. Once again, I was struck by the manner in which personal connections and narrative can make research engaging and relevant.

Meanwhile, stories from literature began working their way into classroom events. A group of students acted out a scene from *Macbeth,* which led to a thought-provoking discussion of the term "blaspheming Jew." Several students, including Anne, were reading on their own for the first time. Roberta and I frequently sought out books on classroom topics, and students, following our cue, also began bringing in books from libraries and from home. Students' presentations on books they had read were becoming more elaborate and their formats more varied. Kirsten frequently tried to engage others in conversations about the historical fiction and fantasies that she read, and often convinced others to read the books she recommended.

By late January, a poetry frenzy was in evidence. Elizabeth frequently collaborated with other students to perform poetry for the class. Maureen shared her own version of a published poem she had almost memorized but lost. Brian and Ted wrote a parody of Poe's poem "The Raven," and their public reading of the satirical poem evoked universal applause. Billy brought two poems to a group meeting to seek help in writing titles for them. André wrote a new poem, "Hate," that struck many of us as profound. Discussions about poetry even spurred philosophical conversation topics, such as the relationship between fate and free will and whether or not humans are innately good.

During January, the social fabric of the class seemed much more tight-knit than before. I observed Patrick touching André's shoulder in a friendly manner as they collaborated on a computer project, Katherine helping a group of girls document their research, and Mei-Ling mediating an argument. Most students were freely moving in and out of dynamically shifting social groups. Disputes concerning boy-girl alliances continued, but were not pervasive.

Interruptions and Eruptions

Although the class was functioning fairly smoothly, hostility began to rumble under the surface of this harmonious hum. I became acutely aware of this discord when I observed Ivy teaching a math lesson in late January. Ivy had taken half the group to an unused classroom to conduct a lesson on fractions; her lesson focused on quizzing the students and getting them to explain the correct answer.

Signs that students were using the lesson to challenge Ivy's authority and power appeared almost immediately. As Ivy explained how whole numbers are represented as fractions and why that concept was important, there were seven rude interruptions and several silly comments. Veronica and Susan continued to say, "I don't understand" and "I don't get it" in loud, challenging tones of voice. As I watched the class climate deteriorate, I wondered if I should intervene and rescue Ivy or allow her to flounder and then help her learn from her mistakes. At that time, I did not realize the smugness of my presumption that I could automatically reinstate order. I finally decided to give Ivy complete authority by merely taking notes and reflecting with her—and, if necessary, with the disruptive students—later.

The climate went from bad to worse as I watched the students become louder and ruder. I simplistically blamed Ivy's "correct answer" approach, assuming that engaging the students in open-ended activities in small groups would have solved the problem. It didn't even occur to me at the time that such a move might merely have relegated the rudeness to small groups. Ivy continued her lengthy explanation and ignored the impudent asides that at least six students continued to make. Bert, Elizabeth, and Doug, who ordinarily treated teachers respectfully, blatantly turned their backs to Ivy and began talking loudly about television programs. Charles, in the middle of Ivy's explanation, catapulted from his seat, announced, "I'm going upstairs!" and left the room. André then began mocking Ivy's explanation of fractions. At this point, Ivy felt she could no longer ignore André's sarcastic comments.

"You wait in the hall!" she said, her voice louder than usual and audibly on edge. André ignored the command as Ivy turned around and began writing more fraction examples on the board.

As Ivy asked more questions, only Maureen, Anne, and Bert attempted to answer. The other ten students, when asked to work out the problems on paper, talked, doodled, or just sat there. Ivy asked another question about a fractions equation, and Anne volunteered an answer. Anne's answer was interrupted when André began calling Bert names.

"Didn't I tell you to wait in the hall?" shouted Ivy, exasperated.

I was feeling more and more uncomfortable. I began to examine my motives. Was my choice to merely observe really in Ivy's best interest, I wondered, or was I fascinated with what was happening, wanting to see just how far the students' resistance would go?

By this time only five minutes remained in the lesson, and Ivy wrote out a math problem that all of the students could probably solve. She looked at me and rolled her eyes.

"I thought we were gonna have time to do more of these together," she told the students.

"But we don't, so let's go!" snapped Elizabeth.

Ivy narrowed her eyes and said that there was still time to work on one more example. Again, only a few students attempted the work. Ivy feebly tried to wrap up the lesson and then dismissed the students.

I immediately made arrangements to talk with Ivy later. When we had a chance to meet, I told her I had debated about whether or not to intervene. She was very open, saying she was glad that I had let her struggle. Her reflections mirrored my thoughts that she had talked too much, and that introducing math manipulatives or drawings would have helped the situation. We also agreed that breaking the students into small groups and then speaking quietly to anyone who was rude might have prevented the defiance, or at least kept it from becoming so blatant.

All along, I felt that Ivy should have insisted upon a civil tone earlier, before the talking became truly disruptive. In the spring, when Roberta and I became unable to ensure a civil tone in class, it became clearer to me that insisting on civility does not always work. Roberta, Ivy, and I all held the view that disruption is a matter of degree, and trying to quash every mutter can be just as detrimental as allowing negative comments to proliferate. The former route allows students no authority in making responsible decisions, and the latter does not acknowledge the leadership role that the teacher must take to ensure that a safe and respectful learning environment prevails. But when does leadership become authoritarian? And what prompts students to consistently choose civil language and actions, rather than monitor their behavior only when teachers are watching?

The Politics of Poetry

Ivy's later teaching endeavors were more successful. She was soon immersed in a series of eagerly anticipated science lessons concerning static electricity and atomic structure. These lessons provided ample time for exploring student questions and for pursuing concrete tasks that helped students understand abstract concepts. By the end of the unit, science logs provided evidence, through sketches, experiment reports, and other records, that most of the students had absorbed many of the ideas that Ivy had introduced.

Poetry continued to fuel learning in the classroom. Infrequent contributors to group meetings, such as Andrew and Charles, were bringing in poems to read aloud and discuss, and more students were bringing in original poems. The poetry often elicited philosophical discussions. When Maureen read her poem about a former, better world, Patrick challenged her nostalgic tone, stating that he thought the past was no better than the present. At times such discussions about poetry became heated, and authors began privileging the interpretations of certain students, claiming those interpretations were the correct ones. On several occasions, Roberta, Ivy, and I reminded the students that poetry is subject to interpretation and that producing interpretations that accurately correspond to those of the author is ordinarily not its chief aim. Although our comments fueled some good discussions, several students continued to publicly favor the interpretations of popular students.

Sharing poetry continued to be a sought-after engagement, and students looked forward to the regular poetry-reading slots in the weekly schedule. In late January, a poetry reading during the somewhat sacrosanct What's on My Mind? discussions provoked a dispute. Billy, whose unrehearsed readings of poetry from an anthology had been less than scintillating, had written the word *poetry* on a slip of paper and put it in the What's on My Mind? box. When his name and the topic were drawn, several students began to protest, arguing that sharing poetry was not the purpose of What's on My Mind? Billy, however, ignored the comments and began slowly reading a long poem in a monotonous tone of voice.

"How long is this poem?" asked a student, whose sentiments were immediately echoed by a resounding, "Yeah, how long is it?"

Billy paused. "Five pages," he said. Objections became so vehement that Ivy, who was in charge of the class that morning, intervened.

"I think you should read only the first part," she said, explaining that What's on My Mind? time was allocated for discussing topics and issues. Billy read the first page and then said, "I'll stop here." When Billy drew the next topic slip for the session, he drew one marked "poetry," with Brian's name on it. Ivy suggested we save that for poetry time. The next topic slip that Billy drew was also marked "poetry," again submitted by Brian.

Brian then confessed that he had written the word *poetry* on several slips of paper and put them into the What's on My Mind? topic box. Since students were not supposed to submit the same topic more than once, this represented a sabotage of the What's on My Mind? procedures. Ivy reached into the box and drew out all the slips. Looking through them, she separated all the poetry slips and announced that six students had submitted more than one poetry ballot.

The students began to debate the issue of the loaded ballot box. The debate was far from over when Ivy truncated the conversation by proclaiming that poetry could no longer be submitted as a What's on My Mind? topic. She justified this by pointing out that a regular poetry sharing time had been established and that, furthermore, those who did not have the chance to read aloud during a given poetry sharing time always had the first chance to do so during the next session.

Elizabeth protested this decision angrily. A wave of similar objections buzzed through the group. Billy angrily stood up, shouted "No!" and headed for the door. Ivy asked him to sit down, yet he continued to walk toward the door until shouts of "Yeah!" from other students compelled him to turn around. Many students joined forces with the seven conspirators who were protesting Ivy's ban on poetry during What's on My Mind? time. Moments before, class opinions had been divided as to the fairness of the scheme. Now, however, the students had banded together in discontent. As tempers began to flare, Roberta returned and ended the session, deferring further discussion of the matter.

More Parent Involvement

Parents continued to visit the class periodically, and their indirect involvement was also in evidence. Henrietta, for example, had been talking with her parents about the video *Roots,* which they had watched in class, and learned that her father had known Alex Haley and had kept their correspondence. Henrietta, with her parents' help, planned an exhibit for the classroom display case, which had already been used effectively by other students in previous months. Henrietta's display, which included family letters and other items related to Haley's work, garnered many questions and conversations.

In early February, Roberta, in response to student interest generated by a presentation on Indian art during Conjunctions week, asked me if I was interested in joining forces with André's father to present our respective slides on India. She knew that I had been to India twice, and André's father had recently taken some slides during a brief research project there. I agreed, knowing that I would enjoy presenting my slides. I also wanted to be there for Dr. Lingle's visit.

Dr. Lingle sent Roberta an e-mail message indicating that he was happy to coordinate the slide show with me. He was also positive about including

Gerald's parents, who had recently given a classroom presentation on India's independence. In her reply, Roberta mentioned that André had been catching up on his work and included one of his recent poems. Dr. Lingle's response expressed appreciation of André's poetry. He noted that André was proud of his work for a change, and was becoming very motivated to write. He also mentioned that he would help André to publish his poem on the Internet, and they did eventually put it on a children's poetry website.

Around this time, Roberta learned that several parents were reading the novels that their children had chosen to read. Some of the students' book talks—brief presentations given to the rest of the class about books they had read on their own—were beginning to reflect home conversations about the books. Children were bringing in many books and artifacts related to class pursuits, and Henrietta's Alex Haley display spurred renewed interest in planning displays.

Parents were becoming more involved in their children's social lives as well. Several parents had driven their sons and daughters to the mall for dates, and Roberta and I heard that a bouquet of roses had been delivered directly to the classroom of a fifth-grade girl. At first we thought this was merely hearsay, but, when other deliveries followed, it was substantiated as fact.

Mob Vengeance

Although the class was increasingly joined in solidarity over class issues that emerged, there were signs that several individuals were on the fringes of the united front. Sometimes the majority would wage verbal attacks on individuals. One such incident occurred when Charles was presenting a large, carefully executed diorama as part of a book report.

Charles, volatile and often defensive in any sort of confrontation, was remarkably restrained during this attack. André, who more and more frequently would initiate rounds of insults in the classroom, began the affront by making a snide remark about the wooden structure in Charles' diorama, calling it an outhouse.

"It's a sawmill!" rejoined Charles, indignant in light of the fact that he had just explained the significance of the sawmill in the book. Others began snickering and criticizing the diorama.

"Why is the tree under the outhouse?" asked Patrick, continuing to bait.

Unable to contain myself any longer, I intervened, pointing out the importance of being supportive of each other's creative work. The public criticisms ceased, but I noticed some furtive whispering as Charles finished his presentation.

It seemed that Gerald, unlike Charles, was no longer being ridiculed by others, at least in public, and it had been some time since he had reported being teased at all. Although his impulsivity and distractibility still resulted in odd behavior and attention lapses, Gerald frequently focused on learning activities for long periods of time, was more socially aware, and happily contributed to many class discussions.

Overall, the class climate seemed more stable. Derogatory remarks such as the openly condescending comments about Charles' work were not the norm, and sometimes outcasts such as Patrick, Gerald, and Charles found willing partners for collaborative projects. Anne and Julie had become friends, and marginally accepted students such as Katherine and Crystal were more actively included in small-group pursuits. There had been no major incidents of defiance since Ivy's math lesson. Patrick interrupted less frequently, and André's rudeness did not follow a consistent pattern. The gossip circle among the girls seemed intermittent rather than constant.

A jarring departure from the calmness surfaced when Hope and Maureen assembled six students to act out a scene from the novel *Slave Dancer* (Fox 1991), which the entire class was reading together. Their enactment of a slave being brutally treated became excessively physical, and Ivy and I were on the verge of halting the skit when it ended. More shocking to me than the simulated kicking and beating—so realistic that it was becoming unsafe—was the class's reaction to the violence and their laughing response to the repeatedly screamed phrase "You nigger!"

The incident, I felt, merited a discussion of the effects that both the word *nigger* and the violence had on me, and why. Ivy, who was in charge while Roberta was out of the room, added to my comments and criticized the language and violence in the enactment. The students vehemently defended the language and simulation of violence, not because it conveyed the horror of the situation, but because they thought it was funny. Disturbed, I refrained from my impulse to deliver a lecture about the callousness of laughing at insults and violence. After all, I thought, doesn't half the world find great enjoyment, even humor, in those dreadful Arnold Schwarzenegger movies? Later, I felt that I had let the subject drop prematurely.

The *Slave Dancer* skit led to a student request that they be allowed to plan and perform skits from *Roots* during class time, since they had seen several episodes from the television series. Roberta agreed to the plan. These scenes engendered some unexpected collaborations. André and Patrick, for example, teamed up to dramatize the sale of slaves. Despite its undercurrent of violence, their performance attempted, in Patrick's own words, "to show that slavery is inhuman." Susan, in a gesture of inclusion, invited Gerald to narrate her skit. Elizabeth and Maureen's scene, depicting the death of the fiddler, was tongue in cheek, and prompted Ivy to again question why a serious scene was played for laughs. The continued use of the word *nigger* in four of the six skits, though contextualized, made me wonder what kinds of experiences might sensitize the students to the destructive potential of the word.

Freedom and Responsibility: Turning Points

By March, Julie's name frequently came up in my conversations with Roberta and Ivy. Her interest in class activities and discussions had surged, and for the first time she initiated, both independently and collaboratively, Internet research, art projects, and writing activities. When she noticed that Anne was lending me copies of the "dialogue poems" they had written together, Julie exclaimed, "Those are the poems I wrote with Anne!" Her unbridled enthusiasm was a welcome contrast to the apathy she had projected during the first few months of school. Julie's mother, in response to Roberta's suggestion, had recently engaged Karen to tutor Julie after school, and this was also boosting Julie's confidence.

Other students seemed to be thriving as well. Kirsten continued to rally others around learning projects, as did Maureen and Hope. Several parents reported that their children had never been happier or more motivated in school.

In early March, the students were asked to clean their crates and update their portfolios. A number of students commented on their work as they sorted through it, while others rushed to complete the job. Billy had major organizational problems, but at least he was making an effort. The only student not attempting to organize his work was André, who was staring into space as he so frequently had done earlier in the year. When I asked André if he was going to get started, Doug cheerfully offered to help him. Ten minutes later, however, I saw André indiscriminately throwing away piles of unsorted paper, not even bothering to use the recycling container.

"Are you sure you don't need any of this?" I asked, pulling some of it out of the trash can.

"No, I don't!" said André emphatically.

André raised another concern later when he ordered flowers to be delivered to a girl in another fifth-grade class. Within the next two weeks, rose deliveries became such common occurrences across the fifth-grade classes that the principal banned the delivery of flowers to students at school.

Around this time, the execution of classroom jobs provided insight into the way that the classroom community functioned. Students had established the jobs at the beginning of the year, and each job was assigned to one student for a week on a rotating basis. Many of the jobs the students had chosen were similar to those chosen in previous years, including secretary, recycling, transparency monitor, teacher's aide, mail carrier, crate checker, water monitor, and runner. Some of the new jobs reflected this group's interest in law and enforcement issues. The snack monitor, for example, was supposed to ensure that students followed the healthy snacks guidelines that, using student input, Roberta had established. When the students created this job, Roberta and I began to debate the fine line between monitoring and policing, but we never fully resolved the issue.

Students in this class neglected jobs far more than any previous class, and we wondered why they seemed less committed to group goals. Early in the year, Roberta had announced that students could occasionally delegate assigned jobs if they had a legitimate reason, such as being in the middle of helping someone or trying to meet a deadline. Sometimes students had delegated jobs out of laziness. By March, jobs were being ignored more frequently, and Roberta had to present this topic to the students during several group meetings. Even after the group unanimously renewed their commitment to the jobs, Billy neglected his job during his week as secretary, and one day defiantly said that he didn't want to tick off the end-of-day community tasks on the overhead as they were completed.

When Crystal became the secretary later in the month, her attitude was similarly defiant. On Tuesday of Crystal's week as secretary, Roberta saw her sitting and doing nothing at the end of the day. Roberta reminded her that she needed to use the overhead to facilitate the day's wrap up. Crystal looked at her blankly and said, "OK." Several minutes later, however, she was talking with someone and Roberta had to speak to her again. This time Roberta was more confrontational.

"You have a responsibility as the secretary," she said. "When I spoke to you before, you indicated you would start checking everybody off. But you haven't done that."

During the rest of the week, Crystal asked others to do her job for her. When Roberta spoke to her about it, Crystal indicated that it really "didn't matter" if someone else did her share of work. Crystal, John, Katherine, Charles, and Mei-Ling were likewise becoming increasingly apathetic about their responsibilities, and, with several exceptions, there was a widespread lack of pride in the performance of class jobs. The smooth functioning of the class did not seem to be a priority for the group. As March wore on, it seemed even less important than before, and the test set bins, the storage crates, and the reading corner were frequently left in a state of disorder. Class resolutions to remedy the situation turned out to be short lived.

The Role of Humor

As with most groups of people, humor can play an important role in facilitating a cohesive community. This class demonstrated a good sense of humor, but by mid-March the teachers began to distinguish between a wholesome humor based on a shared sense of play, incongruity, or absurdity and a more prevalent form of humor based on derision.

An example of levity resulting from genuine playfulness occurred during a discussion of interesting words from *Slave Dancer.* The students were seated close together on the carpet, a configuration that usually encouraged participation. *Tarantella* was cited as an interesting word. Looking for context cues, a student located the passage and read aloud the sentence: "She decided to dance the tarantella."

"Well, it must have been some kind of dance," someone speculated, "but what kind?" As an answer to the question, spontaneous singing and dancing movements broke out among the students, and hearty laughter filled the room. A sense of community spirit reverberated, and the conversation about vocabulary resumed with renewed vigor.

Delight in storytelling or oral reading would often induce laughter as well. When Ivy read *The True Story of the Three Little Pigs* (Scieszka 1989) aloud as an example of a parody, it inspired chuckles along with several enthusiastic responses. "I love that book!" exclaimed one student during a wave of cheerful laughter.

At other times, however, the humor involved victimization. For example, later the same day, Sally looked around to ensure that others were within listening range and then loudly told Julie, "You have stinky breath." This caused a few students to laugh, but Julie, at last more assertive, looked at me and said, "She's rude."

During the unit on stocks, there were many genuinely humorous moments. Learning to understand accounting and principles of economics by making mock investments in stocks, the students sometimes asked preposterous questions or made up jokes about each other's companies. During the verbal interactions that I happened to observe, the fine line between cajoling and merciless teasing was maintained. But I was unsure whether or not the teasing was vicious when I was not around.

Simmering Issues

In the classroom, there was a constant fluctuation between purposeful learning and halfhearted or discarded pursuits. Roberta felt that the shallow or aborted projects often constituted experimentation, a healthy way to "play around" with ideas without committing to predetermined outcomes. In some ways, the inadequately answered or unanswered questions could be likened to an author's scribblings—some turn into important literary endeavors, while others remain dormant or forgotten. Nevertheless, Roberta and I often felt frustrated that perhaps there were too many loose ends, too many projects that weren't sufficiently investigated or completed.

Invitations, twice-weekly sessions during which students could choose between a variety of open-ended activities without the pressure of predetermined outcomes, had, in previous years, given rise to far more ongoing research projects. This was partly because Roberta had not adhered to the Invitations schedule as religiously during this school year; other agenda items sometimes preempted the Invitations slot. In early March, Roberta tried to make up for lost time by planning two lengthy Invitations sessions centered around a Beethoven piano composition. Roberta introduced the first session by reading the picture book *Rondo in C* (Fleischman 1988) while students listened to the piece and followed along with the sheet music. This was followed by a discussion, as well as art and dance activities.

The group's reaction to the first *Rondo in C* Invitations session revealed that many of the students were unable or unwilling to articulate a goal or purpose for their pursuits during Invitations. In addition, the students expressed little interest in what others did during the sessions. None of the small groups tied their Invitations projects to the *Rondo in C* theme that framed it. Boys at a Legos table, for example, began working on constructions related to their previous interest in battles and wars. When asked to talk about what he had done during the afternoon Legos session, Andrew said, "I have no idea what I'm building; I'm just building." Billy's Legos project was intended to show "King Arthur and the Crusades." At another table, Mei-Ling, who spent most of the session chatting, later justified her lack of engagement by saying, "I didn't know what to do."

The children were given a chance to connect their activities with the music during a second *Rondo in C* Invitations session, but, again, the results seemed superficial. Several students began the session angry that they hadn't gotten their "first choice" activity, and André was stridently vocal about his dissatisfaction. When informally interviewed afterwards, students used the words *fun* and *boring* more than other descriptors, indicating that the content of the learning was not foremost in their minds.

Squabbles during the session showed that the students still had far to go in learning how to amicably share materials. There were several quarrels involving who had used the most clay, and I was asked to mediate in a dispute involving Gerald. Gerald had torn off slightly more clay than the others, and probably would have relinquished some if the matter had been addressed in a civil manner. But by the time I was asked to settle the argument, the group had singled out Gerald and had resorted to threats, demanding he give each of them part of his clay. There seemed to be a distorted view of what "equal shares" might mean in this case.

Student reactions to the outcomes of both Invitations sessions tended to be either indifferent or inimical. When Elizabeth presented the painting she'd completed, Patrick blurted out, "Did someone spill the paint?" before she could even talk about what she had done. Although the immediate objection of several students (I heard one voice saying, "That's an insult") may have constituted an attempt to preserve civility in the classroom community, it may also have been merely another excuse to jump on Patrick, especially since a subsequent insult delivered by Billy—"The painting's in some Elizabeth code; only Elizabeth can understand it"—went unchallenged.

The rude inattention to others' presentations we observed at the end of Invitations sessions began to occur during What's on My Mind? sessions. In addition, the discussions were occasionally derailed by unflattering personal comments about other students despite Roberta's objections to such remarks. One such instance provided insight into the group's strategies for settling disputes. When the general topic of sports became a controversial discussion about gender discrimination during basketball games in the P.E. class, a variety of strategies were employed. Elizabeth set off the dispute by complaining about gender-separate teams, which, in turn, led to Billy's complaint that girls "ruined" co-ed games. Billy's remark engendered a range of reactions, from insults fulminated by indignant girls to an astute examination of the issue. Constructive attempts to find a solution—suggestions as to how teams could be divided, Maureen's suggestion that they take the concern to the Student Council, Ben's suggestion that boys actively attempt to pass the ball to girls more during future games—alternated between personal attacks. Charles aggressively demanded that others "shut up" and Brian contended that Hope's attitude was the basis of the problem, provoking Roberta to remind the class that civility must prevail. Seymour, a business student who had been helping out with the previous stock market lesson, then commented that he once had to take aerobics and ballroom dancing and that "guys having to do aerobics and ballroom dancing gave girls a chance to excel." Choosing not to criticize the guest while he was there, Roberta later noted that a belief that girls would automatically perform better in these activities and wouldn't excel in others was a sexist assumption.

Sexism was becoming a frequent topic of discussion among the students. During a guest presentation in which a critical reading of Caldecott award books was encouraged, both regular discussion participants such as Patrick and quieter students such as Crystal identified the sexist aspects of some of the illustrations. The students were less adept, however, at spotting racist implications. Group work, during which students prepared more in-depth analysis of a particular book, yielded excellent mini-presentations that helped students notice racist aspects of some of the picture books.

At this point in the school year, students were able, at least some of the time, to elicit and examine issues from a variety of perspectives. Disruptions flared but faded quickly, probably because rude attempts to suppress individual voices were truncated or criticized by other students.

Leaders with a Vision: *Star Boars*

Throughout March, "What's on My Mind?" sessions continued to invite controversial debates, and personal attacks became more common. In late March, however, a topic was brought to a "What's on My Mind?" session that sparked universal interest and agreement.

Ted introduced his topic, "class play," by explaining that he and Brian had written a spoof on *Star Wars* called *Star Boars.* They were hoping that the entire class would be able to perform *Star Boars.* At least a dozen hands popped above the circle of seated students as questions concerning the play were brought to the discussion.

Maureen, perhaps having a premonition about what would transpire in later weeks, asked, "Is this going to be something totally out of control, or crazy?"

"No," was Ted's immediate answer. "We're going to keep it under control." Already Ted and Brian had assumed that the play would be produced and that they would direct it. Their confidence was not ill founded. Although it was put on hold for a short while, Roberta and Ivy eventually allowed the play to work its way into the class schedule, and Ted and Brian were allowed to direct it.

Bartlett Camp

The end of March was characterized by many special events. The collaborative presentation on India went extremely well. Dr. Lingle, Ms. Katz, and I enjoyed conducting the session together, and the students' attention didn't waver during our two-hour presentation. The stock market cycle was coming to an end and the Science Fair was extremely successful. Ivy conducted a workshop on test-taking, the first of several that she and Roberta had planned to conduct in preparation for the standardized tests, scheduled for April. Meanwhile, the students continued to be absorbed in their Focus Study research, based on topics from the social studies textbook.

As April approached, numerous questions arose concerning the trip to Bartlett Forest. For many students, this would be their first overnight stay away from home, and for most of them the first time to spend five full days away from home. Bartlett Camp, a statewide educational program that has been conducted for decades, takes place in a wilderness area about twenty-five miles from Robinson Elementary. Fifth-grade classes from all over the state are invited to experience a week of outdoor educational activities in the vast Bartlett Forest State Park, staying in cabins built for this year-round program. In this case, all four fifth-grade classrooms from Robinson would depart for Bartlett Forest early Monday morning and return Friday afternoon.

With the exception of Andrew, whose homesickness persisted throughout the week, the students from Roberta's class seemed happier than I'd ever seen them. New alliances began forming right away, both between members of Roberta's class and across the classes, since students from two Robinson classrooms were housed together and grouped heterogeneously throughout the day. Paid educational leaders, permanent staff members, and high school volunteers joined the teachers in a supervisory role.

As anticipated, the dynamics of such a program brought out the best in many of the children and stimulated new waves of inquiry. Some activities corresponded directly to classroom activities. Bird-watching sparked tremendous interest, since Roberta's students had received their grant money and had already begun setting up the bird-feeding station back at Robinson. A Conjunctions session in the fall on surviving in the wild had given Roberta's students a good background for several activities, including the "edible plants" excursion. There had also been some preparation for two of the most popular activities: observing the Hale-Bopp comet and playing "carnivore, omnivore, herbivore," a cross between a scavenger hunt and tag, in which students searched the woods for signs of food and water while on the lookout for classmate "predators."

A communal sense of adventure pervaded the group excursions that I joined on Wednesday and Thursday. During these hikes, I also observed new gender banter, such as girls planning "chance" encounters with boys and boys talking about which of them were "bachelors." When I overheard Kirsten telling Roberta her concerns about leaving her diary in the cabin, I asked her what the worst-case scenario would be if her diary entries were read by someone else.

"Rumors," Kirsten intonated in a deadly serious voice, seeming surprised that I hadn't realized the gravity of rumors. I had already heard the word being bandied about back in the classroom, often accompanied by widespread whispering. Fortunately, judging from student interviews, the rumor mill had not been as dominant at Bartlett Camp as it had been back at Robinson. Students seemed preoccupied with the natural wonders around them. The sighting of a magnificent bald eagle in flight over the lake yielded oohs and aahs, then a hushed silence. The discovery of a "living shell," as Crystal described it, generated excitement, as did the telltale signs of a raccoon: a large half-eaten fish and nearby animal tracks, spotted by Bert.

Inclusion issues became salient throughout the week. Gerald, Charles, and Patrick, victims of exclusion since the beginning of the school year, were being accepted as pair or group partners at Bartlett Camp. I did observe several girls, however, rejecting others. Sally, for instance, refused to be Kirsten's partner during the pairing off for the all-day hike. Kirsten handled Sally's rejection quite well, and I recalled the positive influence she had exerted earlier in the school year. She suggested either rearranging previously chosen partners or a temporary partnership with Sally until they could resolve their differences. As Kirsten and Sally discussed the situation, they agreed to be partners under certain conditions.

Kirsten also provided leadership by furiously writing her thoughts in her journal throughout the hike. It was probably her example that prompted several others to record their thoughts later in the day. At one point, I asked her why she was writing so much.

"I write to think," was her response. "I could tell the thoughts, but the journal understands, and people don't always understand."

During the collaborative shelter-building activity at midday, I noticed that no students stepped forward to organize the group to which I was assigned. Although several students made building suggestions, none were acted on for more than ten minutes. This passivity nearly prevented the group from completing a shelter within the time limit. To ensure successful completion of the activity, I felt compelled to paraphrase the best suggestions and help students delegate tasks. I found the lack of leadership discouraging, and was also disturbed by a group decision to "give up" before the time limit was up. I insisted that the group persevere, and doubled my efforts to gather branches for the shelter. In the other group, the leadership of Sally, Patrick, Kirsten, Doug, and Brian helped produce a splendid shelter that was conceptually sound. My own group's slapdash structure, in contrast, was lopsided and hazardous.

After many miles of hiking, the students were exhausted. Sally insisted that Crystal could make it, and then urged on other stragglers. The hike ended on an extremely happy note, with many of the students rushing to the cabins to recount the day's events to friends.

On Thursday night, each student presented a skit related to a camp experience. Featured performers constituted a "who's who" of the fifth grade, since the popular leaders all had major roles. Many of the skits involved parodies of teachers and counselors; others involved jokes concerning dining room rituals and camp food. The zooming energy as the kids ran to and fro, the intense last-minute rehearsals, the students' delighted screams of laughter during the performances, and the conversations about the skits that lasted well into the night provided evidence that, for many, the performances were a highlight of the week.

❖

Stepping Back: Creativity and Aesthetic Experience

The arts, as communication systems, are fundamental to learning and are avenues to higher-level thinking as much as the "three Rs." They "allow us to step back and see more clearly the world around us" (Graves 1999, 77). Aesthetic expression can stimulate thinking and can nurture what John Dewey (1938) calls a "heightened intelligibility." This intelligibility is within all of us, as Viola Spolin (1983) indicates when she writes: "We must reconsider what is meant by 'talent.' It is highly possible that what is called talented behavior is simply a greater individual capacity for experiencing. . . . This means involvement on all levels: intellectual, physical, and intuitive" (3). Most classrooms downplay the imaginative speculation and experimentation that help synthesize these three modes. Roberta, however, tried to saturate her students in "hands on" activities that could simultaneously engage their analytical thinking and their imagination. She realized that without authentic catalysts for the imagination—animal bones, symphony performances, unfamiliar dialects, dramatic enactments of pain and struggle—the aesthetic experience of the classroom may be confined to coloring within the lines of a ditto or cutting out paper turkeys. The latter activities emphasize product over process. They do not allow students to brainstorm ideas, create without fear of censure, and then seek critical response to their work before refining and presenting it.

An emphasis on product over process fuels competition and may deny many students the opportunity of sustained aesthetic experience. Only those who are selected for the school play, for example, are allowed to experience drama, and only those lucky enough to have parental support learn to play a musical instrument. Students often must demonstrate previously developed talent in order to join the choir, if indeed there is one. Special arts programs usually require uniforms, trip fees, supplies, or special transportation arrangements that some families are unwilling or unable to provide. As testing increasingly drives curriculum, school budgets for field trips, outdoor education, artists-in-residence, guest performers, and other aesthetic experiences are diverted elsewhere, particularly in schools where average student test scores are low. The arts, in cases like these, are not equally available to everyone.

Roberta was highly committed to a process orientation to the arts. Like Spolin, Roberta realized that students cannot become literate in different sign systems such as art, music, and drama without actually being immersed in them. As a result, aesthetic experience in Roberta's classroom took on a variety of forms.

1. Roberta encouraged art, poetry, music, drama, and other creative forms of communication. She valued both the receptive and generative aspects of the arts. She knew that exposure to the arts is essential, but is not enough to vitalize them; they must be experienced. Through their immersion in the arts, Roberta's students learned to balance observing and creating, critiquing others and being critiqued. Both the regularly scheduled poetry sessions and the spontaneous art-sharing sessions allowed children to either critique or merely appreciate each other's creative work. Throughout the year, the easel was always occupied during free time, and students enjoyed making suggestions to painters at the easel and complimenting finished artwork.

As Roberta's class began to eagerly seek curricular enactments of poetry, art, and playwriting, and as the sharing of creative efforts became a regular feature of the class, the potential of the arts became more apparent. The fact that poetry was important enough to generate passionate discussions and arguments was evidence that the students saw poetry as "an instrument for embodied experience" (Rich 1993, 13). Poetry had become both social and vital, something the students wanted to experience on a regular basis. Drama likewise was unleashing its power. The students' passionate enactments of literature, their excitement about *Star Boars,* and the solidarity fostered by the camp skits all show the potential of the arts to unite diverse members of a community. As novels became skits, as music became art, and as parody became performance, the students more actively shifted from one sign system to another. They explored visual and performing arts as means of communication. And through sharing their creative efforts, the students developed a stronger sense of community.

2. Roberta actively demonstrated her own interest in the arts. From the beginning of the school year, she constantly used picture books in the class, and paid close attention to illustrations. By examining the illustrations and eliciting interpretation, she drew students' attention to messages the art conveyed. Throughout the year, classroom topics would often remind her of a picture book, and she regularly shared new "finds" with the class. By spring, many students were also discovering picture books and volunteering to read them aloud to the class. They, too, looked for meaning in the artwork and discussed it among themselves. Art and music (and sometimes dance) were important dimensions of Roberta's Invitations sessions, and the way that she enjoyed making stuffed animals, creating beads from paper, or dancing to Beethoven with the students helped them appreciate the communicative potential of the arts as well.

Roberta also created teachable moments by sharing her immediate response to the visual and performing arts whenever possible. She demonstrated and nurtured the urgency of aesthetic expression. She didn't hesitate, for example, to express a "gut reaction" to a drawing that she was either creating or seeing. She knew that sudden roadblocks or spontaneous insights cannot be "put on hold," but seek immediate response or affirmation. When art, music, and other sign systems are relegated to weekly lessons at best, and when all learning is carefully sequenced and prescribed, the opportunity to respond to the urgency of aesthetic experience may be stifled. By attempting to immerse herself in both creating and reacting to the arts, Roberta conveyed their immediacy and importance.

3. Roberta utilized class meetings to publicly appreciate and critique the creative work of students. As student interest in art and drama came to the forefront during the year, she sought out the creative work of all students, but especially those whose status in the class was marginal at best. She pointed out Andrew's Lego creations, Anne's poetry, and Julie's crafts during class meetings and encouraged classmates to interpret these creative endeavors. She drew a distinction between celebrating a finished work of art and critiquing a work in progress in order to abet revision. Both when admiring and when critiquing, a unique sort of solidarity often emanated from Roberta and her students. Students supported each other most visibly when they were sharing something aesthetic, despite exceptions such as the barbs hurled at Charles when he presented his diorama. By April, Roberta's students were not just interested in artistic expression; they were gravitating toward it and pursuing it daily.

4. Because Roberta devoted less time to music than she did to other sign systems, its communication potential in the class remained less developed. As Blackburn (1998) reminds us, "people not only learn music but learn *through* music" (164, emphasis in original). In Roberta's 1994–95 class, a genuine interest in music prevailed and she devoted much more time to musical endeavors. Those students responded so favorably that, when the departure of one member of the class was imminent in December, the students secretly organized a musical performance as part of a surprise good-bye party. Her 1996–97 class, however, did not have the same background and interest in music, so she pursued it less avidly.

Music was not completely neglected in Roberta's 1996–97 class, however. Roberta occasionally played and discussed music. The *Rondo in C* Invitations led to other music sessions, and the music composed during my songwriting session helped spark later songwriting alliances. Music would reinforce solidarity again when *Star Boars* became an important class project, at one point even becoming a symbol of resistance.

5. Roberta touched upon, but failed to adequately explore, the aesthetic aspect of math. When the school year began, a majority of the students claimed that they disliked math. By January, however, most of them expressed interest in math, voluntarily shared ideas during math activities, enjoyed presenting math stumper solutions, and were developing number sense. The incident with Ivy, however, revealed some residual resistance. Although a variety of factors, from peer pressure to act flippant to the lack of functional outcomes in the lesson, may have fueled their refusal to take the lesson seriously, it is possible that the resistance would not have been so strong if the students had been able to draw or construct conceptual representations. Concrete applications help us perceive math as potentially expressive.

Mathematical ideas have many aesthetic components, from the spiral Fibonacci pattern of pineapple eyes to the geometric aspects of M. C. Escher's tessellations. Math teachers can awaken this aesthetic component of math more often if they address student questions, explore concepts with manipulatives, encourage graphic representation of ideas, and pursue mathematical projects directed at goals other than learning math, such as understanding perspective in art or using architectural principles to plan constructions. Adolescents are often denied the opportunity to apply math in art, architecture, music, and science, and the inherent beauty of mathematical patterns thus remains invisible. Although Roberta's students did communicate their understandings of word problems and tile teasers on a daily basis, Roberta made only a slim connection between math concepts and aesthetic experience, which may have limited the potential of these activities.

6. Roberta, with Ivy's help, pursued an aesthetic exploration of movement, albeit to a limited extent. At the end of the year, a number of Roberta's students, both during interviews and in written comments, referred to her interest in exercise and healthy foods as something they admired about her. The class also talked fondly of the exercise sessions that Ivy frequently led during the ten minutes between specials and lunch. During these sessions, the class was remarkably harmonious and there was a strong sense of shared purpose.

Aesthetic appreciation merges with the health benefits of exercise in athletic disciplines such as dance, yoga, ice-skating, swimming, and gymnastics. Other sports also can be viewed aesthetically. According to interviews with students, skateboarding was avidly pursued by many outside of school, and several talked about how "cool" it looked. School sports, on the other hand, tend to stress competition. Thus, the freedom to explore kinesthetics without the fear of criticism is frequently curtailed. Students who are perceived as weak in particular sports are eschewed or excluded, just as Roberta's girls were shunned during basketball games.

If sports and outdoor activities are pursued without the constraints of winning and losing, their aesthetic qualities can more easily be appreciated. Helen Keller (1955) vividly described the joy and satisfaction of collaborative, noncompetitive exercise, such as riding a tandem and swimming in ponds. Keller, writing about rowing boats with her teacher, Annie Sullivan, felt that Sullivan nurtured a "capacity for rippling delight, gladness and responsiveness to the enchantment of the apple blossoms in spring or the serenity of hay-sweet summer evenings" (93). Such a convergence of an aesthetic appreciation of nature and physical exercise for its own sake, free of competition, is sorely lacking in schools. Roberta and Ivy, however, tried to promote such an appreciation, particularly during the Bartlett Camp trip.

7. Roberta explored aesthetic dimensions of science through nature study. During my first visits to Roberta's class in January 1993, her students were observing class pets, planning magnet experiments, and making paper boats. One group was even wondering about the physics of endlessly reflecting mirrors. This was a refreshing departure from what I call the Teddy Bear Syndrome, symbolized by a proliferation of prefabricated bulletin boards, stuffed animals, and reward stickers in the classroom. The Teddy Bear Syndrome afflicts teachers who falsely assume that commercial trappings are more consistent with a child's imagination than the wonders of the physical world around them. Dewey (1925) similarly criticized the "belief that the imagination is some special part of the child that finds its satisfaction in some one particular direction—generally speaking, that of the myth and made-up story" (61). Science, according to Dewey, can awaken a child's imagination as vividly as fiction, and can also promote enriched and orderly experience. "When nature and society can live in the classroom," writes Dewey ([1915] 1971) ". . . culture shall be the democratic password" (62). His belief has direct bearing upon the relationship between engagement and discipline, as a child who is absorbed in the creative aspects of scientific investigation is less likely to be rude or unruly.

Nature study evokes wonder, and wonder evokes questions. Goldberg (1970/1997) thinks that finding interesting questions is "the single most imaginative and demanding step in scientific investigation" (62). Students whose learning is always guided by teacher questions intended to elicit correct answers may not be easily disposed to ask authentic scientific questions. Unfortunately, natural science is often taught in a textbook void, reduced to getting the right answers to comprehension questions at the end of a chapter.

The leaf study excursion in the fall, the bird observation station, and the Bartlett Camp trip all provided Roberta's students with opportunities to experience nature directly and to sharpen their powers of observation. Because of the leaf study trip, Roberta's students were favorably inclined to pursue follow-up activities in the spring. The grant proposal for the bird-feeding station entailed research into bird habitats and diet, and the students' ongoing research, once the observation station was set up, led to a communal sense of discovery and shared knowledge. During the Bartlett Camp trip, essential aspects of scientific thinking, such as observing, sharing observations, and exploring the tension between "common sense" and "uncommon sense" reasoning (Osborne 1995) were very much in evidence. The "predator game" hunt for water sources, the search for edible plants, and the lookout for animal tracks each called observation and critical analysis into play. Such activities nurtured an aesthetic appreciation of nature and awakened students' imagination within the context of immediate sensory experience. The students did not need contrived bulletin boards and video games to stimulate their imagination; the natural world of Bartlett Forest spurred stories, journal reflections, drawings, songs, and many other creative outcomes. Furthermore, the beauty of science became more evident to many of the children as these concrete experiences helped them explore abstract concepts. When Roberta's students were immersed in nature study, their understanding of the natural world was grounded in experience, inquiry, and the interrogation of assumptions. During such experiences, their learning flourished and a sense of community and shared purpose prevailed.

Goldberg convincingly shows that "the artistic and scientific [vision] are both rooted in the imagination" (1970/1997, 97). He feels that the neglect of aesthetic experience in science education "is the logical consequence of the conception of artistic experience as peripheral to life and of scientific activity as the exercise of skills" (92). That the aesthetic aspect of nature study can lead to important research is confirmed by the recent finding that retinoids in lake water may cause deformities in frogs (Glass 1998). This discovery began as a nature study activity conducted by elementary schoolchildren in Minnesota. When these children found approximately two hundred frogs with multiple, missing, or twisted legs, they initiated an inquiry that spread to other locales. Their questions eventually led to the discovery that frogs in dozens of U.S. lakes may develop deformities as a result of exposure to retinoids, found in pesticides as well as in natural compounds.

A similar process of discovery was in evidence at Bartlett Camp when Bert found the partly eaten fish. At first, the students were fascinated by the physical appearance of the fish. Then they began wondering why the fish was so far from the lake. When they noticed that the missing head had been ripped off, they began hunting for animal tracks. When Bert found raccoon tracks, they were able to confirm that a raccoon had carried the fish to that location. They began speculating on why the raccoon had not eaten the whole fish: Had he been scared off by our arrival, perhaps? The students raised other questions and began searching for evidence to provide the answers. This is an example of how the simple, aesthetic observation of a fish, thrilling in its grisly reality, became a scientific investigation.

Listening to Students: Imagining Possibilities

When interviewing students at the end of the year, I asked them what was significant about the school year. Almost all of the students cited creative experiences such as poetry sharing, Invitations sessions, and the *Star Boars* play as being extremely important. Anne, for example, mentioned that this was the first time she'd ever acted in a play or learned to write songs. Ben, answering the same question, mentioned the creative aspect of creating math problems: "I love the math stumpers. I really like those. That's my favorite thing in math. I can always come up with some kind of funny story in my explanation of the math stumper so it's not just a boring thing." Patrick thought math was important, too, and linked classroom math to his aspirations to be an architect:

> Well, fantasy baseball, I really liked that. I didn't ever think about doing something like that, like keeping track of baseball. I usually just look at scores, how many runs my favorite players got and that's about it. But now I look at other things that they're doing. I was thinking about the Architect Club, because I wanted to be an architect and I want to know more about how you have to be one. I think that's really going to help me because I really want to be one when I grow up, and this made me want to be one more.

Many students also mentioned the Bartlett Camp experience as important. For these students, Bartlett Camp made them appreciate nature in a totally new way. Several students became concerned about environmental protection as a result of their week of outdoor education and wrote letters to environmental organizations.

Several students indicated the chance to "play" with science materials was important. When asked how Roberta encouraged understanding of the science process, Doug described her approach as follows:

> One of the ways is that Ms. Taylor will break us into groups and then let us [explore the materials] the way we want to. That's pretty much why half the

class didn't get the light bulbs to light up at the beginning. She told us to figure out how to light up the light bulb and she gave us certain supplies. And everyone tried to do it a different way. And only three of them worked. So it's better to have more ideas to use, because then if one's wrong, you've got another theory.

This is a perfect example of how brainstorming inquiry questions, experimenting, and ongoing conversations about significance permeated Roberta's approach to science, as well as her approach to the arts.

One student interview made me realize that even limited exposure to an art form can have a significant impact on children. When I interviewed Doug at the end of the school year, he revealed that exposure to music in Roberta's class had inspired him to study a musical instrument:

D: When you do fun stuff, it sort of gets you interested, and you'll do other stuff.

AK: Can you think of an example?

D: I got interested in music, and so [now] I play the string bass. And I enjoy it because it's fun. And I learn more when I'm having fun and still doing the work. Like, my room gets clean a lot faster when I, like, put a game into it.

AK: So you studied string bass before and this expanded your interest, or your school experience with music this year made you study it?

D: My experience with music made me study it.

AK: Oh. So you didn't play before this year?

D: No.

Doug's initiative to study the bass as a result of musical experiences in Roberta's class serves as a reminder that many valuable outcomes of classroom learning are not obvious. By studying the bass, Doug extended his aesthetic experience beyond Roberta's classroom.

Lingering Questions

Why are the visual and performing arts so undervalued in education?

How can the need for more arts instruction be more widely recognized and supported?

What are the similarities and differences between sign systems, such as math, music, and dance?

What is the relationship between survival needs (health, safety, home, etc.) and the need for creative expression?

How can the aesthetic aspects of math and science enhance learning?

How can the arts be utilized to resolve conflict in the classroom?

Further Reading

Teaching the Visual and Performing Arts

Blackburn, Lois. 1998. *Whole Music: A Whole Language Approach to Teaching Music.* Portsmouth, NH: Heinemann.

Dewey, John. [1931] 1980. *Art as Experience.* New York: Perigee Books.

Graves, Donald. 1999. *Bring Life into Learning: Create a Lasting Literacy.* Portsmouth, NH: Heinemann.

Heathcote, Dorothy, and Gavin Bolton. 1995. *Drama for Learning: Dorothy Heathcote's Mantle of the Expert Approach to Education.* Portsmouth, NH: Heinemann.

Heller, Paul G. 1995. *Drama as a Way of Knowing.* York, ME: Stenhouse Publishers.

Hubbard, Ruth S., and Karen Ernst, eds. 1996. *New Entries: Learning by Writing and Drawing.* Portsmouth, NH: Heinemann.

Maley, Alan, and Alan Duff. 1982. *Drama Techniques in Language Learning: A Resource Book of Communication Activities for Language Teachers.* 2d ed. Cambridge, England: Cambridge University Press.

Page, Nick. 1995. *Music as a Way of Knowing.* York, ME: Stenhouse Publishers.

Rohd, Michael. 1998. *Theater for Community, Conflict, and Dialogue.* Portsmouth, NH: Heinemann.

Saldaña, Johnny. 1995. *Drama of Color: Improvisation with Multiethnic Folklore.* Portsmouth, NH: Heinemann.

Spolin, Viola. 1983. *Improvisation for the Theater: A Handbook of Teaching and Directing Techniques.* Evanston, IL: Northwestern University Press.

Spruce, Gary, ed. 1996. *Teaching Music.* London: Routledge.

Upitis, Rena. 1990. *This Too Is Music.* Portsmouth, NH: Heinemann.

Zakkai, Jennifer. 1997. *Dance as a Way of Knowing.* York, ME: Stenhouse Publishers.

Math and Science Education

Adams, Dennis, and Mary Hamm. 1998. *Collaborative Inquiry in Science, Math, and Technology.* Portsmouth, NH: Heinemann.

Atkinson, Sue, and Marilyn Fleer, eds. 1995. *Science with Reason.* Portsmouth, NH: Heinemann.

Carletti, Silvana, Suzanne Girard, and Kathlene R. Willing. 1993. *Sign Out Science: Simple Hands-on Experiments Using Everyday Materials.* Markham, Ontario: Pembroke Publishers.

Chancer, Joni, and Gina Rester-Zodrow. 1997. *Moon Journals: Writing, Art, and Inquiry Through Focused Nature Study.* Portsmouth, NH: Heinemann.

Cornell, Joseph. 1979. *Sharing Nature with Children.* Nevada City, CA: Dawn Publications.

Cromer, Alan. 1993. *Uncommon Sense: The Heretical Nature of Science.* Oxford, England: Oxford University Press.

Goldberg, Lazer. 1970/1997. *Teaching Science to Children.* Mineola, NY: Dover Publications.

Grant, Janet E. 1990. *The Kids' Green Plan: How to Write Your Own Plan to Save the Environment.* Markham, Ontario: Pembroke Publishers.

Lake, Jo-Anne. 1993. *Imagine: A Literature-Based Approach to Science.* Markham, Ontario: Pembroke Publishers.

Ohanian, Susan. 1995. *Math as a Way of Knowing.* York, ME: Stenhouse Publishers.

Ohanian, Susan. 1995. *Math at a Glance: A Month-by-Month Celebration of the Numbers Around Us.* Portsmouth, NH: Heinemann.

Ostrow, Jill. 1998. *Making Problems, Creating Solutions.* York, ME: Stenhouse Publishers.

Reddy, Maureen, Patty Jacobs, Caryn McCrohon, and Leslie R. Herrenkohl. 1998. *Creating Scientific Communities in the Elementary Classroom.* Portsmouth, NH: Heinemann.

Roseberry, Ann S., and Beth Warren. 1998. *Boats, Balloons, and Classroom Video: Science Teaching as Inquiry.* Portsmouth, NH: Heinemann.

Whitin, Phyllis, and David J. Whitin. 1997. *Inquiry at the Window.* Portsmouth, NH: Heinemann.

Williams, Doug. 1995. *Teaching Mathematics Through Children's Art.* Portsmouth, NH: Heinemann.

Zaslavsky, Claudia. 1995. *The Multicultural Math Classroom: Bringing in the World.* Portsmouth, NH: Heinemann.

4

Taking the Law into Their Own Hands

The Launching of *Star Boars*

During the two weeks that followed the Bartlett Camp trip, students repeatedly requested class time to rehearse *Star Boars.* Standardized testing and several other prearranged activities that couldn't be rescheduled left little time for play rehearsals in mid-April, but Roberta did schedule a few rehearsals and helped the students prepare for them. Ted and Brian had photocopied the script and distributed copies to everyone in the class, and the rehearsals were fairly orderly even though the classroom area set aside as the rehearsal stage was too small, creating both congestion and confusion. Kirsten was taking on a greater leadership role, and Brian and Ted appointed her to be the "stage manager." This three-person coalition had taken responsibility for the planning and direction of rehearsals. The children were intensely involved in each rehearsal, closely observing and responding to many details of the production.

None of the teachers had realized that exclusion from the play was becoming a problem until April 23. That day, Brian announced that he was seeking a volunteer to play a new character that had been written into the play. Although John was one of several students who already had dual roles, he volunteered and was chosen on the spot, without an audition.

"Why does John get the part?" asked one of the students crowded around the stage.

"His hand was up first," answered Brian.

Then Gerald asked a question, his voice ringing out loudly and clearly. "Does everybody have a part?"

Not realizing that it was a rhetorical question, I was the first to answer.

"I think so," I said. "Don't they?"

Gerald answered his own question and mine.

"Not me," he said. "I don't have a part. I don't want a part."

This surprised me, because Gerald had vocally supported production of the class play from the beginning, and he had been very excited about earlier rehearsals. Wanting to get to the bottom of this, I first set out to determine whether anyone beside Gerald was not in the play. I walked around, asking each student about his or her role in the play. It turned out that Jessica was the only other student not acting in the play. She did, however, have a non-acting role.

Many events consumed the following days. Students were working on their final Explorers Club research projects. All fifth-grade classes were participating in a math project that involved simulating the operation of a small business. The project would culminate in a field trip, during which students would use token money to actually purchase items from each other. Invitations were still being offered twice a week, and the students always looked forward to the open-ended arts, crafts, music, and science activities.

As Ivy's ten weeks of student teaching drew to a close, Roberta began planning a good-bye party for her. After school one day, as she told me about the party, she realized that she had not slotted time for a play rehearsal during the coming week. We began to talk about *Star Boars,* which led us to discuss the ramifications of Gerald's exclusion from the play. Roberta wanted to get more facts from Gerald before taking further action. We then talked about some of the cliques that had formed and expressed concern about the way that Gerald and several other students were being treated.

A joint activity related to the upcoming field trip revealed that negative norms were not only evident in our classroom, but had been established in other fifth-grade classrooms as well. During a planning activity involving students from the other fifth-grade classes, I heard a number of students from the other classes make disparaging comments about each other, and I asked them to be more respectful. Later, however, the insults started up again when André began quietly singing a rock song as he worked. Two students told him to shut up, and he reacted by crossing his eyes. Patrick's twin sister, Colette, who was notorious for her vitriolic mouth, glared at him.

"So how long have you been constipated?" she spewed. "Is this the third month you've been constipated?" A few minutes later, another girl called André a "dork" for no apparent reason.

I remained at a distance and documented the social interactions for a while longer. The conversation continued to be characterized by disrespectful remarks made by students from the other class, and eventually I felt compelled to intervene and tell them that the name-calling and insulting remarks had to cease.

Ivy's good-bye party struck a harmonious note that contrasted with the discord of the field trip planning session. Ivy had brought plant seeds for each student as a parting gift. She had specially chosen each packet of seeds according to the child's interests or personality, and the seeds were accompanied by a note explaining the choice. Although Ivy summarized the notes when presenting the gifts publicly, many students wanted to read their personalized notes aloud so others could hear what she had written. After several volunteers read their notes aloud, everyone circulated to scrutinize each other's seed packets and notes. The students, as they had done for Karen, had prepared good-bye notes, gifts, and a booklet in which everyone had written a special memory of Ivy. Ivy seemed genuinely pleased by her send-off, and the students loved the personal touch of the gifts. Like Karen, she had left a positive mark upon the class.

A Brewing Tempest

When the next play rehearsal took place, Roberta still had not had a chance to talk to Gerald's mother about his exclusion from the play, but I had spoken separately to Gerald, Ted, and Brian about it. Gerald indicated that, even though he had decided not to be in the play, that he "*might* want to be in it." When I mentioned to Ted and Brian that it seemed Gerald wanted to be in the play, they passed off his nonparticipation as incidental. When I said that including everyone in the play might be an important issue, they agreed to write him in. Unfortunately, I did not pin them down to ascertain how and when.

Having sensed that rehearsals were becoming unwieldy, Ted, Brian, and Kirsten had prepared some rules for play rehearsals, along with consequences for violation of those rules. After the directors had read the rules and consequences aloud, the other students began talking loudly. For the first time, the talking prevented the class from proceeding with the play practice. After five minutes of loud, chaotic talking, Billy began flicking the lights off and on, Maureen began ringing the hand bell, and several students asked their neighbors to be quiet. The noise level, instead of abating, began to increase as Maureen again rang the bell, this time shouting "Be quiet!" Billy grabbed the bell from Maureen and began ringing it himself.

Roberta and I looked at each other and realized that we both were waiting to see if the students could manage their own rehearsal. Our exchanged glance also conveyed an amazed exasperation that the class could be so unruly, particularly in response to an activity they had been supporting so keenly.

When Charles began screaming for quiet through a handmade paper megaphone, Roberta approached him.

"You know what," she told him quietly, "if you walk around with a megaphone like that it just gets louder in here."

The loud talking continued for a minute or two as Roberta circulated to quietly request silence. Once the din began subsiding, Kirsten announced that only when there was complete silence would the rehearsal begin.

"She's going to be a great lawyer," commented Jessica as the last murmur of talking faded to a whisper.

As the play practice progressed, the need for clearer stage directions was repeatedly iterated by Susan, Elizabeth, and Kirsten. Each time, Ted responded by taking a look at the directions in his script, whereas Brian usually reacted defensively, arguing that the directions had been clear and didn't need to be changed. Susan, taking on a stronger leadership position than ever before, began a self-appointed role as assistant director by calling for some scenes to be rehearsed a second time when she had specific suggestions for improvement. Billy's attempts to exert control, in contrast, were thwarted by flat rejections from others.

For the first time, there were signs of disengagement during the rehearsal. Mei-Ling and Sally were arguing about Sally putting her foot on Mei-Ling's chair, Jessica was talking to her neighbors, Patrick was reading a novel, André was making faces, and Gerald was at the periphery of the crowd, picking his nose. Still, the majority were focused on the enacted scenes, and certain lines that the children had already heard close to a dozen times still evoked loud laughter. The lines that made the students laugh the most involved insults; their favorite lines were a series of derisive "Do you know . . ." lines delivered by Hope, such as, "Do you know you're an idiot?"

The inattentive students began to engage when, as the introduction to one of the scenes, a recording of dance music was played and the entire cast began to dance. All the students, including Gerald and Jessica, happily gyrated until the music ended. Students were similarly delighted with their song about "Harvey the Hamster," a character played by a stuffed animal. The song had just been added to the play, and they sang it confidently, with glee. Roberta and I looked at each other, surprised that the entire class had managed to write and learn this song, presumably during recess time, without our knowledge.

Throughout the rehearsal, logistical problems cropped up. Charles noted that a scene had been misnumbered and, with my help, brought it to everyone's attention. Susan asked about props and costumes, and Hope pointed out that she was already working on props. Several suggestions concerning props were then proposed, and Hope wrote down the recommendations. Ted talked about the need for everyone to keep a check on their rapid delivery of lines. The positioning of students not actually onstage was discussed, and a solution was proposed and accepted.

Several students then questioned the internal consistency of the script. Susan, for example, pointed out that it was not clear what happens to her and the other characters in the final scene.

"Do we die or live on?" she queried.

"You live on," said Ted with a tone of finality. Ted's interpretation, however, was later challenged and the script was changed accordingly.

After discussion of several more issues, the play rehearsal resumed. The only student in the room who was not closely following the script was André. When I asked him where his script was, he said he "didn't need it." The next day, he admitted that he had lost it, and was given a new copy.

Roberta called for a debriefing after the rehearsal. Brian, Susan, and several other students stressed the need for quiet and order. Hope then began talking about the delivery of lines, again bringing up the need for slow, clear speech.

"Yeah, Billy says his lines too fast," pointed out Ted, and Billy immediately disagreed.

Kirsten mentioned that she wanted to use the auditorium for rehearsals, but that there had to be "reasonable quiet and control" before they could do this. This comment engendered a rash of accusations concerning who had been talking the most, with several students turning on Patrick. Patrick changed the subject.

"What about costumes?" he said. Hope answered by claiming that she was already in charge of costumes, and then told the group her ideas concerning how props and costumes could be arranged for easy access during the play. Brian brought up his concern that the actors had not memorized their lines. Before this subject was addressed, Ted backtracked to the topic of costumes and requested that Roberta grant the students a "costume day" to work on them. Roberta responded with hesitation, saying that it seemed too soon to add costumes and props, since the problem of disorderly rehearsals had not been resolved and lines were not yet memorized.

Then Brian brought up the overriding concern that the disorder had raised.

"The lack of cooperation is preventing the actual production from happening," he announced. Without explicit approval from Roberta, Brian, like many others, had assumed the play would reach the production stage.

"There are only five weeks left in the year!" Ben reminded everyone in an alarmed tone of voice.

This sobered everyone into a temporary hush. After the brief silence, however, issues concerning the play were again introduced and, to a large extent, hammered out. Hope fielded questions and comments concerning costumes, and many ideas were proposed, along with possible sources for materials. The management of offstage players was again brought up and more guidelines established. Patrick made some very specific suggestions concerning sets.

"I know that Elizabeth and some other people are good artists," he said, framing his suggestion with an uncharacteristically thoughtful compliment. "Maybe they can paint the sets. We can have blackouts between scenes and stagehands could move them."

Elizabeth used this opportunity to suggest that the script be modified to make it clear when actors might be available to move sets.

"Shouldn't it be clear," she said, "when people should come offstage and when they should be onstage?" Brian then went through the script for a full ten minutes, detailing where the actors should be at certain times. Most students wrote notes on their scripts.

The concern about offstage talking was again brought up. One student suggested that those offstage remain seated. Susan suggested that Roberta be responsible for maintaining quiet offstage. Patrick announced that Sally had just told him that her uncle might be able to donate wood for set construction. Maureen brought up the offstage noise yet again, but no solution was devised. When there was a pause in the flurry of conversation, Roberta spoke up.

"It did seem loud and chaotic today," she calmly stated, "but a lot was accomplished. I was wondering if you realized how long it took to run through the whole play."

The directors, Ted and Brian, spoke first, guessing fifteen and twenty minutes, respectively.

"It took forty-five minutes," Roberta told them, hastily adding, "but my comment wasn't negative. In spite of the talking, it took *only* forty-five minutes." She recommended that they be more cognizant of the time and to list everything that needed to be done. Realizing that more planning was needed, she seconded a proposal that the discussion continue after P.E. and lunch.

At one o'clock, suggestions continued to bubble up; the children's fervor about the play had not died down. Some suggestions were heeded, some were challenged and negotiated, and others surfaced only momentarily before drowning in the flood of comments.

During the discussion Henrietta spoke up loudly and clearly for a change, saying that the issue of who was onstage and who was offstage needed to be monitored by those in charge.

"I know sometimes I made a mistake about when people are supposed to be on stage," confessed Kirsten, taking responsibility for some of the confusion. "I'll try to be more understanding."

"I was wondering," snapped André, "why Kirsten gets to boss everybody around."

"She gets to because she's the stage manager," said Brian.

"Then she should be offstage," Hope noted.

"She's also a director," claimed Brian, and several students looked surprised or confused.

"No she's not, she's a stage manager," clarified Ted.

"Today I was in a really bad mood," began Kirsten, apparently feeling the need to defend herself at this point, "and I know I sounded like I was trying to boss everybody around—"

"I know you think Kirsten's a psycho maniac murderer," said Ted, trying to defend her by taking a humorous angle, "but—"

"I wasn't finished," asserted Kirsten, cutting him off. "I wanted to say that I'm going to be better about that, but with all that noise and confusion, we didn't really know what was going on."

"Can I be a bodyguard for somebody?" said Patrick, as usual trying to shift the attention to himself.

"Can we rehearse two scenes at the same time?" asked Billy.

"No!" shouted Brian, countering Billy in a hostile manner as he had during earlier power struggles.

Kirsten paraphrased Billy's suggestion in a mediation attempt. "I think he means getting two scenes ready at the same time, to save time." Billy confirmed her interpretation.

"When I was in a play before, the director always said, 'Remember to enunciate,'" contributed Doug, changing the subject.

"That means speaking clearly," clarified Patrick in a pedantic tone.

"We probably should do voice warm-ups," suggested Hope, again providing a practical perspective by contributing her theater experience.

"We have some evaluation forms," said Ted, who had, with others, drafted and photocopied the forms to keep track of all the issues that had emerged during the day. "They can be about today's practice or about all practices."

The students were soon immersed in the evaluation questionnaires. Roberta and I were handed forms as well. The entire rehearsal had raised many questions for both of us, and we talked about our questions extensively after school. It was the first time we had fully realized what a unifying force the play had become despite the chaos that had threatened the rehearsal. We also talked about the students' assumptions that the play would "go public" and wondered if enough time in the school year remained for this to really happen. In addition, we wondered if the leaders who had naturally emerged as the play progressed—most notably Brian, Ted, Doug, Kirsten, Billy, and Hope—could successfully steer the entire group.

Roberta and I were also concerned about the cryptic nature of the script. The satire was often lost on us, but we realized that this could perhaps be attributed to the fact that I hadn't seen the film *Star Wars* in twenty years, and Roberta had never seen it. Roberta vowed to rent the video—or see the new version being released in the cinemas—soon. Meanwhile, we continued hashing out what, to us, was confusing about the script. We were uncertain as to how much our adult perspectives needed to prevail. The independent student ownership of the play that we'd seen might foster the kind of community we had been working toward all year. We realized, though, that our guidance would likely be necessary to oversee the project and help the students tie the many loose ends. Our main concern was that the leaders not silence those who disagreed with the majority but were reluctant to express their opinions.

"Many students understand democratic principles now," said Roberta, "but they use them to serve their own ends."

The Play's the Thing: Continued Engagement

I took extensive notes on the science and math activities that transpired during the last days of April. Many of these activities were characterized by an unusually frequent sharing of resources, from the bubble-making supplies to the geoboards. Boys and girls were mingling more in small groups, and during these sessions there seemed to be very little talk about girlfriends, boyfriends, dates, and going steady. On several occasions, formerly silent students called for collective responsibility to solve problems; Katherine, for example, decried the terrible mess at her group's table and insisted that other group members help her clean it up. Amidst the myriad of ongoing projects, a new law inquiry emerged when Brian suggested another Calvin and Hobbes trial. The subsequent planning discussion was a remarkable synthesis of concepts learned earlier in the year, when civil law was a hot topic.

The initiative that characterized the math and science projects, the responsible clean-ups, and the Calvin and Hobbes trial was also in evidence during the April 30 *Star Boars* rehearsal. André was the only student who kept forgetting his lines, and several students politely suggested he study them before the next rehearsal. Students speedily resolved a dispute over the handling of the music during the bar scene by deferring to Hope and Henrietta. Several students protested the violent treatment of the stuffed animal in the play, and the group resolved to handle Harvey the Hamster more carefully. A murder scene was criticized as confusing and unconvincing, and the staging refined through several revisions. Andrew, whose nonspeaking role as "the box" was an important one, had been as silent as his character during rehearsals, but this time he spoke up about the need to control the staging of all scenes involving violence. Students immediately began discussing how to stage the scenes involving fistfights. Notably absent during the discussion was André, who, halfway through the rehearsal, had retreated to the corner of the room to work on his painting at the easel.

André's lack of participation became one of the primary topics during the class meeting that followed the rehearsal. A number of students were peeved that André had not been ready for his cues.

"André wasn't on top of it—he wasn't even looking at the script," said Patrick, who had been sparring with André even more than usual.

"I know half my lines," André protested.

"But you needed your script," insisted Ted.

At last André confessed that he'd lost his script again.

"That's a penalty!" shouted one student, and then several students echoed the cry "Penalty!," invoking Ted and Brian's consequences to anyone who broke the play rules. There had been no precedent for implementing the rules and consequences, even though Ted and Brian had placed a copy in each student's mailbox. After a few more minutes of discussion, the class agreed to waive André's penalty this time and arranged to have another copy of the script made for him.

Students then began questioning whether or not those who weren't in a given rehearsal scene should be required to watch that scene. The vocal members of the group insisted that everyone should be paying attention and providing feedback at all times. When Gerald agreed, Roberta and I simultaneously remembered that he didn't have a role in the play, even though he had been participating in the group scenes with everyone else.

"I really liked this [rehearsal]," said Billy, echoing other students who had mentioned how well it had gone. "And I know that I need to slow down my lines."

"I couldn't hear Veronica," added Susan. "I think people should be interrupted at some points in the dialogue if you can't hear them."

More discussion followed. Props and costumes were discussed in detail, and there was a debate concerning how the lines could have been clearer, louder, or better timed. Ted delivered the final analysis.

"Everybody was better today," he said, conveying a sense of pride.

"Except me," said André, sounding meek for a change.

"Yes," said Ted, hastily adding a positive tag to his criticism, "you've done better than this."

Hurtful Humor

The settlement of conflicts during play rehearsals had become quicker and smoother, but during other activities there were small signs of rebellion against authority that created, rather than addressed, class problems. Several students ignored small requests that Roberta made to ease class functioning, and she had to speak to these students individually. Students began to pay less attention to the schedule, and transitions were getting loud and unruly. The only time the class seemed to be completely attentive and cohesive was when *Star Boars* was mentioned.

The level of disrespect in the class became apparent during a special presentation on Friday. The archaeologists who had worked with Roberta's students earlier in the year had planned a follow-up presentation, again introducing major concepts to the entire group and then splitting the class into separate groups for more in-depth workshops.

The all-group workshop started with an introduction. Then students were given a chance to roam around the room in order to handle the artifacts and ask the presenters questions. During this time, I heard a surprising abundance of negative, sarcastic remarks. Students practically ignored the archaeologists at the bones table as they roughly handled the artifacts, making flippant comments.

"This is a cracked something," said Andrew as he picked up a bone and carelessly tossed it back onto the table.

"Let's just put 'em in a pile and say they're bones," said Charles, starting to put them in a precarious pile.

André grabbed a skull and began playing with it.

"You're gonna break it, André," cried Patrick, trying to grab the skull from André's hand. As André began running, trying to keep the skull away from Patrick, I intervened. I asked all four boys to step aside and reminded them that the bones were not their property and that they needed to be careful with them. In spite of my admonition, André hung on to the skull for a while, wanting to ensure that Patrick did not get his hands on it. Later, I saw André throw it recklessly onto the table. I pulled him aside and spoke to him sternly, wondering if further intervention was necessary.

Doug and Sally, unlike the others at the table, had some genuine inquiries concerning the bones. Doug wanted to know if some of them belonged to a cat, and this gradually led into a discussion about the large eyes of nocturnal animals. Sally wanted to know more about vertebrae. Although André, Patrick, Charles, and Andrew listened to part of this discussion, by the end of the short session they were already playing with the bones again, pretending they were bomber planes.

The boys' antics were interrupted by an announcement that students should split up for small-group workshops, each held in separate rooms. I joined a group in a room down the hall, where the students were already looking at a replica of a Neanderthal skull. The archaeologist leading the session had planned two activities. First, students were asked to examine the skull and sketch the way the original head and face might have looked. Patrick, André, and Sally began drawing "creatures" and making insulting comments about the activity. I asked these students to step outside and talked with them, chuckling to myself as I noticed that André was wearing a T-shirt that said, "I'm not insensitive, I just don't care." When the four of us returned to the group, several other students had begun making snide comments and drawing silly faces. The presenters, observing that some students had attempted to follow the directions, began discussing those students' drawings with the group. This redirected the attention of the disrupters, and soon all but Ben and André were asking interesting questions concerning anatomy, diet, tools, and other relevant topics. Roberta entered the room and, noticing that André and Ben were talking, separated them before moving on to another room.

The second activity dealt with the order of primates. The presenters began to explain that a volunteer "primate" was going to go into a large cage and try to use a rake to get some food outside the cage, and the rest of the students were going to observe and, later, ask questions. While the archaeologists explained the activity, at least six students began talking loudly about unrelated topics, and the glare I shot in their direction quieted only two of them. One of the presenters took control at that point and specifically requested full attention, which was granted, but only temporarily. By the time the presenters finished their directions, Sally, Patrick, and Billy were blatantly talking.

The simulation began. Charles, the volunteer primate, pursued his role appropriately as he manipulated the rake, but most of the other students detracted from the rake-fetching simulation by talking among themselves and yelling out teasing comments. By the end of the activity, most of the students were practically shouting insults at Charles, using the obvious ape theme.

Just as I was about to barge in and reprimand the whole group, the archaeologists announced that the time period was nearly up. The students quieted down for the brief wrap-up discussion and dismissal. I decided I would talk to all of the students later, but asked Sally, Patrick, and Billy, the most flagrant offenders, to stay and reflect on their behavior. They freely admitted that they had been rude, but seemed to think that the rudeness was justified because it was "funny." I finished the conversation feeling that the problem had not been resolved, and that it should be addressed further at a later time. I had not realized that this incident was a precursor of mutiny.

Cloudy Horizons

As one project followed another in the classroom, the disruption during the archaeologists' presentation seemed like a distant, isolated occurrence. A new literature study was beginning, and most students were actively gathering information about their Explorers Club topics. The students' enthusiasm and their mobilization of resources earmarked visible growth in their ability to conduct and present research.

On Monday, Roberta and I circulated during an Explorers Club session. We took note of student progress and helped students identify new information sources, tie together information already gathered, and plan presentations. During the session, I was astonished by a brief classroom visit from a University of Florida professor. On the World Wide Web, Patrick had learned about this professor's class on rock music and had e-mailed him questions concerning the rock group Nirvana. The professor, who happened to be in Riverdale for a conference, had come to the classroom during the Explorers Club work time to hand-deliver a copy of a research paper on the band, written by one of his university students. Later, Roberta and I both laughed at the irony that Nirvana was a topic we had tried to discourage Patrick from pursuing, judging the topic as trivial and thinking that resources on the subject would be limited.

The students I interviewed later in the week were extremely enthusiastic about their Explorers Club research. My only surprise was that this class, unlike Roberta's classes of previous years, had mostly pursued individual, rather than collaborative, research projects. Individuals, however, had consulted others as they worked, and the congenial class climate that had prevailed during Explorers Club sessions seemed to linger during my Friday morning observations and interviews.

Unfortunately, the pleasant atmosphere did not last. After lunch, Gerald, who had been acting rather despondent all morning, told Roberta that some of the boys were saying terrible things about him. Roberta asked him to specify which boys were involved, and the two of us immediately met with Gerald and the accused to discuss the matter. The insults had evolved, it seemed, from an occurrence at Bartlett Camp. At the camp, some feminine hygiene pads had been found in the pocket of Charles' coat, which was actually his mother's coat. Gerald, using the misnomer tampons, had joined the others in teasing Charles about the discovery. Since then, Charles had been spreading rumors that Gerald had "run around naked," "pooped in his pants," and "climbed into other boys' sleeping bags" during the camp week. After Roberta asked what had happened, the boys involved—Doug, Ted, Bert, Charles, and André—reported the rumors as if they were fact, and Gerald was visibly distraught to hear these rumors once again. Roberta and I insisted on establishing evidence for these accusations, and the "evidence" turned out to be hearsay.

Charles tried to justify the vicious rumors and, in the course of doing so, inadvertently revealed his role in creating the rumors. "It serves you right," he said, "since you said stories about me."

"Now I know how it feels," said Gerald, turning to Charles, "and I'm sorry I said anything to you."

Apologies were less forthcoming from the others. They felt that belief in the verity of the accusations, regardless of the lack of evidence, justified their actions. Bert, perhaps the most consistently positive student in the class, turned the tide of the conversation by apologizing, denouncing his own complicity as wrong.

Ridicule again became an issue later in the day. Jessica had been imitating another girl in the fifth grade who had pronounced the word *tornado* as "tornader." Her imitation was generating peals of laughter. I acknowledged the humor, but cautioned them against branding someone as unintelligent because of accent or dialect. I told my own story about coming to Indiana from Georgia as an undergraduate and being called ignorant because of my use of "y'all" and my pronunciation of vowels. Since "Ebonics" (a popularly coined term for African American English) had been in the news recently, one girl brought up that topic. The view espoused by the four girls present was that African American English represented ignorance and was worthy of mockery. Despite my disagreement and my examples of instances in which stereotypes based on language could be damaging, Jessica insisted that it was OK to imitate accents and dialects in any circumstance. She refused to admit any exceptions, and her clan of supporters rallied to her cause. The discussion was unpleasant; it left me disturbed at the tenacity of Jessica's hostility and the blind loyalty of her supporters.

A Maelstrom of Hostility

The calm that characterized the group meeting on May 6 belied the tension that would build, and eventually break, later in the day. In the morning, the group meeting was loosely structured, except for some procedural matters concerning literature groups that needed to be discussed at the end.

The meeting began with Roberta requesting bird observations. During the discussion about bird sightings, a student noted the appearance of a blue jay and many students dashed to the window. Still new, the completed bird station was generating a great deal of excitement at the slightest provocation.

"The blue jay is eating the seeds!" squealed Anne. Her delight at what, to me, was such an ordinary occurrence, made me chuckle.

"There's a squirrel!" piped another excited voice.

"We'll use a gun to get those squirrels out of there," said Billy, whose continued preoccupation with firearms bothered Roberta and me, but amused many of the students.

After a few minor class concerns were discussed, Maureen ended the meeting by talking about her visit to an orthopedic specialist to learn more about her scoliosis. The students had not heard of scoliosis, and were interested in Maureen's explanation. She had brought up the topic in order to propose that she teach her back exercises to the rest of the class during "stretch time," which, now that Ivy was gone, was no longer a ritual during the ten-minute window between special classes and lunch. The class unanimously agreed to try the exercises.

Later, when Maureen attempted to lead her exercise session, the leadership strategies she often used as a presenter and as a What's on My Mind? discussion leader did not work. The other students simply would not listen to her. She calmly requested quiet, circulated to get people to pay attention, and tried flicking the lights and ringing the bell. Nothing worked. She then raised her voice, pleading with everyone to at least try the exercises.

"You said earlier you wanted to do these exercises, didn't you?" she said, exasperated.

I was the only adult in the room; Roberta was in the hall talking to some students about a social problem. As Maureen showed us the first exercise, I was one of only six people trying to hear and follow her instructions. The others, instead of lying on the floor as requested, were sitting or standing. Most of them were talking loudly, blatantly ignoring Maureen's attempts to teach the exercises. Loud conversation between Kirsten and Elizabeth, for example, was punctuated by defiant glances in Maureen's direction. Several students retreated to the reading corner.

I sat up. "You're interrupting the exercise session," I told Kirsten and Elizabeth.

"People can interrupt in class," rejoined Kirsten, "but they can't do it in the play. Besides, Mr. Koshewa, you have no power to send anyone to the office."

I told her that my power should have nothing to do with whether or not they extend Maureen some common courtesy. Meanwhile, Maureen had gone to the reading corner and was exclaiming, "I wonder what would happen if the teacher hid behind the bookcase like this!"

When Roberta returned to the room, I told her how out of control things were getting (not that she needed to be told). She stood up and demanded the students' attention in a calm but loud voice. After the students quieted down, she announced that she was appalled at the inconsiderate behavior of most of the class, and if Maureen was willing to try again, she was going to give everyone a chance to do the exercise session in a positive manner after lunch. Over lunch, Roberta and I met with Maureen to discuss the matter.

The lunch meeting was interrupted by another discipline issue. The teacher on recess duty sent four boys back to the classroom to discuss an incident that had happened during after-lunch recess. Brian, Doug, Ted, and Andrew had discovered a toy horse on the playground and had broken off its legs. Although each of the four boys admitted that they had participated in the destruction, they did not feel that their vandalism warranted further action. Their reasons sounded more like rationalizations: Brian and Doug argued that since the horse was lying on the ground, it must have been discarded; Andrew claimed that since they didn't know who the owner was, they hadn't really done anything to harm anyone; Ted dismissed their destruction of the horse as irrelevant because it was "just a cheap toy." None of these reasons acknowledged the issue at hand: the damage of someone else's property. During the meeting, Roberta attempted to elicit a solution to the problem from the students themselves. Since this was not forthcoming by the time the bell rang, signaling the end of recess, Roberta asked each of the four boys to propose a solution to the problem in writing and bring it to class the next day for further discussion.

After all the students entered the class, Maureen, her enthusiasm punctured but not drained, made a valiant attempt to teach the exercises again. The room was quiet, but occasional mumbling and grumbling indicated that the students were not interested in the stretches. Having chosen to watch the students this time rather than participate, I observed that many of the children's attempts to do the exercises were, at best, half-hearted. They did, however, make it through the activity with some measure of compliance and a minimum of distractions.

When the exercise session ended, Roberta called a group meeting. The meeting began in a civil manner, with Roberta asking the students to compare the first and second exercise session. André described the first session as "crazy."

"Do you think having the teacher there made a difference?" asked someone in the back.

"Yes!" someone shouted.

"Why?" asked Maureen.

"Because I'm biting my hands," replied André, scrunching his face and crossing his eyes while pretending to bite his hands. He looked around quickly to see who was laughing, and then continued in a more serious vein. "Because we knew we'd get in trouble if we goofed around too much."

"How did you know that?" asked Roberta. Her question unleashed a chorus of answers, indistinguishable because so many students were talking at once.

Roberta let the furor die down and then quietly cited two concerns. First of all, she said, she wondered whether, and if so, how, their behavior was affected by her presence in the room, explaining that she didn't feel that her being there should make a difference. Second, she wanted the students to articulate "our basic rules," since, at the beginning of the year, "we talked about the fact that everybody kind of knows the school rules so we don't really need to talk about them. But I think this class has a lot more difficulty knowing, and maybe showing respect for, those rules."

Suddenly two students began shouting at each other. Roberta said that she didn't have much of a sense of humor at the moment and that she was "frustrated by saying the same things to the same people all the time." She then suggested the discussion return to comparing the two exercise sessions.

Patrick began, "At first, it wasn't enough time; it took us a long time to get organized."

The students began to discuss why the first exercise session had been unruly and whether or not it was Roberta's presence in the room that made the second session different. Several students maintained that it did make a difference. Serious comments were punctuated by so many flippant ones that Roberta solemnly reminded everyone that we were conducting a group meeting. There was a silence lasting thirteen full seconds before a hand went up and Roberta called on Maureen.

"I was just wondering why—I want to hear everybody's perspective on why the second time was more, I guess, tame, and more effective." Maureen paused before continuing, "If you were one of the people who acted differently, why did you act differently?"

There was another long silence. Several hands went up, and Roberta asked Maureen to call on someone. She called on Doug.

"Well, I wasn't here for the first one, but the second one, it was still pretty loud." Several students then jumped on Doug for commenting on the second session if he hadn't been at the first.

Maureen retained control of the conversation and politely repeated the question. Ted answered that it was because the teacher was there.

At this point, a number of individuals posited that the signal for obtaining quiet was at fault, and the discussion veered to possible alternatives. "What's the best signal?" asked Maureen.

"A bullhorn!" shouted André. This comment was followed by many loud bullhorn noises.

Maureen tried to field other suggestions for quiet signals, but her questions were interrupted by loud shouts from different areas of the room, including Patrick loudly telling someone that "sticking out your tongue does not help!"

"I think Ms. Taylor is open to ideas about how to get quiet," continued Maureen, trying to maintain a semblance of control. "I think that anything that works is OK with me."

Maureen's comment unleashed a fury of remarks. Since so many people were talking simultaneously, I couldn't pick out all of the comments from the audio recording, but many were silly, prompting immediate put-downs from others. After a short while, the group had settled down long enough for students to speak in turn, but there was general disagreement about which signal might be most effective.

"Do something that gets everybody's attention but that everybody hates," suggested Ted, "like scraping down the chalkboard." Unrestrained laughter filled the room, and again at least four students began speaking at the same time, making it impossible to hear individuals. The disorderly talking continued for several minutes. When it quieted down, a vigorous argument started concerning whether or not the bell should be the official signal for quiet. While some students took this debate seriously, others continued to make light of it.

"Instead of using a bell," said André during a lull in the debate, "we could actually bring in a cow." More laughter erupted, and everyone began talking at once. When the group quieted down, the conversation turned to an important point.

"People who are going around saying 'be quiet' are making noise too," said Brian. Ben's subsequent attempt to broaden this issue to one of respect erupted in yet another free-for-all in which André again tried to play the class for laughs, mocking the idea that anyone deserved respect.

"Let's stop right now," said Roberta. "Does anyone else feel completely outraged by André yelling out in the middle of this?" The surprisingly widespread reaction was an immediate "No!" Many students resumed talking at once. Several voices attempted to explain that André's comments were funny, and therefore shouldn't bother anyone.

"It's not just André," said Roberta. "It seems that this is the sort of thing we're talking about, where everybody just acts like they have complete authority to do whatever they want and no one is respecting the group process. I want to hear what Ben has to say."

Ben then suggested that they sing a Bartlett Camp song as a signal for quiet. This led to a new eruption of suggestions that continued for several minutes. Kirsten inserted a criticism of Maureen during a quiet moment, pointing out that Maureen had shouted when trying to get everyone quiet during her exercise sessions.

When Patrick repeated the suggestion that they all sing the "Harvey the Hamster" song as a symbol for quiet, the class burst into song, and the laughter that followed set off another melee of talking.

The meeting had again become a shouting match. It took several minutes for the pandemonium to subside. When it did, I raised my hand and Maureen, who was still trying to orchestrate the discussion, called on me.

"More than a few people," I admonished, "are making noises or comments, including some insulting remarks, that indicate the problem is not being taken seriously. The present interruptions, including those trying to maintain control, constitute the problem we're actually talking about." I then pointed out that I had waited for a pause and raised my hand to get the floor at that very moment. I also emphasized that since each individual can control his or her own behavior better than that of others, quiet listening and patient waiting sets a better tone for group meetings than screaming demands for quiet. I identified four main problems: "remarks that indicate people don't care, the constant interruptions, the lack of a mature way to conduct discussions, and exerting your own control to get everyone quiet." I then invited student responses to my comments. Again, the serious responses were interspersed with flippant remarks and personal disputes.

Watching the class get off course again, Roberta demanded quiet and then asked me how individuals are kept from dominating my university seminars. I confessed that sometimes individuals did take over class discussions, but mentioned good strategies for preventing such domination, such as relating the topic to silent members' interests or by asking quiet students their opinion.

After a few students muttered comments, André spoke out audibly.

"Mr. Koshewa was talking about us, like, not being mature and stuff. I mean, we're only ten or eleven and stuff—do we really have to be that mature?"

"The answer to that question is," I replied, "how do you want to be treated?"

André made a babyish sound, and his neighbors chuckled.

"What is the way, then," Roberta asked the class, "to control an immature person who doesn't want to take responsibility?"

"Take away their teddy bear," answered André. As anticipated, the class laughed.

"My whole philosophy about how I treat children," continued Roberta, "and how I believe in giving people choice and letting them take responsibility for their learning, that whole foundation right now is kind of shaky. And what I'm hearing from the people who aren't taking this seriously is that you don't want to be treated the way I want to treat you."

Elizabeth then raised her hand, explained that she wanted to go back to something earlier in the conversation, and said, "Some people—I don't want to mention any names—" but before she could finish, other students jumped in to accuse each other of misdeeds.

Roberta waited for a pause and continued.

"We're hearing a lot of rude things that are indicating 'I don't care about you.' I've tried to show that I care about you, and I'd like to have that same kind of respect."

Kirsten then tried to bring in an example from literature, describing a fantasy novel about a culture in which people's actions are based on revenge. Maureen, however, had read the book and claimed that Kirsten "got it wrong." She then took over Kirsten's synopsis, turning it into a long drawn-out summary. Kirsten's attempt to wrest back the floor was successful only when she used classmates' names in a hypothetical scenario about revenge. This evoked more laughter. The discussion had once more become a forum for personal attacks.

Realizing that the class meeting was going nowhere, Roberta told everyone to sit in their seats and write a reflection on the discussion. She also told them to mention what they thought their individual responsibility was in the matter, and added that she was expecting complete silence during this writing session.

Sorting Through the Debris

After school, Roberta and I read the written reflections and were stunned at how pervasively the students denied the disorder and rudeness of the class meeting, or took no responsibility for the problems. We realized for the first time that behavior totally unacceptable to us was now acceptable to most, if not all, the students in the classroom community.

Most of the students who acknowledged the excessive talking and rudeness blamed others. Only six students used the pronoun "we" or "I" when describing the interruptions, insults, and excessive talking. Three of the worst offenders had the audacity to claim that they were trying to make others quiet. Patrick and Billy were frequent scapegoats, even though they were no more disruptive than at least a dozen other students. Jessica's composition was a good example of the many papers that conveyed a holier-than-thou tone. Jessica felt that the class had done "pretty well," and blamed others for being "disruptive," even though she herself had loudly interrupted and complained vociferously about having to write. She went on to defend herself by claiming that she always behaved responsibly, offering as evidence the fact that her mother allowed her to take babysitting jobs. Less defiant talkers also defended themselves. Outright denial that disruptions had occurred appeared in nine of the responses; these students thought that the group meeting "went quite well" or had been "good," "OK," "fine," or "nice." Several students who admitted that the meeting had been chaotic or out of control implicitly or explicitly stated that the humorous aspect of the disruptive comments justified the chaos. Sally, who had also talked out of turn and insulted others, reacted defensively to André's remark about maturity:

> I thought we had a relly good meeting besides Patrick & Billy. When André said "Some of us aren't mature because we're only 11 & 12 y.o." I think he ment a little not mature not babies. I fell relly bad on Mrs. Taylor's part because she trys to organize relly cool things but people always interupt her. Espesilly Patrick & Billy. I think Mrs. Taylor had a relly different way of teaching and we'll never be able to take advantage of that if every one talks out of turn and don't respect that.

Elizabeth, who defended herself by claiming she was "trying" to be more responsible, astutely identified the peer pressure behind the interruptions and insulting comments:

> I think that our class's biggest weak spot is being non-chaotic. I'm not really sure if I'm being more responsible but I'm trying. I think some people (possibly me) really feel like if they don't talk out and make funny remarks, people won't like them.

Kirsten, ordinarily a champion of individual rights and, until recently, always respectful to teachers, wrote that "I felt that [the meeting] was OK. . . . Why can teachers interrupt and we can't?"

This last question exposes the extent to which the issue had become one of rights. The students' perception of what their rights were had begun to ignore the balance between group and individual rights, as well as the right of the teacher to ensure that learning is unhampered in the classroom.

During our discussion of the papers after school, Roberta and I talked about the ramifications of what had happened. We tried to analyze the social dynamics at play that were allowing the poor class climate to fester. Roberta mentioned the early signs, the most prominent one being what she described as "the field trip from hell" at the beginning of the year. This reminded us of the next morning's field trip. We decided to proceed with it as planned despite a sense of apprehension.

Our analysis of the day's events turned to individual students. We discussed Kirsten, whose positive leadership qualities and strong sense of justice throughout the year had taken an unpredicted turn. We were both surprised at her defiant behavior. I then told Roberta about my recent interview with Katherine, in which she told me that her opinions weren't valued, and that she often felt excluded from conversations. Like Katherine, we had become outsiders in the class community:

RT: I'm feeling right now that we don't share common values with many of the students in here. So I'm just wondering about how to come to some kind of understanding so that this will work. It's so disappointing to me. If I wanted to talk about what's really important in people, I think it's respect for each other.

AK: I don't think you can learn unless you have the idea that other people have things that are important to say and you give that space.

The conversation then turned to parenting: what Roberta learned through her own parenting, how parents summon respect, and how parent attitudes toward the "peer culture" might be influencing the children in the class. We talked about how the "blusterers" usually have the lowest self-esteem, even though they're trying to project confidence. I expressed my feeling that being "lectured" fails to build self-esteem, and Roberta said she heard herself, during the discussion, saying things about how she was feeling as a way to make people ashamed. "I don't intend to make people feel shame either," she said, "because that's kind of how I grew up—being shamed." She was surprised at how easily she had slipped into that mode, saying that she didn't believe that was the way to really be heard. We decided that lectures might command listening, but they tend to silence the listener. Some students were shaming others into silence even more forcefully. They were demanding, rather than engaging, attention and were not hearing other people in a way that nurtured voice.

The conversation then shifted from the right to be heard to property rights. The broken horse problem was far from solved, and we reflected on the values its destruction symbolized. Roberta commented that it was "interesting that today was the day of the breaking of that toy." I noted that none of them had actually taken a moral stance. We continued to talk about the issue.

RT: I think there should be a consequence for it. I'd like for them to meet the person whose toy it was.

AK: We need to put a face on it, you know, that makes it—

RT: Doug said he had lost figures on the playground earlier in the year. I could just imagine how he'd feel if people had picked them up and broken them. But he wouldn't say that it would bother him.

AK: I wonder how much of it was safety in numbers. If it had just been one or two of them—

We both acknowledged the problem-solving aspect of teaching, but wondered if we were addressing it effectively. We wanted the boys to recognize their vandalism as a problem but had not yet succeeded. Roberta noted that the students we usually depended on to recognize and solve problems, such as Kirsten, Hope, and Elizabeth, recently had been creating, rather than solving, problems.

After hashing out many other issues and ideas, we finished planning the next day. The long class meeting had led to the cancellation of math and Invitations sessions, and students wanted more play rehearsal time. Roberta felt that, in addition to the morning field trip to see an excerpt from a high school musical, we should include a group meeting, a math lesson, and play practice in the day's schedule. She also decided that individuals who had not completed the week's math assignments should have to work on them during play practice. The students, we agreed, should help decide how to schedule these plans, as they usually did. We were hopeful that the students would start the next day on a new foot and help us establish a positive tone.

❖

Stepping Back: A Commitment to Justice and Equality

Martin Luther King, Jr. once said, "Most people are thermometers that record or register the temperature of majority opinions, not thermostats that transform and regulate the temperature of society." What Roberta and I were witnessing at this point in the year was an unwillingness of students to transform and regulate the classroom community. Individual students were being ignored and excluded, highly vocal students were being allowed to dominate class discussions, and rude, insulting behavior was becoming more and more common. On the other hand, students were seeking and considering the points of view of every community member via the play evaluation forms, generously sharing both school and personal supplies, and encouraging each other's artistic efforts. These contrasts between irresponsible and responsible behavior show that moral development is not linear and sequential, but contextual. Roberta and I, however, were concerned that there wasn't more stability, and upset that many students were not striving to be supportive and inclusive. As an undercurrent of sultry defiance disturbed the calm and collected tone that normally prevailed, it was becoming more unpredictable when—or even whether—we could count on the children to make good decisions concerning self-rule.

The unabashed willfulness was the worst aspect of the transformations we were witnessing. Gerald's exclusion from the play, Charles' victimization during the archaeology workshop, and the destruction of the toy horse were all examples of inequity, of blatantly privileging one's own interests. In retrospect, it was clear that Roberta and I had not thought out what really constituted rights within the context of the classroom. We were being excluded, in many ways, from the community, but were unsure how to provide leadership and yet grant the autonomy that we felt students needed to decide what is right and ethical. As our role in the community became less important in the children's eyes, we began to assume control more actively—by using approval and disapproval strategically, by determining the agenda more often, and by demanding that students reflect, rather than inviting them to do so. This approach eventually backfired.

Experiencing these difficulties so late in the school year, Roberta and I were keenly sensing our failures. When I reflected on where we might have gone wrong, both Roberta's strengths and weaknesses became more apparent. Her curriculum continued to spur learning and to address important issues and problems, yet she failed to effectively articulate student and teacher rights within the context of the present conflicts. Roberta strived for equality, but, as classroom events vividly reminded us, striving for equality through democracy should not be equated with its attainment.

1. Roberta continually brought up issues of fairness with students, parents, colleagues, and policymakers. Whether discussing possible restitution for a misdeed or encouraging students to write a letter to the editor of the local newspaper, she initiated discussion about what is moral and just. Roberta's commitment to equality and justice, and to discussing those issues in class, is consistent with the "connectionist" perspective that Jesse Goodman (1992) advocates, a perspective that promotes "moral compassion, social responsibility, globalism, antiracism, [and] antisexism" (151). Roberta, like Beane and Apple (1995), wants students to "be 'critical readers' of their society . . . to ask questions like these: Who said this? Why did they say it? Why should we believe this? and Who benefits if we believe this and act upon it?" (13–14). In order to discuss questions such as these with other teachers, Roberta organized informal professional study groups. These study groups gradually began to attract some of the more reactionary teachers in Riverdale, and together the teachers shared the ramifications of important social issues and how they might be addressed in the context of their own schools.

Beane and Apple (1995) challenge the assumption that democracy promotes equality, cogently pointing out that democracy has been used to both defend and oppose unjust practices. They give as an example the "contradiction between the movement for greater school achievement on the one hand and the resistance to equitable spending for all schools on the other" (6). A truly democratic approach to school reform needs to ascertain, as Gutmann (1987) suggests, who has the authority to make decisions about education and how far-reaching those decisions should be. Questioning the authority to make decisions about education is especially important in light of the current "movement to turn our schools, and other public institutions, over to private greed and political self-interest" (Beane 1998, 10). The current inequities in education will only be challenged, however, if teachers are interested in such issues and discuss them with students, parents, colleagues, and members of the greater community.

Teacher commitment to equality issues does not always manifest itself in ways that lead to effective classroom commitments to equality. Roberta and I, for example, failed to tackle the inequity problems fueled by popularity until they became unbearably oppressive. And despite our belief in democratic practices, we began to restrict the role of democracy in the classroom when the entire community began following the unethical lead of the most influential students. Important issues of democracy and equality can easily elude teachers, even teachers who, like Roberta, are committed to examining them.

2. Roberta tried to promote fair educational practices by becoming politically involved. Her commitment to democratic classrooms propelled her to work, as a volunteer, for the Indiana State Board of Education to help write new assessment materials that would include authentic writing samples. Roberta questioned the value of standardized tests, feeling, like Frank Smith (1995), that standards "are best achieved without standardization" (90). Yet she hoped that her work could prevent the worst possible scenarios from occurring.

Already Roberta felt restricted by state mandates. Although she asked students to research aspects of the Columbus era in order to meet state policy guidelines, the decision to make Columbus a central topic of the curriculum had nothing to do with her. Yet, because of state requirements, Columbus became more significant than other important social studies topics. As Levy (1996) points out, "every curriculum choice, every pedagogical method, every assessment, reveals what we consider important" (154).

Roberta jumped at the chance to write state assessments that would serve as alternatives to traditional multiple-choice exams. By working to include authentic writing and other contextualized assessments in the state exams, Roberta was hopeful that better approaches to teaching reading and writing would spread, since testing increasingly drives instruction. Unfortunately, the new assessments that Roberta worked on were abandoned before implementation because of legislation reinstating multiple-choice test formats. Still, she did not regret the exchange of ideas that her volunteer work generated, and has not given up hope that such assessments will eventually replace multiple-choice tests.

Roberta also believes that mandated achievement tests, by emphasizing isolated, rather than collaborative, learning, reinforce authoritarian approaches to controlling students. Many teachers are expected to raise test scores, in spite of the fact that curriculum geared toward testing reduces student participation in classroom learning (Darling-Hammond and Snyder 1992). As Angell (1991) succinctly states, "autocratic teaching methods are in part the result of pressures to demonstrate professional competence—pressure to produce higher test scores, pressure to cover more material, pressure to impart 'correct' values, pressure to maintain order and quiet in the classroom" (258). Although it is faulty to presume that higher test scores, a single moral perspective, a uniform knowledge base, or quiet order are indications of learning, such assumptions underlie the standards movement and tend to promote autocratic approaches to learning and teaching. This is why Roberta continues to speak out against the test mania induced by the standards movement.

Roberta's belief in the importance of political involvement is consistent with that of DeStigter (1998), who feels that democratic classroom goals should "reach beyond localized settings and [extend] the habits of democratic communities to, for instance, school boards, state legislatures, and federal courts" (41). With curricular mandates increasingly restricting teacher autonomy, political awareness and involvement have become essential. Wolk (1998) thinks that one reason women have historically been teachers and men administrators and legislators is the compliant role that women have been expected to take. "To break that pattern," he writes, "teachers must see themselves as educational *activists*, as critical questioners, as professionals who make issues of freedom and control, regarding both themselves and their students, central to their daily work" (74, emphasis in original).

3. Roberta believed in different outcomes for different students, and acted on this belief by welcoming special-needs children in her homeroom. She regularly volunteered to include special-education students in her homeroom class. In fact, the first year I conducted research in Roberta's class, she had a "cluster" class containing more than the usual proportion of children with disabilities. By the end of the year, these children had grown in ways their special-education teacher could not have imagined. The special-education teacher who worked with Roberta that year became inspired to radically change her teaching and to pursue courses for a master's degree to further what she'd learned about inclusion and collaboration. During the 1996–97 year, however, Roberta's success with special-education students was not as clear-cut. Gerald, the only student formally diagnosed as having special needs, was experiencing some measure of social integration and was enjoying school for the first time, yet he was often excluded or mistreated.

Roberta strongly believes that everyone has the same right to learn, regardless of gender, age, skin color, socioeconomic status, language background, sexual orientation, and other aspects of identity. In developing a unique relationship with each student, Roberta does not assume that identifying characteristics such as ethnicity, learning disabilities or socioeconomic status will interfere with students' learning. Instead, she expects all children to demonstrate effective learning strategies in her classroom, and, to a remarkable degree, they do. She worries, however, that the pass/fail implications of state benchmarks, the exclusion that voucher schools and charter schools can perpetuate, and mandates that particular reading programs be used with every child will widen the gulf between the "haves" and "have-nots." Such measures contradict what Short, Harste, and Burke (1996) call a "theory of difference," which values different experiences, different perspectives, and different outcomes in education. They question "the assumption that the function of education is to teach a common set of concepts to everyone" and argue that "people can have a good educational experience even though they are not learning the same thing" (350–351). Roberta felt that the state tests weren't valid because they were not based on what students know and the way that they spend their daily lives. These tests did not show if students were interested in learning, able to use a variety of resources, or able to communicate what they have learned. The state test percentiles produced profiles of students as above average, average, or below average, yet, as Wolk (1998) aptly states, "there is no such thing as an average child" (19). Children whose low scores may be a result of home problems, lack of enrichment experiences, disabilities, limited immersion in the English language, or even just a bad day are often deemed inferior when they obtain below-average test scores. Roberta resents the tyranny of test scores and feels that learning is validated best "in the contexts of the activities being assessed—in the school, workplace, home, and on the street" (Murphy, Shannon, Johnston, and Hansen 1998, 30). In Roberta's classroom, there were many times when students were learning different things in different ways, and her ongoing observations of and conversations about learning outcomes allowed her to assess each child individually. This approach facilitated the accommodation of special-needs students.

4. Roberta's Literature Studies, Writers Guild, Explorers Club research, Focus Study projects, and other curriculum components promoted a sense of equality in the classroom, and were relatively unhampered by the social unrest the class was experiencing. Despite the conflicts that occurred, students were ordinarily willing to collaborate to meet mutual goals of discussing novels, publishing, investigating, and reporting on self-selected social studies topics, and researching topics of personal interest. Disrespectful behavior was becoming more common, but when the students were busily engaged it was rarely the dominant mode, and never did the students completely neglect or abandon their academic pursuits. Furthermore, the peer and teacher recognition students were getting for their writing, their research presentations, and their artistic endeavors allowed them to develop interests and talents outside the scope of curricular mandates, highlighted their strengths, and countered the powermongering that was rearing its ugly head.

Literature Studies, Writers Guild, Explorers Club research, and Focus Study projects promoted equality through choice. Although Roberta guided some students to choose books within the scope of their current reading proficiency and helped them narrow or broaden their research topics, her provision of choices helped students develop their interests and base their inquiries on prior knowledge. Since these components of her curriculum were process oriented, students could create products that reflected their present levels of learning, in the form of literature circle questions, classroom publications, or research presentations. Those who needed more help than others could rely on the collaboration opportunities the curriculum provided.

5. Roberta insisted that students present ideas and strategies for solving problems. Even though spates of inattention and outbursts of rudeness had increased, Roberta did not take sole responsibility for addressing these problems, and this shared responsibility eventually paid off. At this point in the year, however, Roberta was taking a more prominent role in conflict resolution in part because the students were having more problems. The broken horse incident provides an example of the way Roberta shared responsibility for student problems. Roberta used her authority to demand that the students come up with some form of restitution, but she helped them devise the final solution of offering the owner money to pay for a new horse.

Roberta also projected her authority to schedule a second exercise session after Maureen's first session had gone awry, but she presented it as a chance for the students to somehow solve the disruption problems and make it succeed. Although there were no disruptions during the second session, most of the students were not committed to making the second session work, as the subsequent discussion revealed. The students' attempts to solve their own problems with minimal intervention were becoming less and less effective; the situation would have to become worse before it became better. The value of Roberta's refusal to take sole responsibility for student problems did not reveal itself until the final weeks of the school year.

6. Roberta failed to sufficiently elicit silent voices. All students had opportunities to speak up in Roberta's class, but they may have needed more safeguards before mustering the courage to counter prevailing social forces. Roberta had tried to establish a safe environment, but students whose views differed from those of the majority didn't feel safe enough to "buck the crowd." She encouraged silent students to speak up, but she did not always find ways to ensure that they did. Some mechanisms she could have tried include individual, written solutions to problems, more discussion of solutions in pairs or small groups before class meetings, not calling on anyone until quite a few students raised their hands, and more insistence upon waiting until everyone had a chance to speak before moving on to new class meeting topics.

A social democracy depends on equal participation, but this assumes that neither majority nor minority views will exert undue influence. Conservative views of democracy often extol majority rule at the expense of minority opportunity. As Gutmann (1987) reminds us, the integrity of democratic deliberations can be preserved only if decisions are made in accordance with principles of nonrepression and nondiscrimination. Such principles are often invisible when a classroom community is in the throes of a majority rule vote. On the other hand, if majority rule is rarely used, students may not fully understand that individuals cannot always be accommodated if group goals are to be met.

Roberta, at this point in the year, had not clarified the role of voting and majority views in the classroom. She had not insisted that everyone have a say when dominant students railroaded decisions during classroom discussions. Furthermore, she had failed to explicitly teach better listening strategies. Wolk (1998) recommends that, at the beginning of the year, teachers require each speaker to restate or summarize the previous comment during class meetings. This strategy, along with others such as soliciting written opinions or allocating a maximum number of individual comments until everyone has said something, might have coaxed more participation from silent members of Roberta's classroom.

As I interviewed students at the end of the school year, I learned that there was a general resentment of authority in all the fifth-grade classes. Roberta and I, of course, were not unaware that the dominant leaders in her own class were having a negative impact on the community, and we were discussing possible ways to regulate their power. We knew, however, that our concern needed to be viewed as a problem by other members of the community before the group would autonomously regulate its tyrants.

7. Roberta continually brought up issues of justice and equality, but had failed to think of these issues in terms of student and teacher rights. It was still not clear in our minds what distinguished student rights and privileges in the classroom, and debate about this distinction occurred too late in the school year to undo the damage that had already been done. Students were beginning to abuse their rights, but, at first, this abuse was insufficiently addressed. I was just as guilty of this neglect as Roberta was. Indeed, I had not thought through my own rights as a teacher-researcher in the classroom, which is one reason that I found it particularly disturbing that Kirsten had not seen me as a teacher. Even though my researcher role was often in evidence as I observed and took notes, I had led many small-group and whole-group sessions, and the students knew that Roberta and I consulted each other on many matters. Kirsten's dismissal of my power as insignificant made me wonder why I hadn't earned more respect. Was I seen as less powerful simply because, as Kirsten implied, I couldn't "send anyone to the office"? Perhaps some students really gauged Roberta's power in terms of behavioral consequences she almost never enforced. Or was Kirsten simply testing me, and at the same time trying to ascertain the limits of her own power? I had, perhaps, failed earlier tests by not conveying my behavioral expectations more actively. The traditional role of the teacher still seemed to loom large in many students' minds, yet another important reason that a focused examination of student and teacher rights within Roberta's class was long overdue.

As Gathercoal (1997) has shown, legitimate educational purpose and preventing serious disruption of the educational process are compelling state interests. Student actions in Roberta's class were beginning to disrupt learning, and some sort of teacher intervention seemed necessary. But what kind of disruption merits intervention is contextual. Some schools forbid practices such as chewing gum which, in itself, does not ordinarily impede learning. Teachers must juggle the needs of the individual and the group when deciding when to intervene. As Paley (1992) writes, "so much of teaching straddles the moral fence: Should I or shouldn't I? Is it right or wrong, fair or unfair?" (73). By allowing strong leaders to abuse the rights of others, and then restricting each student's right to speak and move around appropriately, Roberta demonstrated that what constituted student rights and what kinds of intervention would address their abuse were still not clear in our minds.

8. Roberta persisted in demonstrating calm, civil behavior. She consciously tried to model what Gathercoal (1997) calls the "language of civility." Yet the language of civility was not in evidence among the students to the extent that we desired or expected. Our philosophy, however, would not allow us to abandon our own implementation of this standard of conduct, even though we briefly contradicted our beliefs by dealing with discipline problems in an authoritarian manner. We believed in equality and tried, at least until our tolerance broke, to treat the students in as egalitarian a manner as possible.

Roberta's calm demeanor is not a calculated technique; it is part of her character. As Ohanian (1994) writes, "the greatest defense against vulnerability is not a prepackaged fast-fix management system; it is competence. Teachers must be intellectually, spiritually, and physically competent—basically able to deal with kids" (182). Roberta weathered problems in a dignified manner because she completely conveyed civility. Competent teachers like Roberta may occasionally lose composure when they're caught off guard, but overall they communicate calmness and self-restraint.

9. Roberta avoided rewards and tried to distinguish between restitution and punishment when dealing with behavior problems. Jesse Goodman (1992) provides an example of the ambiguous relationship between restitution and punishment when he describes a series of events involving a student he calls Bruce, at a school where discipline efforts "were seen as opportunities to teach children to be responsible for themselves and to their fellow human beings" (112). Bruce raised safety concerns when he walked across a room divider and encouraged others to do so, and a "crisis meeting" involving the student and two teachers was held. As a result,

> it was decided that Bruce would have to be supervised [remain in sight at all times] after school by the weekly "after school" teacher for one month, and for the next two weeks he would be expected to keep the library [the site of his transgression] clean and put books away after school. In addition, he was to address the students at a Family Meeting to discuss what had happened. (112)

This incident shows the fine line between restitution and punishment. What the adults perceived as restitution was likely perceived as punishment by Bruce, especially since cleaning and putting books away are irrelevant to the issue of ensuring safety concerns. On the other hand, there is not always a clear-cut restitution, once a misdeed has occurred, that can serve as an alternative to other types of consequences.

Roberta avoided using academic tasks as rewards or punishments, because she believed this practice sends subliminal messages concerning those tasks. Many teachers, for example, dangle valuable educational experiences such as field trips as rewards for good behavior, conveying the idea that worthwhile educational experiences are frills. Teachers still use academic tasks as punishment as well; some, for example, assign written essays or copied sentences as punishment, which frames writing as negative.

Rewards reinforce a sense of competition that inhibits risk-taking and promotes failure in those who feel they don't "measure up." As Nicholls (1989) has shown, children who fear poor performance will avoid the task, choose an easy task where success is assured, or choose a very difficult task that could shift the locus of failure to the difficulty of the task. An emphasis on performance can also prompt confident students to choose easy tasks. For example, reading programs that reward a large quantity of completed books encourage strong readers to race through short books that don't challenge them.

Behavioral rewards convey the message that material gain should be a primary reason for making positive moral choices. True morality, however, is contingent upon doing what is beneficial to oneself and to others regardless of whether one is rewarded for doing right or punished for doing wrong. A moral conscience is unlikely to develop as a result of school awards or grades; it must be nurtured through enlightening social experiences. This is why Roberta valued restitution, such as direct contact with the owner of the broken horse, over punishment.

10. Roberta may have promoted equality more effectively, both in the classroom and beyond, if she had pursued service learning. Roberta's first attempt to implement service learning was unsuccessful. In 1995, her students embarked upon a project designed to help an elderly couple in the community with daily chores and tasks. It turned out that the couple was less in need of help than originally thought, and the project petered out. During the 1996–97 school year, Elizabeth and Maureen conducted a bake sale to raise money for a local land trust, but, like the project with the elderly couple, their endeavor did not place students in direct contact with the truly needy.

Service learning extends social responsibility beyond classrooms, and may be most effective in situations involving people in great need, such as the homeless, ill, and severely disabled. I am convinced that the strong sense of equality among the students in Roberta's 1993–94 class was nurtured by the presence of a number of students with disabilities. The students that year developed a sense of fairness and an emotional sensitivity unparalleled by later classes. Roberta's students learned to care about classmates with pronounced disabilities. Their attitude and conduct showed that ideals of equality emanate from caring and are enhanced by responsible social participation (McEwan 1998).

Service learning projects have the potential to deflect self-centeredness. If Roberta's 1996–97 class had helped the needy, they might have become more critical of social inequalities, both in the classroom and beyond. As Arnove (1980) writes, those with knowledge and power may serve "dominant groups, working to legitimate the social order; or . . . they can participate in collective struggles to transform an unjust society" (18). Conversations about justice and equality can be highly effective, but sometimes there is no replacement for actually witnessing inequality by helping those most affected by it.

Listening to Students: Inequality and Peer Pressure

In my interviews with Roberta's students, I tried to ascertain what was inhibiting fair democratic practices in the classroom. Several interviews addressed which students seemed to have power in the classroom, and why. Both popular students, such as Ben and André, and unpopular students, such as Katherine and Anne, equated power with popularity almost as if the popular people constituted their own social class. Ted was another student who equated voice and popularity:

T: I think that mostly popular people tend to take the spotlight and take over. But the people who aren't as popular never get a voice. But maybe if they were heard they would have a significant role and people would understand them. People just might have never given them a chance.

AK: Why do you think people give special consideration to people who are more vocal?

T: Because they think if they stick with them, they'll be popular too and they don't want to be left out. But they need to be open to everybody. People need to realize that everyone needs a voice.

An interview with Susan revealed how powerful the popular students had become:

S: People are mad about things. I know a couple of people who have personal grudges against Ms. Taylor.

AK: And what do you think the source of that is?

S: Well, one person at Bartlett Camp really got mad at Ms. Taylor and ever since then she's been really mad at her.

AK: About what? She told her not to do something?

S: Yes, she told her she was out in the limbo dance, and she was calling Ms. Taylor cuss words afterwards. People just have personal grudges because they think they've turned in their work and Ms. Taylor says she doesn't have it, so they say, "She's just being mean to me" and then they have a personal grudge against her.

AK: To me, there's also a problem with, I don't know if you'd call them grudges—

S: Resentfulness?

AK: I don't know if it's resentfulness, but negative attitudes towards individuals in the class. Like Gerald, for instance. . . . When he asks if he can join their group, people say no. It just seems like those issues of rejection are kind of scary.

S: But I think it's also that some people just aren't interested in [others]. And about Gerald. He's a very sweet boy, but I think people just don't like him because he's different.

AK: That's really what I'm saying. How can people respect differences more in general?

S: People are mean to him because he's different than them. He's just as bright but he has—I don't know. He talks a lot and—I don't want to tell personal things about him.

AK: But another student in the class, too, was just telling me that people call her fat.

S: Katherine. People who are fat really have a hard time with that because people just crawl all over them, and with some people it's not their fault.

AK: So how can people band together in a community to respect differences more rather than make people feel left out because they're different?

S: Well, I think it's because if you like someone, like if you walk with Gerald, instantly the whole school will know and they'll all say you're going out with him. So people are afraid to be with people.

AK: So you think gossip is the main reason?

S: Well, there are people who are popular and then there are people who have personal grudges against you. I mean, I know a couple of people who really hate me. And so, when they see you walking with another person, then they think "Oh yes, I can get Susan really embarrassed." And so they spread it all over the school. So people are really cautious about doing things with boys, or with people that people call mean or fat or ugly or stupid.

AK: So do you think it's not worth the risk, to risk that?

S: No, I don't. I think it *is* worth the risk, but I don't think other people think it is. I think some people would if they felt it was safe, but they really value public opinion and they don't want to risk that.

Gerald was quite aware of the social conditions Susan was describing. In the following interview excerpt, he describes the social exclusion he had experienced:

AK: You said that sometimes people leave you out. But do you feel like that all the time in the classroom?

G: No, only when they don't let me play with them or something. A long time ago they used to call me the "f" word or something like that.

AK: But they haven't done that this year?

G: No.

AK: Why not? What's changed?

G: I don't know. Maybe they just, like, forgot all that stuff.

AK: Do you feel more accepted, then, this year?

G: Kind of. It's like, at Bartlett Camp there were always, like, these rumors about me. And some of them even reached over to the other side of the camp.

AK: Do you think it affected the way people treated you, or did people still treat you well?

G: They keep on annoying me, [saying] I actually got in someone's sleeping bag, but I just jumped on his bed.

In addition to discussing the teasing and taunting we were witnessing, Roberta and I had been talking about the fact that so many students failed to speak up for their rights or for others whose rights were being denied. When I presented this issue to Crystal, who rarely spoke up for her own rights, she explained how topics of conversation were sometimes used to exclude her:

AK: Do you think it would help if you tried to speak more?

C: I'm not sure. A lot of people think what I say is really stupid and they aren't interested.

AK: So you think it's a lack of interest in what other people have to say that's causing it?

C: Yeah.

AK: How do you think people can become more interested in people that don't talk as much?

C: I don't know. There's a lot of stuff I don't know about my class. Some of the things they're talking about I have no idea about.

AK: Like what?

C: Like Patrick talking about all this stuff he sees on MTV. And André and Ben are talking about stuff that I never know. And it makes it seem like they're just talking to each other. And it's just that some of us are put into this group.

In my questioning, I focused on the lack of interest others expressed in Crystal's opinion. A closer look shows that uppermost in Crystal's mind was her own perception that she was viewed by others as stupid. This self-perception shows that the fear of peer disapproval can silence voice as much as, if not more than, a perceived disinterest.

After my interview with Crystal, I began to notice other subtle forms of exclusion in the class, and felt negligent that I hadn't detected them before. I observed, for example, that students sometimes looked at Mei-Ling strangely when, as the only nonnative speaker of English in the classroom, she produced nonstandard forms of English. In an interview, Mei-Ling told me that she didn't mind people asking about her Chinese identity, but when they focused on her Chinese identity as being "funny," "strange," or "different," it bothered her. Likewise, she was bothered by Chinese people who thought her oddly "un-Chinese." In both circumstances, assumptions of inequality lurked beneath the stereotypes. Her experiences indicate that equal treatment does not mean treating everyone the same, nor does it mean focusing on differences. When I asked her what equal treatment meant in her view, Mei-Ling gave specific examples:

M: I've been to three schools. The one in New York they're really nice people. But when I came here these people made fun of me and say like "Tell me some stuff in Chinese." And I just say no 'cause I don't feel like it. If they want to see how to say in Chinese, if they mean like to learn Chinese and take lessons, I feel like it. But people here say like "You look Chinese but you don't act Chinese." I lived in New York and I didn't spoke Chinese a lot. I felt left out from people that knows Chinese . . .

AK: So you felt different from both Chinese people and American people who were asking you to speak in Chinese?

M: Yeah.

Mei-Ling's dilemma of being classified as not American enough in one community and not Chinese enough in another shows that equality frequently has to be negotiated at the personal level. What equal terms might entail in a diverse community can only be determined if these issues are openly discussed. Although issues of equality and fairness came up in Roberta's class, their relevance to the exclusion of unpopular or different students was not being adequately probed.

As peer pressure to exclude certain students increased, so did resistance to Roberta and, for that matter, to any authority. Throughout the fifth grade, a complex stratification was being constructed in which "cool" people were at the summit and "nerds" at the bottom. This was occurring not only in Roberta's democratically oriented classroom but in the other fifth-grade classes as well, according to my interviews with teachers, students, and the principal. The fact that Roberta's class may not have been any more civil than the other fifth-grade classes indicates that we cannot assume that democratic approaches will automatically uphold aims of equality.

Lingering Questions

What is the relationship between democracy and equality?

How can democracy protect against undue majority or minority influence?

In what ways might the disempowered need more than an equal share in a fair and just community?

What kinds of assessment are consistent with a theory of difference?

What kind of bilingual education policies promote equality and fairness?

What can help teachers distinguish between restitution and punishment?

Further Reading

School Reform

Apple, Michael W. 1995. *Education and Power.* 2d ed. New York: Routledge.

Contento, Sandra. 1993. *Rituals of Failure: What Schools Really Teach.* Toronto: Between the Lines.

Dewey, John. [1915] 1971. *The School and Society.* Chicago: University of Chicago Press.

Glasser, William. 1969. *Schools Without Failure.* New York: Harper & Row.

Greene, Maxine. 1995. *Releasing the Imagination: Essays on Education, the Arts, and Social Change.* San Francisco: Jossey-Bass Publishers.

Kohl, Herbert. 1994. *"I Won't Learn from You" and Other Thoughts on Creative Maladjustment.* New York: The New Press.

Meier, Deborah. 1995. *The Power of Their Ideas: Lessons for America from a Small School in Harlem.* Boston: Beacon Press.

Mercogliano, Chris. 1998. *Making It Up as We Go Along: The Story of Albany Free School.* Portsmouth, NH: Heinemann.

Ohanian, Susan. 1994. *Who's In Charge? A Teacher Speaks Her Mind.* Portsmouth, NH: Heinemann.

Postman, Neil, and Charles Weingartner. 1969. *Teaching as a Subversive Activity.* New York: Dell Publishing Company, Inc.

Shannon, Patrick, ed. 1992. *Becoming Political: Readings and Writings in the Politics of Literacy Education.* Portsmouth, NH: Heinemann.

Standards and Testing

Azwell, Tara, and Elizabeth Schmar, eds. 1995. *Report Card on Report Cards: Alternatives to Consider.* Portsmouth, NH: Heinemann.

Berliner, David C., and Bruce J. Biddle. 1995. *The Manufactured Crisis: Myth, Fraud and the Attack on America's Public Schools.* Reading, MA: Addison-Wesley.

Calkins, Lucy, Kate Montgomery, and Donna Santman, with Beverly Falk. 1998. *A Teacher's Guide to Standardized Reading Tests: Knowledge Is Power.* Portsmouth, NH: Heinemann.

Murphy, Sharon, with Patrick Shannon, Peter Johnston, and Jane Hansen. 1998. *Fragile Evidence: A Critique of Reading Assessment.* Mahwah, NJ: Lawrence Erlbaum Associates.

Ohanian, Susan. 1999. *One Size Fits Few: The Folly of Educational Standards.* Portsmouth, NH: Heinemann.

Taylor, Kathe, and Sherry Walton. 1998. *Children at the Center: A Workshop Approach to Standardized Test Preparation, K-8.* Portsmouth, NH: Heinemann.

Zemelman, Steven, Harvey Daniels, and Arthur Hyde. 1998. *Best Practice: New Standards for Teaching and Learning in America's Schools.* 2d ed. Portsmouth, NH: Heinemann.

Teaching for Justice and Equality

Apple, Michael W. 1990. *Idealogy and Curriculum.* 2d ed. New York: Routledge.

Bigelow, Bill, and Bob Peterson, eds. 1998. *Rethinking Columbus: The Next 500 Years.* 2d ed. Milwaukee: Rethinking Schools.

Edelsky, Carole. 1996. *With Literacy and Justice for All: Rethinking the Social in Language and Education.* 2d ed. Bristol, PA: Taylor & Francis.

Gathercoal, Forrest. 1997. *Judicious Discipline.* 4th ed. San Francisco: Caddo Gap Press.

Gaughan, John. 1997. *Cultural Reflections: Critical Teaching and Learning in the English Classroom.* Portsmouth, NH: Heinemann.

Henkin, Roxanne. 1998. *Who's Invited to Share? Using Literacy to Teach for Equity and Social Justice.* Portsmouth, NH: Heinemann.

Kozol, Jonathan. 1991. *Savage Inequalities: Children in America's Schools.* New York: Crown.

Lehr, Susan, ed. 1995. *Battling Dragons: Issues and Controversy in Children's Literature.* Portsmouth, NH: Heinemann.

Lewis, Barbara. 1991. *The Kid's Guide to Social Action: How to Solve the Social Problems You Choose—and Turn Creative Thinking into Positive Action.* Minneapolis: Free Spirit Publishing.

Paley, Vivian. 1995. *Kwanzaa and Me: A Teacher's Story.* Cambridge: Harvard University Press.

Pradl, Gordon M. 1996. *Literature for Democracy: Reading as a Social Act.* Portsmouth, NH: Heinemann.

Shapiro, H. Svi, and David E. Purpel, eds. 1998. *Critical Social Issues in American Education.* 2d ed. Mahwah, NJ: Lawrence Erlbaum Associates.

5

Democracy and Anarchy

Freedom of Speech

After Maureen's exercise fiasco on Tuesday and the mutinous class meeting that followed it, Roberta resolved to shore up her leadership and make her expectations more explicit. On Wednesday morning, May 7, she started the day by announcing that beginning class on time would be a new goal, since making the most of each moment was going to be vital until the end of the school year. The resulting student questions attempted to clarify the parameters of this new expectation and the students' role in monitoring it. Some students felt that they shouldn't have to monitor their time at the beginning of the day. Roberta stressed that she wanted everyone to work toward this goal as an exercise in collaboration. If we can't achieve this small goal, she rationalized, how can we achieve grander goals that involve using time wisely, such as finishing Explorers Club projects, preparing for field trips, and producing the play?

The morning meeting did not move on to bird observation reports as expected because no one, including the students who had volunteered to report observations that week, had made any. The meeting topic instead shifted to the musical we were going to see, since the students still had questions about the trip, and about the musical itself. When she had answered the questions, Roberta gave a little speech:

> This morning I was looking to see if you looked at the chart as you came in and paid attention to what needed to be done. Because people didn't, there wasn't opportunity to do those extra things that we usually do, such as observing the birds. About yesterday . . . I really believe that in order to have

> choice and freedom, you have to be responsible. My conclusion is that there are an awful lot of people who are not being very responsible in here. And that's not just the people who are not doing what needs to be done; other people aren't taking responsibility for helping them get those things done either. . . . We'll [continue to] offer choices, on a limited basis. If people are being more responsible, we'll add more choices. One of the things that will determine whether or not we're going to have play practice is whether or not people turn in their math assignments this morning.

She continued by mentioning that a student had just asked her permission to fill the water dispenser. Since the ten minutes allotted to class jobs was over and it was time for the play rehearsal to begin, she had said no. The person whose job it was to fill the water dispenser had not done it, she explained, and therefore there would be no water in the classroom today. "Ten minutes," she explained, "is a short amount of time, but if I'd seen people trying to get those things done, we could have taken longer."

Andrew, obviously concerned about the possibility of missing play practice, publicly justified not having done the math homework by saying he had "worked on it over an hour, and couldn't get it." Roberta asked who remembered that bringing in evidence of this could constitute completing the assignment, even if the solution wasn't obtained. Most students raised their hands.

The discussion then returned to the ten-minute morning time. Students began making excuses for not getting their jobs done, such as late buses, alarms not going off, and too many things to do in the classroom. Roberta acknowledged these concerns as legitimate and asked the class to suggest solutions to these problems. She highlighted the most practical suggestions, reiterating her expectations that all class jobs be completed within the first ten minutes of class.

After the meeting, the students were calm and orderly until they boarded the bus to head for the high school. Once on the bus, they began talking loudly. Within five minutes of the ten-minute ride, many students were shouting rather than talking and a number of students were turning around in their seats or moving to other areas of the bus. Given the orderly conduct on the bus to and from Bartlett Camp less than a month before, the extent of this disorder was alarming. Susan, ordinarily a fairly compliant student, screamed loudly and abrasively for no apparent reason other than attracting attention, and Roberta immediately got up and spoke to her firmly. Others began to act unruly, and Roberta and I found ourselves hopping up to speak to offenders several times. When the bus arrived, Roberta addressed the whole group. She announced that the bus behavior had been totally unacceptable and that she wanted absolute silence from the moment we left the bus until we were seated in the auditorium. She then mentioned the hard work the high school students had put into the musical and reminded the students to show appreciation for their work by being respectful and attentive.

Although the absolute quiet that Roberta had demanded did not occur, the students said very little as they filed to the auditorium. Their resistance to her authority was expressed by hostile looks and defiant whispers. Before entering the auditorium, Sally and Hope attempted to run off to the bathroom without permission, and Roberta reprimanded them before letting them go. Inside, Roberta and I had to negotiate disputes about seating. Fortunately, they were quickly resolved and the students waited quietly for the play to begin.

The production was surprisingly sophisticated. The program lasted about forty minutes, and during the production, all of the students' eyes were focused on the stage. Although they seemed to be appreciating the musical numbers—some of them were swaying or tapping their feet—only a few students applauded after each song. Even after the last number, fewer than ten of Roberta's students clapped, and one of those who didn't was, surprisingly, Hope, the student in the class who had acted in professional theater and had talked about audience behavior during discussions about *Star Boars.*

Roberta again demanded silence on the bus trip home, and the students complied. The silence, however, seemed more glum than contemplative. Roberta and I acted like watchdogs, and we foiled four students' attempts to shift seats. Glancing at each other, Roberta and I nonverbally conveyed our frustration that our natural style of participation had been replaced by surveillance.

It was a disjointed afternoon. Roberta cancelled the play rehearsal due to the prevalence of incomplete math homework and the amount of time it had taken to finish other work. So the bulk of the afternoon was consumed by the math groups. My own math group had been orderly but listless. After the extended math session, Roberta attempted to shift student perspectives by calling a class meeting and asking the students to answer the following question: "What worked well in our community today?"

Students didn't seem ready for the shift. Instead of positing what worked well, students talked about what shouldn't have happened. Maureen, for example, brought up negative comments other students had made about their classmates' clothes. Two more students made other complaints before Roberta intervened, hoping to turn the tide of the conversation by focusing on positive actions.

"We had some good examples of caring in our [math] group this afternoon," she said. "Maybe some people in our group can talk about specific things that happened."

Students cited the absence of problems rather than positive actions: People didn't make fun of each other, no one got mad about anything, and people didn't "goof around." It took a concerted effort on Roberta's part to elicit examples of kindness, support, or responsibility toward others. She added her own observations to the few sketchy examples brought forward, such as the fact that someone, at the end of the math lesson, had gathered and carried back all the math materials of a student who had gone to the bathroom. At this point, Kirsten destroyed the emphasis on the positive by accusing Roberta of restricting their freedom of speech:

K: This is a little off the subject, but I just wish we could be frank at school because you feel that sometimes, well if I say that I find this book really boring, if I tell the teacher that, she'll get me in trouble. So you can't really express your opinion because you're afraid somebody will get you in trouble.

RT: What you're talking about is not a totally different thing, as you're talking about freedom. And what I'm talking about is responsibility. One thing I want to say is that I'm not happy with the enforcement that I've been doing today, but it's going to continue until I see people doing things that are responsible. I think that you have a lot of freedoms, but one of the things I was thinking was that tomorrow still there won't be drinks, there won't be snacks, there's no getting up out of your seat unless you have permission—all of those things, until you earn those things back again.

Kirsten was unwilling to let go of the freedom of speech issue she had raised. "In the constitution of the United States," she said after being called upon, "it doesn't say 'You have freedom of speech if you don't say anything wrong or bad or something'; it just says you have freedom of speech—"

Billy began to interrupt Kirsten.

"Hold on a second," cautioned Roberta. "I think Kirsten is talking about something very important."

"If somebody doesn't like what you wrote in the press," Kirsten continued, "you can still write it because you have freedom of the press."

"Can someone respond to Kirsten?" queried Roberta.

Ted brought up school rules concerning "cussing," positing that students really did not have freedom of speech.

"We don't completely have freedom of press either," Elizabeth said, returning to the second issue. "I read in the newspaper that people can sue magazines for writing stuff about them."

"Well, they can if it's not true," said Patrick.

"We're supposed to have the freedom to write whatever we want, but we don't," said Brian.

The discussion suddenly became a chorus of competing voices, as had happened so frequently in recent days. Roberta jumped in.

"Excuse me," she said forcefully. "Because we have been unable to talk without raising hands, I'm going to enforce that right now. And I want to hear from more people, even people who aren't usually participating. If you have something to say, put your hand up." Andrew, not a frequent discussion participant, raised his hand and was called on to speak.

"I think about the freedom of speech thing," he said, "you can say pretty much whatever you want as long as it's not offensive. If you're not being mean to anybody—in school, there's just no cuss words—but in any other place, if you're not being mean to anybody, you can say cuss words and stuff like that. But if you totally cuss someone out, then they have the right to get mad at you and stuff like that."

Roberta remarked that Andrew was pointing out the distinction between the protection of ideas and protection against harassment. She then brought up the three branches of government to demonstrate how the protection of freedom, in many instances, depends upon interpretation. She brought up the students' own trial to discuss the limits of freedom. Several students made relevant connections, and the topic of freedom of speech kept returning.

"A couple of years ago, I tried that freedom of speech thing against my mom," said Doug. "She told me that the laws don't apply to us, as children."

"Why not?" shouted André in an indignant tone of voice.

"One thing I try to do as a teacher is apply the laws to you. And that's why I feel like I've given a lot of freedom that you may not have had other years in school. But when I saw that people weren't behaving responsibly—actually, André said it yesterday."

"I did?" André asked, puzzled.

"You were saying 'If we don't choose to behave responsibly, you'll have to treat us differently.' "

"Oh, yeah."

"So you've had a day of being treated differently. I was watching to see how things went when we rode the bus to the high school. I had said before we went that I wanted you to be on your good behavior. But on the bus ride there it was way too loud. I asked people to sit down, and I turned around and they were standing up again."

André raised his hand.

"Yes?" queried Roberta.

"Can I use the bathroom?" he said in a sarcastic, babyish voice. Loud laughter echoed through the room.

"This is really shades of yesterday," Roberta admonished, her voice expressing frustration, "where everybody gets into a laughing thing about something I consider very serious right now. So what's the answer? We had loud people on the bus when everybody was supposed to be quiet." She nodded at Elizabeth, who had raised her hand.

"I just want to say that sometimes people get blamed for things that aren't entirely their fault," Elizabeth said. "Like this morning, we didn't get water today because my computer wouldn't print out my homework. So I was late for school, and when I got here I tried to get the water but it was time for our meeting."

"The hardest thing for me," responded Roberta, "is not making exceptions. And there won't be exceptions tomorrow, so this is a warning."

The freedom of speech discussion continued, unabated.

"One thing you can do is strip us of our privileges, but I don't believe that talking is a privilege," said Patrick. "Does anybody here agree that talking is really a privilege?" he continued, addressing the rest of the group.

Suddenly, every student seemed to be talking at once. The only student whose voice was audible above the din was André, who shouted, "We have the right to say whatever we want!" This brought on loud cheers and more talking. Several voices suggested singing the hamster song as a quiet signal. In spite of a few "shhhh" sounds, the talking continued until four or five children started to loudly sing the play's song.

"Harvey, Harvey . . ." The entire class joined in, and had nearly completed the first line when Roberta interrupted.

"No," she shouted. "That is *not* how we are going to get quiet in here. And André, no, you do not have the right to say whatever you want."

"Yes I do!" he snapped back without hesitation, and began talking to Ben.

"Wait," said Roberta, talking quietly but risking yet another power struggle. "You just said 'I do' and you started talking. And I said no, you don't, and be quiet. Hope, I'm sorry I skipped you." André glared at Roberta, who nodded at Hope.

Hope then put forth yet another excuse, saying that since the school buses were usually loud and unruly on the way home, that they thought that's how they could act on the way to the high school as well.

"Let me go back to my earlier question. Why do you think I asked the whole class to be quiet on the bus?" said Roberta.

André was the first to raise his hand, and Roberta nodded in his direction.

"What I was trying to say before is that normally outside of school we have the freedom to say whatever we want and I would think that in school we'd at least have the freedom to talk. It's really a right!" As he loudly proclaimed the final point, he jumped up.

"Excuse me, sit down," said Roberta. "You've made your point, and I've written it down, that you think it's a right to talk."

The students then went back to Roberta's question, and several publicly agreed that to control the talking of a few, perhaps it had been necessary for her to mandate quiet on the bus. At this point, Roberta, realizing it was nearly the end of the day, closed the meeting. As the students got ready to leave, they were unusually loud and disorderly. A kicking incident on the way out the door rendered the day's end even cloudier, and the friendly good-byes that usually characterized the end-of-day departure had been replaced by stormy scowls.

Roberta and I began reflecting on the day almost immediately. We started by mentioning how André and others were grabbing power and how we might stem this. We discussed the rudeness and defiance that were dominating class interactions. Then we wondered if spelling out the rules more clearly, emphasizing procedures, and attending to other organizational concerns might quell the atmosphere of anarchy. We also devised a handout that began as follows:

REFLECTIONS ON THE STATE OF OUR COMMUNITY

> There can be no degree of democracy without some kind of order. It takes a different kind of order in a crowded classroom than it does in other circumstances. What are some of your rights and how are they maintained?

Under this were two columns. The word "rights" was the heading over the left-hand column and "How are those rights maintained?" the heading over the right.

Although our planned reflection on what defines and protects a right was potentially constructive, we were still lacking a clear, legally grounded picture of this in our own minds. We had not adequately discussed the fine line between rights and privileges, and the students were often equating the two. Worse, we felt that we were back to square one with the class as we exacted compliance but hoped for respect. We thought of the recent toy horse incident. The boys who had been involved had come up with a plan to try to identify the owner and offer to buy a new horse, but it seemed that they had done this to comply with Roberta's demand for restitution, not because they really shared her concerns about what they had done. Compliance, we noted, can be demanded, but respect cannot. Knowing that disrespect was rampant at the moment, we worried that the situation might get worse before getting better.

Maintaining Rights

The ten-minute beginning of the day was more productive on Thursday, but the deadline to complete all tasks during the allotted time was not met. Roberta noticed that a small group of students who weren't getting ready for the day seemed to shun those who were. We had decided to provide some silent work time in the morning, since students were in the final stages of their Explorers Club projects, with several scheduled to make presentations that day. This work time was quiet and productive, with the notable exception of four students who basically did nothing, not even after gentle reminders.

After forty minutes of silent work time, the students were asked to convene to answer the question, "What was different this morning?" In spite of relevant comments, there were significant disruptions. Sally threw a crumpled paper at Mei-Ling and involved others in the dispute, for example, and comments were shouted out. Roberta asked several of the "blurters" to write down their questions or comments until there was time for them to contribute.

The discussion was less than satisfactory, but eventually Roberta felt that it was time to move on. The rest of the day was devoted to work time for independent projects such as the Explorers Club research. Many students worked on their projects, but loud talking and flare-ups between individuals continued.

I was unable to be in Roberta's class on Friday. On Friday afternoon, Roberta and I met to reflect upon the week and to plan the next one. The day, Roberta reported, had not gone well. The kids had been ostensibly quiet, she said, but there were many signs of resistance and she had felt on her guard all day as she tried to convey a sense of authority. The students, she reported, attended to morning tasks when school began but did not put forth a concerted effort to meet the ten-minute goal. The class meeting in the morning highlighted, as before, important issues concerning rights and responsibilities, but she had gained no further ground in garnering greater commitment to smooth group functioning. Presentations throughout the day showed that a number of students had worked hard on their projects, but again there were few questions and the children seemed less keen to support each other's learning than they had been earlier in the year.

The "rights and how those are maintained" writing assignment yielded some fascinating results. All but one student wrote "talking," "speaking," or "speech" as a right. Although what some students listed as rights exhibited hostility and insubordinance (such as "not to be bosted around" and "the right to know why someone in our community is in a bad mood and taking it out on you"), most of the listed rights and the accompanying explanations of how they are maintained were reflective and deep. As we looked over the papers, Roberta commented that many of the mechanisms for maintaining rights that the students had cited in their writing were not in place. Many students understood that protecting group rights involved individual responsibility, but few seemed committed to shouldering such responsibility.

We began to make plans for Monday, since I had been slated to substitute teach for Roberta on Monday and Tuesday, and this plan could not be changed. Carol, a friend and former colleague of mine, would be visiting me until Wednesday and, since Carol had favorably impressed Roberta during a classroom visit in October, Roberta was happy to have her team-teach with me during those two days. Going over the plans, Roberta and I naïvely felt that the suspension of the students' rights still needed to be maintained until the students were consistently civil.

Stormy Monday

By the time the students arrived Monday morning, Carol and I had already mobilized for the day's activities: Job cards had been rotated, the video camera (for taping the Explorers Club presentations) had been set up, independent math work was ready, notices were in student mailboxes, and the day's schedule had been posted. The students drifted in and attended to their morning tasks with varying degrees of intensity. Some students simply started conversations and didn't attempt to organize for the day at all. Some greeted Carol in a friendly manner, while others ignored her.

Since two of the buses had arrived late, not all students were in the room by 9:00. Due to the circumstances, I allowed for some extra preparation time as the late bus students drifted in. Around 9:15, I pointed out that we still were not ready even though the deadline for completing jobs had been extended. A number of individuals reacted defensively. The antagonistic climate did not ebb when I handed out the directions for the math activity. The handout turned out to be the wrong one, and the students became very confused about what they were supposed to do. When my error was revealed as the source of the confusion, several students responded angrily and began to talk loudly. Within one minute, at least nine students were pounding on the desk, clapping, and stomping. The group seemed fiery enough to kindle another rebellion. I demanded quiet and told everyone to write a reflection on the start of the day: what they had done as individuals, as a group, and as a class to try to meet the morning deadline. My instructions were met with hostile protests. The last comment—"Another reflection? Enough is enough!"—resonated in the lull that followed. Although the comment actually reflected my own sentiments, I doggedly stuck to my guns.

As we circulated, Carol and I observed that the responses were almost universally angry and most, including the students who had been most disruptive, denied individual responsibility. "Mr. Koshewa said I needed to get my work done," wrote Susan. "How can I get my work done when we continually have to stop to raise our hand?" Patrick claimed he was reading the whole time, except when he commented on the "torture" of having to write a reflection. "I'm relly mad that this is going on over last week," wrote Sally. "We had a bad group meeting. And we do more good stuff than bad. . . . This is just water under the bridge. Everyone is mad. There's nothing more to say." One student wrote that "if Mr. Koshewa hadn't talked half the time, we could have used our time more efficentienly." Only four students admitted they had talked, "stomped," and clapped. One of these four nevertheless wrote that "the classes actions I think were pretty good and I think we had fun we hadn't had for a week." Another wrote, "We were loud but not as loud as ussual." The class had been writing in silence, but the steam being vented through their pencils almost hissed.

Realizing that we needed to move on, Carol and I decided to collect the papers and begin the next activity. Roberta had been reading *The Rifle* (Paulsen 1995) to the class the previous week and we had planned another read-aloud session and discussion. The group was completely focused as I read the novel. The discussion went well too, as the students probed issues of craftsmanship, ownership, and war. They also raised questions concerning nineteenth-century life and commented on the characters. At last, I thought, the students were reviving the kind of discussions that had generated peak learning experiences earlier in the school year. I was hoping that the Explorers Club presentations would build upon the more positive climate that was developing.

André's attentiveness as the video camera operator allowed Billy's presentation to start on time. Billy had prepared an informative poster for the presentation, had written some notes, and had brought in some resource books he had used. He introduced his topic, the human brain, by telling us how he got interested in the subject, but instead of thoroughly presenting his material, within minutes he embarked upon a laughing fit that put an end to the calm mood. Many students began laughing, talking to each other, and moving to different seats. Billy then began a skit that consisted of a string of jokes loosely related to the topic of the brain. His clownish gestures and goofy faces overshadowed his research. He was sabotaging his own presentation by playing it for laughs, as he was eliciting more talking than laughter.

The traditional question-and-answer session that followed did not go well. The questions, on the whole, were sarcastic and frivolous, mostly focused on Billy's fictional skit. For example, one student asked why the characters he'd assumed in the skit had been so "mental." More rhetorical questions followed.

Veronica's presentation followed Billy's, and although she maintained a serious tone, her presentation, like Billy's, was far from substantial. Her topic was zodiac signs, but despite the many resources she had found concerning history and astronomy, the content of her presentation ignored those resources and was limited to a horoscope flip chart that attributed certain personality traits to each sign of the zodiac. Questions about the presentation were exclusively centered around the alleged personalities ascribed to the students' individual horoscope signs. One horoscope description had included the words "rude" and "silly." André's question, "How do they decide if somebody is rude or silly?" represented a legitimate questioning of resources, yet was dismissed by Veronica and the rest of the class. I paraphrased the question and asked Veronica to talk about the resources for her horoscope information, but she wasn't able to cite the source of her horoscope descriptions. After this, students who hadn't known their sign wanted to hear the descriptions again. Veronica started rereading the long descriptions, this time giving the calendar dates for each sign. By the time she finished, the students had become talkative and restless.

After the two presentations, Hope and Henrietta were slotted to read a picture book they had written together. Hope, until recently, had been the most respected member of the class, someone who could always command attention. Furthermore, her oral interpretations of picture books had always captivated the class. This time, neither the usual enthusiasm for Readers Theater nor Hope's ability to take charge were in evidence. Instead, at least half of the students were shuffling papers, talking, and, in one way or another, ignoring the girls' presentation.

Hope and Henrietta's read-aloud had to be interrupted because of the scheduled library period. Carol and I, after witnessing the apathetic audience, were surprised when many students asked if the girls could continue after lunch. We agreed to this, happy to see some enthusiasm.

When the students entered the library, they began racing to grab the seat of their choice, shouting loudly. I asked everyone to leave and re-enter. Dorothy, the librarian, shook her head, commenting that this group had been very difficult recently. The students entered again, this time calmly and silently. I returned to the classroom.

According to Dorothy, the calm atmosphere broke down just before I returned to check on the students, about five minutes later. When I entered the library, I saw Ben shouting loudly and throwing Doug's notebook around as he played "keep away." I called him into the hallway, instructed the students out of their seats to sit down, and waited for order to resume before going to the hall to talk with Ben. Ben's general tone was that he "didn't do anything wrong." I insisted that he *had* done something wrong, but neglected to focus on a solution to the problem right away. After a few minutes, he calmed down, but he stubbornly continued to justify his actions. I allowed him to return only after he agreed to apologize to Dorothy.

When the library period ended, Dorothy handed me a list citing those who had disrupted her class: Ben, Patrick, Bert, André, Brian, and Doug. The appearance of Bert and Doug on the list was alarming. Bert and Doug, at least before the toy horse incident, had been two of the most responsible class members. I privately told each of the six students to come to the classroom during after-lunch recess to discuss the matter.

The after-lunch meeting started calmly, but early in the session, Ben was summoned to the office. The social worker was there that day, and wanted Ben to attend a session with Sally since the two had been having problems with each other. Bert, Brian, and Doug were eager to rectify the library situation, and proposed that they apologize to Dorothy and that their parents be notified if there were any future problems during library class. André and Patrick reluctantly agreed to the plan, but it was clear that they weren't taking their rude behavior very seriously.

After lunch recess, Carol and I asked Henrietta and Hope to finish reading their story. Then we began a math lesson involving cylinders. The activity allowed movement and talking, and the students happily slipped into a positive mode as they compared measurement methods and results. Some students eagerly wrote in their math journals with a gusto that had been noticeably absent for almost two weeks.

Toward the end of the math lesson, I noticed that Sally was missing, and went to look for her, leaving Carol with the group. Sally was in the hall, chatting with a student from another class. When I asked her what she was doing, she said she was "waiting for a session with the social worker."

"Who gave you permission to wait here?" I asked.

"Ms. Waters," said Sally.

"So Ms. Waters asked you to wait all this time in the hall until you could see the social worker?"

"Yes," answered Sally in a condescending tone of voice. I suspected she was lying, but gave her the benefit of the doubt and went back to class.

Writers Guild, the next learning session, started out productively. We began by brainstorming genres of writing as a way to begin a new writing cycle. An orderly raising of hands helped us construct a large web using ideas from the whole group. After we finished the collective web, each student set to work quickly on their individual webs. The intention was for students to choose a genre and a possible topic, then formulate a writing plan for their first draft. Many, however, began working together on a draft instead of finalizing an individual plan as directed. Rather than negotiate at this point, I pulled rank once again.

"The directions were to work individually," I said. "You need to make an individual plan and work silently."

Students began to bristle, and a few voices paraphrased the question, "Why can't we work together?" I told them that before any kind of collaboration would be considered, they each needed to have their own web.

Many students, one step ahead of us, silently began to write collaborative "individual" webs that mirrored those of their intended writing partners. They also began talking, and our attempts to quiet them down and get them to write individual plans were unsuccessful. Those who wanted to collaborate began to put forth elaborate justifications for working together.

Carol and I glanced at each other. We were exhausted from dealing with these power struggles, and my previously sore throat was now raging and raw. Swept up in a battle about following our directions, we had lost sight of a greater victory: The students, by working together, were exploring the social context of writing. Once we realized that all students were engaged and working, we breathed a sigh of relief.

"Shall we just go with the flow?" Carol asked me.

Before I could answer, the intrusive bellowing of a behemoth lawn mower just outside the window drowned out all other sounds. The deafening roar immediately provoked a simulated laser battle among several boys, in which the mower noise mingled with their own sound effects. One look between Carol and me finalized our decision to negotiate; after calming down the laser fighters, we circulated and, shouting above the din of the lawn mower, told students that they could write collaboratively. The only students who stayed in the *Star Wars* mode were Patrick and Ben, and their laser battles finally led me to send them into the hall. Meanwhile, the commotion had shattered our hopes of a calm afternoon.

After about fifteen minutes, as the lawn mower gradually ambled away, the racket receded. Mercifully, the day was nearly over. We devoted the remaining twenty minutes to clean-up, and, happily, the atmosphere was one of hustle and bustle. The anger and resentment had, for the moment at least, dissipated. The clean-up went reasonably well, except for a handful of students who did not clean their area until I supervised them. As the students finished cleaning, I went into the hall to talk to Patrick and Ben. Ms. Waters was passing by at that very moment. She asked the boys what they had done, and Ben sarcastically responded that they "were just doing what we were supposed to." Ms. Waters reprimanded Ben for his tone of voice and said that if they had been behaving correctly, they wouldn't be in the hall. She then asked the two to write out a consequence for future problem behavior that night or spend the next day in her office. Silenced but far from contrite, the two boys returned to the classroom, and I stayed by the door to talk to Beth. I then learned that she had not given Sally permission to miss class for a meeting with the social worker. Beth said she would talk to Sally immediately. I asked Sally to come to the hall to speak to Ms. Waters, but didn't stay with them since the bell was about to ring and I wanted to attend to the other students before their departure.

As Carol and I said good-bye to each student on the way out, we sensed that the students had lowered their defenses and were more relaxed—until, that is, the last students filed out. Sally, who had joined the end of the line after her brief discussion with Ms. Waters, paused to say, in a snippety voice, "I'm so sorry there was a misunderstanding about Ms. Waters."

"I don't think it was a misunderstanding, Sally," I answered. "You very clearly told me that Ms. Waters had asked you to wait in the hall." The line began advancing, and before I could pull Sally aside to finish the conversation, the interruption of a scuffle allowed her to slip out the door. Ben, defiantly licking a gigantic sucker, had become impatient with the slowly advancing line. As he shouted, "Hurry up, stupid" at Crystal, he angrily kicked her, practically knocking her over. This was the final straw for me. I marched Ben to the office, called his mother, and told her what he had said and done. She expressed concern and said she wanted him to come straight home instead of going to a friend's house for skateboarding as previously planned. I told her Ben was next to me, so she asked to speak to him. His "I didn't do anything" speech obviously didn't work, as he was silent and glum when he handed the phone back to me. I spoke briefly with his mother again before hanging up. "I'm sure we'll have a better day tomorrow," I said, as we shook hands and parted.

After school, Carol and I agonized over many questions. Carol raised the most salient issues by asking, "Do we have to throw out our beliefs about good teaching in order to 'crack down'?" and "Which battles are worth fighting at this point?"

Both of us felt strongly that our approach to the class had not been consistent with our basic beliefs about learning and teaching. We regretted our hard-nosed approach to the writing lesson, and realized that we'd lost a valuable opportunity to compare solitary and collaborative writing strategies. We had not explained our rationale for the directions, nor had we listened to their ideas concerning how they might collaborate.

The policing we had done all day had not felt good to either of us. "Laying down the law" and making so many decisions for students was not our style, and we were setting ourselves up for power struggles we may not have been able to win. By trying to prohibit all talking and movement, we realized, we were demanding a learning environment that we ourselves would abhor. Perhaps, we noted, the students were correct that the freedom to talk is a basic right, as long as it does not interfere with learning.

As we continued to reflect on the day, we agreed that the open-ended math activity had gone well. We realized that our high expectations had, at least for that brief time period, been met. We resolved to extend our trust and to expect reciprocation. As a starting point, we compiled the students' reflections on "Rights," synthesizing their comments as follows:

May 13, 1997 Expectations for Reinstating Rights

Right	**Guidelines**
Talking	Use low voices Take turns Speak in a positive manner Respect quiet signals
Moving around room	Work at your table Move around responsibly
Drinking water	Be orderly Get water unobtrusively
Using computers	Use on a sign-up basis only Give infrequent users a chance

Armed with our plan to reinstate some basic rights and to trust the students to act responsibly, I presented this plan to Roberta over the phone that evening and obtained her stamp of approval.

Reconsidering Rights

Carol and I started the next morning on a positive note, even though I felt consumed by the flu. As soon as all the students were in the room, we put up a list on the overhead of the positive actions we had observed the day before:

helping each other with classroom work, low voices, pleasant comments, and a conscientious clean-up. I informed them that we would begin the class meeting at 9:04, thereby extending the deadline by four minutes. The students seemed invigorated by the extension of the deadline, and began efficiently organizing for the day. At 9:04, the tasks were done, the students were in their seats, and the class meeting began. We passed out the "Expectations for Reinstating Rights" handout and announced that, based on their own ideas about rights and how they are maintained, we would reinstate the rights of students to get water, talk quietly, leave their seats, and use the computers. We then went over the handout and asked for feedback.

The discussion began noisily, with several indignant students assuming that some people would "get in trouble" for offenses and others wouldn't. Carol and I assured the students that our goal was to be fair, to ensure everyone's rights, and to avoid punishment. The group calmed down and a reasonable discussion ensued. The positive mood, however, was interrupted by Sally, who made an "anonymous" swipe at Gerald by saying that she would "appreciate it very much if some of you would stop doing some of the nasty things you do as far as picking your nose and stuff like that." Gerald, ironically, rarely picked his nose these days, since I had talked with him extensively about the problem weeks earlier, and we had arranged for me to make a secret, nonverbal gesture that had worked well as a reminder to stop. It seemed to me that the purpose of Sally's comment was to assert her "right" to put others down. Her comment was followed by applause, and I announced that we would move on to another subject.

Kirsten then spoke up, saying that everyone was angry and that they needed to talk during work time. I stated that today we would try to meet that need by allowing for more talking, but that I expected all conversation to be quiet, courteous, and positive. I then brought up the quiet signals, noting that one student had mentioned that the light-flashing signal wasn't working because of the bright sunlight streaming through the windows. Advantages and disadvantages of ringing the bell were debated. Maureen suggested the class use the hand signal used at Bartlett Camp, since that had worked well there. Music was suggested as another signal. I expressed my concern that turning on music might be easily abused, favoring the hand signal. Veronica then said there likewise was no assurance that hand signals, though they worked at Bartlett Camp, would work in the classroom. André, reinforcing previous comments, noted that "any signal could be abused." Applause followed his comment. Realizing the students were about to mount a campaign for music as the signal, I agreed to the music plan, saying that I would start by using the signal, and, if it worked, would later extend its use to the students. The group unanimously agreed to this plan. To end the meeting, I posted the schedule and said we would stick to it as long as the morning went smoothly. Immediately, there was an undercurrent of conversation about the play rehearsal scheduled for the afternoon.

After the class meeting, it seemed as if a spell had been broken. The students became relaxed and friendly. As the morning progressed, the atmosphere continued to be peaceful and productive, although minor disputes between individuals kept us vigilant. The music worked reasonably well as a signal for quiet, even though it became less effective during the coming days and was eventually abandoned in favor of the hand signal.

The only truly unsettling incident of the morning occurred during a second class meeting just before lunch. Charles, who occasionally suffered from migraines and usually put his head down at his desk when they occurred, was singled out by the group for being at his seat, instead of sitting on the floor with the others. André vocalized the concern publicly.

"How come Charles gets to be at the table?" yelled André. His question was followed by a chorus of "yeahs."

"He has a headache," I said, and dropped the matter, not realizing that the incident would simmer until it reached a boiling point. As the somewhat routine class meeting resumed, there was no immediate evidence of the heated buildup. Five minutes later, the meeting ended and the students disbanded for lunch. I sought out Sally to obtain some closure on the lying incident, but she refused to admit that it was more than a "misunderstanding" on her part. I ended the conversation by saying I felt it was more than a misunderstanding and that I wanted her to help me rebuild my trust in her. I then let her go to lunch.

About ten minutes later, while walking down the hall, I heard loud chanting and screaming coming from the lunchroom. Apparently, the entire fifth grade had been cheering a fistfight that erupted between Ben and Charles. Charles, according to several witness accounts, had been heading to a lunchroom table with his tray of food when Ben sprinkled milk down his neck. Charles then tossed an entire carton of milk in Ben's face, and within moments they were engaged in a violent tussle. At that point, the rest of the students began screaming, pounding, and even jumping on the tables. When I entered the cafeteria Ms. Waters was restoring order. She lectured the students, telling them that they would have to sit quietly in the lunchroom during recess time. She told Charles and Ben to stay in her office for the rest of the day.

When the students returned to the classroom, there was a distinct change in morale. Some students were cursing, some were loudly rehashing the event, and others were glumly silent. Instead of addressing the anger, Carol and I attempted to corral the group for presentations.

Henrietta and Hope, who had been researching gender issues in picture books, had set up an elaborate display of two dozen books during the lunch period. When the students finally settled down, the girls stood by their display, ready to begin. As Henrietta picked up one of the books, a domino effect sent the books crashing to the floor. Understandably, this generated laughter. When it happened the second time, there was more hilarity, but the girls, who had taken pains to set up the books carefully both times, were flustered. By the time they actually started the presentation, the class was again restless.

The audience eventually settled down, but the remaining presentations were flat and there were few student responses. Even the brief play rehearsal seemed perfunctory. The students seemed languid and indifferent as they left the class, although there were no overt signs of hostility.

Reinstating Rights

Roberta's return on Wednesday was marked by a subdued but peaceful atmosphere. During the morning class meeting, most students said very little at first, but those who did were using a calm and pleasant tone of voice. Kirsten managed to sour the atmosphere, however, when she raised her hand and said, "Ms. Taylor, I don't mean to be rude, but I don't like the sound of your voice today."

"That *is* rude," responded Roberta sharply, "and it's unnecessary."

During the rest of the day, student accountability was, at most, erratic, in spite of the fact that student rights had been restored. Students were civil, but were not particularly friendly and seemed to take no initiative. Many students asked Roberta when they would be able to practice the play, and she promised to discuss it with me within the next couple of days.

We were not able to discuss it that day, however, because we had an appointment with Dr. Lingle after school. He had called the meeting because André, according to Dr. Lingle, was "feeling victimized." He cited the library incident as a recent catalyst, claiming that André "always wants to stay in at recess" because being reprimanded had traumatized him and he was now too embarrassed to play with his friends. He then justified André's continued failure to complete homework by saying he was smaller, younger, and less physically fit than the other boys. After listening to Dr. Lingle paint a picture of André as weak and powerless, Roberta said that, although he may be powerless in some situations, he was not at all powerless in others. She cited some examples of André using his influence in the class to demonstrate caring, and then said that, more often, he chose to set an example by being silly and callous. Furthermore, she claimed, he was capable of completing assignments. She then asked some direct questions about André's behavior at home, and Dr. Lingle eventually revealed that André "needs coaxing to get him to do things," and that he almost always needed two or three reminders before following parent directions. He then confessed that he and his wife couldn't get André out of the door in the morning without physically pushing him. The reason for all this recalcitrance, according to Dr. Lingle's analysis, was that André was "uninspired" by school. Roberta suggested ways for Dr. Lingle and Dr. Martine to make expectations clear and suggested withdrawing privileges, such as TV and trips to the mall, in the event of noncompliance when it came to important matters such as being ready to leave for school. Dr. Lingle agreed to try these measures, but closed the conversation by reiterating that André was "uninspired" about school these days and needed to be "inspired" in order to accomplish anything. After Dr. Lingle left, Roberta and I felt similarly uninspired.

Thursday was a pivotal day. For the first time in weeks, neither Roberta nor I needed to remind anyone to complete their morning jobs, and class was under way by 9:00. The homework of all but four students (including André) had been turned in. Many students participated in the morning class meeting, a contrast to recent meetings in which a few students dominated. Most of the day was consumed by Explorers Club presentations, and a high level of engagement was sustained throughout each presentation. Even Charles' presentation on the anaconda, which, unlike the others, was disorganized and rambling, elicited a respectful wealth of questions and comments.

The highlight of the day, for many of the students as well as for Roberta and me, was Anne's presentation. Before this school year, Anne had hated school, did not read fluently, had no close friends, and was extremely disorganized and unmotivated. I thought about her recent enthusiasm and her complete absorption in the Harriet Tubman books she had been reading in recent weeks. Roberta and I had shared several animated conversations with her about the material she was reading. We never imagined, however, that she could make such an eloquent and moving presentation.

Anne eagerly walked to the front of the room and propped up an evocative poster depicting Harriet Tubman as an adolescent. She faced the class with a confident smile and said, "Harriet Tubman was . . ." Stopping in midstream, she grabbed her index cards and finished the sentence ". . . born in 1820." Then, to our surprise, she put aside the notes and painted a vivid picture of Tubman's childhood in slavery and later accomplishments. When she finished, the vigorous applause and the abundance of questions and comments attested to the quality of the presentation.

As significant as Anne's presentation was, it was not the event that turned the tide of the classroom community. Instead, it was a decision that Roberta and I made at the end of the week.

"You know," I said to her after school, "we're going to have to decide whether or not we're going to make a commitment to *Star Boars.*"

"I was thinking the same thing," she responded. "It will take a lot of work, we'll have to abandon a lot of other things we'd hoped to do, and we may not even be able to perform it before the school year ends. Are you willing to try it, though?"

"Yes," I said, and sealed our fate with that final word.

Stepping Back: Class Meetings

Unfortunately, Roberta, Carol, and I saw the students' failures, squabbles, and contentiousness as threats to the stability of the class, rather than seeing them as opportunities to refine our approaches to classroom discipline and democracy. As a result, we resorted to authoritarian practices despite our gut feeling that these practices didn't correspond to our beliefs. Our authoritarian stance did achieve some degree of compliance, but the price we paid was an element of discord and volatility that undermined the benefits of that cooperation. In essence, several features of our "crackdown" were ultimately detrimental: curtailing choices, instituting group punishment, denying speaking rights, not directly addressing the conflicts, and truncating deliberation processes. These features of the crackdown actually threatened democratic processes. Class meetings, however, acted as a safety valve for democratic practices and ultimately compensated for these temporary restrictions. Only in retrospect did Roberta and I understand that some of our strategies had threatened democracy, while other strategies had preserved the integrity of class meetings, helped re-establish order, and eventually restored the positive morale of the class.

1. Roberta thwarted democratic practices by curtailing choices and invoking group punishment. On the morning of the field trip to the high school, she made it very clear that choices would have to be earned, and warned the students that irresponsible behavior could threaten the opportunity to rehearse *Star Boars.* The threat of group punishment inherent in this message was reinforced by Roberta's ruling that no one could have water because of Elizabeth's failure to fill the dispenser before class. These pronouncements, as the students themselves explained to me two weeks later, turned Roberta's remaining supporters against her. Students who had tried to get ready in the morning, had completed their math work, and would gladly have filled the water dispenser for the benefit of the whole group were deprived of water privileges and the chance to work on the play. In addition, her reasoning that the students had not been trying hard enough to get the morning tasks done was viewed as an unfair accusation by a vocal few who had indeed put forth an effort to get ready. Those more inclined to be cooperative immediately sympathized with those whose privileges were withdrawn for legitimate reasons. As a result, the students most responsible for the problems gained power by their ability to incur consequences on the entire group.

Students were making choices that were impeding equal participation in the class, and Roberta was compelled to somehow restrict those choices. Unfortunately, like many teachers, she suspended many choices at once and found herself veering into an authoritarian role. At the time, Roberta and I failed to understand Freire's (1998) position that "because I reject authoritarianism does not mean I can fall back into a lack of discipline, nor that, rejecting lawlessness, I can dedicate myself to authoritarianism. . . . One is not the opposite of the other" (64). Both Roberta and I established decrees that eliminated choices and closed off criticism. Since the crackdown punished the entire group and was not negotiated through student input, the students saw it as unfair and authoritarian.

2. Roberta thwarted democratic processes by not adequately probing freedom of speech issues. During the crackdown, she demanded complete silence when quiet talking would have been appropriate. Furthermore, when Roberta responded to Kirsten's remark about her voice, she merely commented that it was rude and moved on. Though Roberta's reaction did provide a parameter for the class, the time might have been ripe for a more extensive discussion about what is and isn't acceptable classroom speech, and why.

Few teaching strategies differentiate the way we treat adults from the way we treat children more than attempts to control talking. The argument that adults are generally able to monitor and control their talking better than children is valid, but there are occasions when groups of adults are not easily silenced. Delivering a decree exacting absolute silence until further notice would likely induce the same hostility among adult groups as it might among children. Although it was important for Roberta to exert her control over shouting during the bus ride to the high school, her demand for complete silence was perceived as a denial of rights. The bus behavior actually represented several continua of behavior, from ordinary talking to screaming, from leaning into the aisle to jumping from seat to seat, from compliance to defiance. Like other zero tolerance policies, our decree represented a rigid view of rights, and falsely assumed that all violations were equally detrimental. Zero tolerance policies tend to construe humans as nonthinking entities who will fall like dominoes once one person has "gotten away" with violating a rule. Roberta and I, by forcing everyone to be completely still and silent, were treating all bus offenses as equally disruptive. When we policed the bus to catch violators, we bred collective resentment.

Gathercoal (1997) provides a legal perspective of freedom of speech when he writes that "not every form of student speech is protected by the First

Amendment; basically *only ideas are protected*. For example, profane language, indecent gestures, and bigoted statements directed at someone and intended to harass have no protection" (170, emphasis in original). As Roberta and I began to analyze the proliferation of insults in the classroom and how we were addressing them, we began to formulate our own definitions of free speech. After we reinstated free speech, we shared some of these definitions with the class. As we actively solicited student definitions through conferences, interviews, group meetings, and written responses, the parameters of free speech became clearer to us all. These parameters, however, might have been clearer from the beginning if we had understood that the state interests of protecting health, safety, property, and legitimate educational purpose constitute a fundamental set of criteria for legally denying the constitutional rights of students (Gathercoal 1997).

3. Roberta thwarted democratic processes by refusing to allow ample time for deliberation concerning classroom decisions. During the crackdown, the students' perception that their rights had been denied was reinforced by Roberta's refusal to publicly debate issues and policies. She exacerbated the drinking water situation by refusing to discuss the implications of the new rule. The fact that Elizabeth may have had a legitimate excuse for not filling the water dispenser made Roberta's decree appear even more extreme. When the students defiantly chanted the "Harvey the Hamster" song, the song was a symbol of group solidarity and autonomy. By singing the song, they were defying Roberta's suggestion that they all should be treated alike by, paradoxically, acting exactly alike. By allowing no exemptions to the time limit for completing jobs, Roberta conveyed the idea that equal treatment means treating each person the same way. As Gathercoal (1997) notes, exceptions to rules are important "because they recognize the legitimate differences among members of the group. The group must learn to trust that decisions regarding exceptions will be fair for all" (47).

What constitutes fair, equal treatment cannot be ascertained without extensive debate about specific incidents of inequality. As the students themselves indicated in interviews, class meetings were sometimes rendered ineffective because insufficient time had been allocated for hearing every possible side of the issues at hand. And even when many opinions were voiced, not all opinions were deliberated. As Elshtain (1995) reminds us, "A compilation of opinions does not make a civic culture; such a culture emerges only from a deliberative process" (29). Students hesitant to participate either felt they had no opportunity to voice an opinion or that their opinion was disregarded. Freire (1998) feels that when students feel they are heard, they are more open to teacher ideas and develop what he calls democratic dispositions: "It is through hearing the learners, a task unacceptable to authoritarian educators, that democratic teachers increasingly prepare themselves to be heard by learners" (65). Authoritarian approaches, such as the zero tolerance policies Roberta and I implemented during the crackdown, effectually quashed debate altogether and made students feel unheard.

Obviously, some veto power over the group's rebellious teetering into anarchy was called for. But the fact that Roberta's quietly spoken requests garnered a large measure of compliance, even during the crackdown, indicates that extensive deliberation of the conflicts and possible resolutions could have been orderly. Furthermore, such deliberation might have instilled more student ownership over discipline decisions, even if Roberta had the final say. Support for differing ideas could have replaced the need for consensus. If hearing different viewpoints, rather than voting and consensus, is a frequent focus of deliberation, class meetings need not entail the tyranny of the majority, nor must they lead to sacrificing the many at the hands of individual students—or the teacher.

4. Roberta thwarted democratic processes by not confronting harassment and conflict resolution more directly during class meetings. Teachers, of course, cannot avert or discuss every conflict. But Charles' actions during the lunchroom incident indicated that he had been harassed too often, and the extent of this bullying had not been sufficiently understood or addressed. During the lunchroom incident, the mob mentality of the fifth graders showed that social support for bullying permeated the entire fifth grade. Social forces beyond the confines of the classroom were affecting the students: Fifth graders from other classes were bullying second graders on the bus, some students had witnessed vandalism and drug incidents at middle school events, and some students' parents were unable to discipline them at home. Utilizing class meetings to learn about and resolve conflicts beyond the classroom might have minimized the adverse effects they were causing.

Roberta also could have confronted conflict more effectively during class meetings if she had learned more about the students' use of the relatively new Conflict Council. The Conflict Council was a group of volunteer students who, with the help of the part-time counselor and the principal, helped students resolve their problems through mediation or arbitration. At Robinson Elementary, the school psychologist trained volunteer students to mediate for the Conflict Council. When students went to the Conflict Council, adults were ordinarily not involved. As Beth, the principal, described it, the students "have to come up with their own solutions rather than those being imposed by some authority figure, like myself or a teacher or whatever. The solutions last longer, I think, because the kids have come up with them themselves." During the crackdown, Roberta was not yet referring students to the Conflict

Council, which resulted in fewer opportunities for students to directly confront harassment and conflict. Students who had been involved in lunch and recess disputes had been utilizing the Conflict Council, but neither Roberta nor I had kept abreast of these disputes, nor had we sufficiently understood different approaches to conflict resolution.

Although Roberta did indeed implement conflict resolution strategies, she was not always conscious of her approaches. Levin (1994) contrasts conflict resolution and traditional discipline approaches, explaining that traditional discipline approaches invoke rules, rely upon "time out" tactics of isolation, or "impose an adult's ideas about a solution on the children rather than significantly involving the children in finding a solution of their own" (58). According to Schellenberg (1996), there are five main approaches to conflict resolution: coercion, adjudication, negotiation, mediation, and arbitration. When coercion and adjudication approaches are used, the most powerful party in the dispute determines the outcome, either through force or decree. Roberta tried to avoid using coercion and adjudication to settle conflicts, but she often utilized negotiation, mediation, and arbitration. When she relied upon negotiation, she sought voluntary agreement by encouraging all participants to air their views, but a formal vote was not always taken. Mediation and arbitration involve a third party, the difference being that, in arbitration, the third party makes the final decision. Sometimes Roberta allowed student leaders of group meetings to take on a mediation or arbitration role, while at other times she took on that role.

Experience in helping children come up with their own solutions is essential, but it should not be assumed that solutions will eliminate further problems. Christensen (1994) feels that struggle is at the heart of a thriving community. "Students won't always agree on issues," she writes, "and the fights, arguments, tears, and anger are the crucible from which a real community grows" (14). Meier (1995) reminds us that "democracy is not always convenient, and rights do require sorting out. . . . It is often in the clash of irreconcilable ideas that we can learn how to test or revise ideas" (7). Even if teachers do not have experience in conflict resolution, they can support group attempts to solve problems. A belief that problems are barriers that should be eliminated in order for learning to take place is not consistent with conflict resolution precepts. A traditional view of discipline problems needs to be replaced by a belief that problems are opportunities for growth, and thus need to be confronted and discussed.

5. Roberta preserved the democratic environment by persistently holding class meetings. Throughout the school year, class meetings were an important feature of Roberta's classroom, and even during the crackdown she did not completely abandon them. During the first couple of months, Roberta made a concerted effort to field debates and demonstrate their value. She concurred with Amy Gutmann's idea (paraphrased in Darling-Hammond and Ancess [1996]) that "citizens must have the knowledge and skills to be able to intelligently debate and decide among competing conceptions, to weigh the individual and the common good, if they are to sustain democratic ideals" (153–154). Roberta frequently demonstrated ways to effectively run class meetings, such as paraphrasing what others have said and soliciting opposing views. Sometimes, as Anderson (1998) suggests, she redirected "gripe sessions" by asking questions such as, " 'How can we make things better?' or 'How can we help Johnny with his problem?' " (19). During the crackdown, students neglected many of these strategies. Roberta and I later realized that debate concerning individual and group gain needed to be explicitly addressed more often, keeping in mind, as Goodlad (1997) does, that maintaining a balance between individual and group rights is an ideal, not a norm.

The class meetings concerning the play rehearsals provide a perfect example of how student-run meetings ran the gamut of effectiveness. At times, the students effectively solved their problems during these meetings, but at other times they mismanaged the meetings, discouraged equal participation, or came up with solutions that did not entail maximum benefit for all. Roberta nevertheless had faith that relinquishing teacher control over class meetings would allow the students to experience how to run successful meetings in a way that directing them herself wouldn't have provided. On the other hand, she sometimes did intervene when class meetings were unproductive.

The rebellion in Roberta's class forced us to examine the role of class meetings in the curriculum. The depth of the conflict that precipitated the crackdown was first revealed by the deterioration of the meetings. As the conflict intensified, the importance of effective class meetings became more apparent. If Roberta had given up on class meetings rather than found ways to make them effective again, we might not have witnessed the remarkable community-building power that the meetings would exert during the last two weeks of the school year.

6. Roberta maintained the integrity of class meetings by not using them to promote her authority. She frequently brought her agenda to class meetings, but allowed students great latitude in making decisions about meeting issues. The snack situation was a case in point. Roberta proposed parameters for healthy snacks during a September class meeting, but genuinely sought the students' support through persuasion. Majority rule supported Roberta's position and prevented minority voices from having undue influence upon snack choices. Only in September, when the student snack monitors were most vigilant, and in May, when students were actively attempting to defy authority, was there a pattern of children abusing the guidelines. When compliance became a class meeting topic, however, Roberta genuinely wanted to examine the issue rather than simply maneuver popular students to put pressure on the others to comply with the guidelines.

Class meetings can provide an effective forum for persuasion, but if there is an undercurrent of favor seeking or threat, the persuasion becomes manipulation. The motives that underlie the reasons a meeting is called, as well as the way it is conducted, must be examined to ascertain the fine line between persuasion and coercion. Who benefits, and in what ways, from democratic decisions based on consensus should also be scrutinized. A teacher's faith in democratic processes may, at times, need to be tested by her ability to accept a majority rule decision that she doesn't feel is in her best interests, or in the best interests of the entire group. Kohn's (1998) assertion that teachers must accept unwanted outcomes of democratic deliberations, given that deliberations were not discriminatory or repressive, is a bitter pill to swallow, but allowing poor decisions to run their course may be the only way to ensure the hardiness of democratic processes in the classroom. Veto power on the part of the teacher should be invoked only to protect the compelling state interests of property rights, health and safety, legitimate educational purpose, and prevention of serious disruption of the educational process (Gathercoal 1997).

7. Roberta held class meetings for a variety of purposes: to discuss issues with or without a particular outcome in mind, to share compliments, to plan projects, to make decisions about the curriculum or social concerns, to solve problems, and to follow up on prior solutions. The many functions of class meetings became more evident during the last two weeks of the school year, when student-called class meetings occurred at least once a day. Only then, in the midst of *Star Boars* planning, did students utilize class meetings for a variety of purposes: they offered critique and compliments about acting, made plans, and solved conflicts.

Too often, teachers utilize class meetings simply to obtain consensus. As Lyotard (1988) claims, consensus in itself is not unjust or inadequate, but, taken as a community goal, it fails to recognize the contestation that underlies all decision making. Consensus can be an avenue for attaining justice or a mechanism by which the healthy articulation of different theories and goals is suppressed. Short, Harste, and Burke (1996) critique the fact that democracy in education has often been interpreted as a need for consensus, which has reinforced the current emphasis on curriculum guides, standardized tests, behavioral objectives, and national standards. Too much faith in consensus can undermine the value of uncertainty and downplay the differing perspectives within social groups. In Roberta's class, however, consensus was not a primary goal of class meetings.

The reinstatement of rights in Roberta's class marked a turning point in the school year and had a major impact on class meetings. It led to renewed student ownership over class meetings and to a new openness to minority views. Just as Anne revived the excitement of sharing Explorers Club research with her dazzling Harriet Tubman presentation, individuals would soon imbue passion and life into class meetings. These meetings, in turn, would vitalize the remainder of the school year.

Listening to Students: The Complexity of Democratic Decisions

The students' renewed interest and passion in each other's work provided a glimmer of hope that the tide had turned. But the recent problems were still fresh in our minds. When class meetings were becoming more disorderly, it became clear that the insult culture was interfering with effective democratic practices. Kirsten's insulting remark about Roberta's voice symbolized a growing student perception that "honesty" should preclude courtesy, and that individual rights should outweigh collective norms. As negative thoughts were publicly aired, the insult culture was tightening its stranglehold, gaining more and more social approval. Ben, during an interview, commented on the "jokes" that had been proliferating:

AK: Isn't it possible that you could be funny to some people and not to others at the same time? It seems to me that was kind of the problem last week. Some people thought things were funny that other people thought were hurtful. . . . I guess my question is, can't the criteria for what's funny or what's nice be different for different people, in which case, how is it decided what really is funny or nice?

B: For one, you have to make sure that if you're going to make a joke about somebody or say something not kind to the other person, you have to be in the right environment to do that. Like, everybody's joking around and you just crack a joke about somebody. Usually, if somebody says something like that to me, I'll laugh because usually it's funny. I'm not really sensitive like some people are. If somebody cracks a joke about my family or something like that, I'll laugh if it's funny and everything. And then I'll find a good comeback to get 'em back and they'll easily laugh too.

Ironically, Ben was rarely as nonchalant about insults as he claimed to be. Although there were occasions when he laughed off derisive remarks or thoughtfully considered others' feelings, he usually took offense at others' insults and reacted with commensurate viciousness.

Anne was the butt of derision early in the year, but managed to find her voice through curriculum. Anne's persistence in choosing an "unpopular" topic for her Explorers Club research shows that Anne saw the open-ended nature of Explorers Club as an opportunity to develop her voice. At first, no one was interested in her topic and she could find no one to collaborate with her on the research. An interview with Anne shortly after her presentation showed that she had chosen the topic despite peer disapproval:

AK: You really delved deeply into that topic; what motivated you?

A: Ever since second grade, I've always wanted to study Harriet Tubman. So I said "This is a perfect time to study Harriet Tubman." I asked if anybody else wanted to do it with me, and they said no because they thought it was dorky to do Harriet Tubman. So I just did Harriet Tubman by myself.

After the presentation, however, questions flourished and the topic did not die. As students began discussing the inequalities Harriet Tubman experienced, many points of view emerged. During the following weeks, students actively sought Anne out to learn more about the topic and periodically talked about her presentation. In Anne's "What I Will Always Remember" booklet, five students wrote about the Harriet Tubman presentation. At last, Anne's voice had been actively heard.

Anne did more than find her voice in the classroom; she also learned to view voice as a means for preventing the abuse of majority rule:

AK: What about the whole idea of democracy and majority rule—has that worked very well in here?

A: One time when we were deciding if people wanted to go outside for math, a lot of people, sixteen or eighteen people, raised their hands to go outside, and the rest of the class raised their hands to stay inside because they don't like all the bugs. So everybody had to go outside. And people who didn't want to go outside thought that wasn't fair, because they always have to do what the other people think and do. During the trial of Calvin and Hobbes, a witness lied and the jury didn't even notice. We tried to point that out but they weren't even listening to us. Some people in the jury didn't like me at that point, so they voted for the other team. That isn't fair.

AK: So you're saying that majority rule doesn't ensure fairness?

A: Yeah.

AK: So what does make sure that people are fair and honest?

A: They need to tell what they think.

AK: Who? The people who disagree with the majority?

A: Yeah. I think, in the jury, I think they should have went back in for a retrial. It was an unfair decision. She was not guilty of throwing a snowball and breaking his nose.

AK: So in cases like that, people who disagree have to have more opportunities to talk about it?

A: Yeah.

AK: What if the majority still isn't convinced? Is it still fair to go with majority rule?

A: After a while, I guess.

Hearing the voice of shy students took continual work throughout the year. If I had not conducted interviews with the students, I might never have heard the unique and profound views some of the quiet students held. Only three students—André, Charles, and Ben—were not very reflective during interviews, saying little. Many students revealed remarkable sensibilities during interviews, and their articulation of those sensibilities sometimes re-emerged during class meetings. Susan, for example, offered astute social analysis during interviews and would later refine her views during class discussions. When she returned from a multiple-day absence shortly after Maureen's disastrous exercise session, Susan quickly noticed how strong the peer pressure had become:

S: When I came back, suddenly the whole class was mad. I had six people come up to me that day and just sit there for about half an hour and tell me all these different things they were going to do. . . . Some people were going to act up as much as they could. People were really mad. And I just didn't know what to do. And I kind of felt that that was the wrong thing. But . . . people don't want to tell on each other normally. . . . And there are a number of people who act like they can own the classroom. . . . Some people do what they want just because they want to be liked by them and some people don't. If you don't, you're not popular, but it depends on how much you really want to be popular.

AK: And what makes someone popular these days?

S: They dress like everyone else. They act really sassy and they act like the teacher is not the teacher, but just someone that they can obey or disobey. That's how you become popular.

AK: It seems to me that the problem is not just in Ms. Taylor's class but all over the school.

S: This has been going on for a couple of years now.

AK: Oh, so you think it happened when you were in third and fourth grade, too?

S: Well, the people who were popular then are still popular now, and they still try to run the classrooms.

AK: Why do you think that's what makes people popular?

S: Because people think, "Oh, they can do these things. They can tell the teacher no. Oh, these people must be really cool; let's do what they do."

AK: So it's because they're bold?

S: Yeah. . . . the rest of the classroom is sort of divided. There are the people who are popular and there are the people who just really do whatever the teacher wants them to do and then there's the group that's not really sure. They're kind of mad at the teacher and yet they don't want to be really sassy. I think it's them that's having the hardest time right now. I know that some people are still mad at the teachers; I've heard them say so.

Popularity, characterized by following trends and exhibiting defiant behavior, seemed to be guiding student leadership in the fifth grade. And the group punishment had made normally compliant students angry enough to support the defiant, powerful ones. The powerful students, however, exerted undue influence and did not really seem concerned about the rights of their followers. This was one reason that majority rule was no longer a productive basis for group decisions in Roberta's classroom.

Many of the students were beginning to realize that majority rule was not ensuring fairness in the class. Patrick, for example, did not see voting as the ideal way to seek equality:

P: Sometimes it's not fair for a vote because some people might just like this one thing instead of thinking about what it will do. Take voting—a lot of people would just vote for their friends. Some people would just vote for something because their friend thought of it—

AK: Without even considering what?

P: What it's about or what they're going to get out of it.

AK: What they're going to get out of it, meaning the individual or the group?

P: Kind of both, 'cause when you're in a group each person gets something out of it, and as a group as a whole you get something out of it, too.

AK: I was interested because you were saying voting is good most of the time but not all of the time, and since you said not all the time I'm trying to figure out which times it wouldn't—

P: Well, maybe if you're voting on a better piece of art or something. If you don't understand what the art's about, would it be fair for you to vote on it, to [decide] that this one's better? If you don't know what it's about or what it means, then how can you vote on it?

AK: Then you're saying that enough background information and understanding have to happen before voting?

P: Yeah, because if you don't understand what you're voting about, people will just pick eeny-meeny-miney-mo, oh, let's just get that one.

AK: But what if people understand the issues but still decide to vote for whatever will benefit them rather than everybody?

P: Well . . . before people vote they should learn more about it and really choose which one they think is best. But you can't always guarantee that with people, because people have opinions.

AK: So if you can't guarantee it, what else can you do to make sure that everyone's opinion is heard and considered?

P: Having people take suggestions, give suggestions. Finding out exactly what a person's going to do, why they're doing it, should they be doing it.

AK: So more discussion time and analysis?

P: We vote just off the bat, I don't think that's fair all the time. Do you want this person or this person to be president of the world? I'll take the one on the right.

AK: So you think decisions that affect the classroom need to be deliberated?

P: Not necessarily the whole classroom, any time. It doesn't have to always be the whole classroom.

Several other students also mentioned the importance of time for deliberation; Jessica, for example, claimed that sometimes class meetings were cut short before all points of view were heard.

When I brought up the issue of problematic group decisions with John, he discussed the role of unanimous agreements during group meetings:

AK: What happens when the majority decides on something that might be mean or decides that they want to exclude people?

J: Then it should be that everybody has to agree on something.

AK: Unanimous, you mean, instead of majority?

J: Yeah, yeah, yeah.

AK: How do you decide when something should be unanimous rather than majority?

J: Well, like, if it's something really important, it should be unanimous.

AK: Like what, for example?

J: Like having our rights and everything, like going to the bathroom when you need to, getting up and getting drinks.

John's assumption that unanimous agreement can overcome the limitations of majority rule fails to address the important fact that some groups can unanimously make decisions that are detrimental to group members or others outside the group. But as we know from legal precedents, sometimes this is inevitable. Poor decisions, however, may occur less frequently if, as the students themselves suggested, deliberation is inclusive and thorough.

Maureen was another advocate for thorough deliberation:

> You should think about everybody's point of view and get in other people's shoes before you say something that you think might hurt them. You could think, "Well, gosh, what would I do?" . . . You have to check and make sure that things are just. If you don't discuss things with people, they'll never know what happened.

Other students pointed to the importance of leadership in guiding majority rule. Brian, for example, used the disruption of What's on My Mind? sessions as an example of a situation in which teacher intervention was justified:

B: If you've got a majority and decide that you know what's right, and the majority's on the wrong side, then the person who has the most power, the teacher, she should automatically appoint the right one, like no talking during What's on My Mind? You should just know not to be talking during that and such.

AK: So the leader should have the right to veto majority decisions?

B: Yeah.

AK: What if that person abuses the power?

B: Um, if that person is abusing the power then it can get tooken away, probably.

AK: Who would take away the power of the teacher, though?

B: A principal, maybe. There's always somebody that can take over the power but it's kind of like Congress and the president. The president's head man but he can't do all he wants because it has to be approved and all.

Some students thought that majority opinion justified curtailing individual rights. Crystal, for example, thought that nose-picking should be outlawed in the classroom simply because she didn't like it when Gerald did it. When I asked her, however, if nose-picking really interrupted learning or otherwise interfered with others' rights, she acknowledged that it didn't. She was reluctant, however, to waver from her position that the majority should be able to regulate individual actions of which they disapproved:

C: If it's something gross, I would like to have the majority agree on it, because it's kind of disgusting. . . .

AK: [If you were so concerned about the rudeness of nose-picking], why didn't you get mad when people were interrupting? Isn't that also equally rude, or not?

C: Sometimes I do get mad and go "Be quiet."

AK: So you do tell people to be quiet sometimes.

C: Because sometimes they interrupt you and everything.

AK: So what's the best way to ensure that a community's a good one?

C: I don't know.

AK: What's going to make the democracy and the majority rule and the cooperation positive? What makes it positive?

C: Well, I guess it's people are questioning.

Crystal's final statement was, I feel, highly significant. It showed that, despite her belief that majority opinion should curtail individual rights, Crystal also believed that majority decisions should be open to question. She seemed to understand that allowing individuals to contest and debate majority decisions helped limit the abuse of majority rule. Like many of the other students, she valued the ongoing deliberation concerning what constitutes individual and group rights and how both can be protected.

Students felt strongly that the protection of individual and group rights was an important outcome of class meetings. Doug, for example, brought up the abuse of group rights when several students began hogging the computer that had Internet access. After a class meeting drew attention to the issue, several students discussed the matter among themselves and a solution was devised. During an interview with Doug, he referred to the solution as an example of student-imposed guidelines to ensure fairness:

AK: Do you think there's any way to ensure that everybody has their fair share [of classroom resources]?

D: Yes, that's why we came up with those little sheets of paper for the computers. We have all these times that would be OK with the teacher and we made, like, a graph of times. And you have to sign up for that time and space.

AK: Who thought of the sign-up system?

D: Ted and Brian.

AK: And it's worked pretty well?

D: Yeah.

Doug also felt that the Conflict Council was extremely important. He described Conflict Council procedures as follows:

D: If you're having a problem, you go to the principal and they call on two conflict managers. There's two kids from each class, and they'll call in two conflict managers, like at recess. They help you resolve your problem and you have to agree on certain things, like you can't speak directly to that person, because there's always the possibility of another fight. You have to speak to the conflict managers. And you have to agree on a bunch of rules and stuff.

AK: That you come up with?

D: No, that the conflict managers come up with. They have a sheet that they have to read to us, and we need to agree on the rules.

Unfortunately, Roberta and I did not always implement conflict resolution approaches, especially during the crackdown. Neither did Beth, even though, as the principal, she had established and supported the Conflict Council. Despite her belief in the program, Beth responded to the rebellious outburst in the cafeteria by making the children sit in assigned seats during lunch. This authoritarian move, designed to divide and conquer, had the opposite effect: Students conspired with friends to snub unpopular individuals and cliques became stronger. A taped conversation I had with Hope and Jessica provides student perspectives of this reaction:

H: Now all these groups are being split up and have to sit somewhere else, say, for example, [I have to sit with] somebody that I've never gotten along with . . . so that brings up more fights. You can see people sitting but not being nice to that person. A lot of times I'll just see people sitting there like this: "When will lunch be over?"

J: Yeah, they won't even look at the other person, they're so disgusted by them.

AK: What I hear both of you saying is that people are still really angry at having to sit in certain places in the cafeteria.

H: Yeah, it really makes you feel like you're in jail. Like, I can't sit by Jessica or people I hang out with. Jessica's at the complete opposite end of the table with this whole mob in between. And then I can't see my other friends anymore. And we're not allowed to get up and talk to them. We're not allowed to yell across the lunchroom, for obvious reasons.

Student perceptions might have been different if students had helped devise their own consequences for the cafeteria riot. Assigned seats and imposed quiet were meant to deliver a message that chaos would not be tolerated, but the new order reinforced cliques and peer animosity. Obviously, squashing chaos and tolerating it are not the only alternatives to disorder.

Roberta realized that classrooms with a wide latitude of student choice may entail a certain degree of disorder. The 1996–97 school year, however, was the first year of her career in which disorder was accompanied by disrespect. My interviews with students indicated that Roberta was highly regarded by most of the students throughout the school year, the disrespectful incidents and conspiracy against her notwithstanding. Even during the crackdown, she obtained a large measure of compliance without resorting to common teacher tactics such as raised voices, bribes, and threats. Nevertheless, problems of disrespect and bullying kept emerging. If Roberta and I had been more familiar with conflict resolution theories and strategies, we might have relied less on trial and error when trying to resolve these problems. Fortunately, class meetings became an important mechanism for conflict resolution during the last two weeks of the school year, and the students at last turned their attention to the disorder that was interfering with democratic practices.

Lingering Questions

How should teachers distinguish between classroom rights and privileges?

How can class meetings effectively address social issues such as popularity, bullying, and compliance?

What kind of preparation is needed to establish conflict resolution programs?

What should inform decisions about the time allocated for class meetings and deliberation?

What kinds of experiences help students consider the relationship between individual and group rights?

When are behavioral consequences justified, and how closely do they need to "fit the crime"?

Further Reading

Democratic Classrooms and Schools

Apple, Michael W. 1993. *Official Knowledge: Democratic Education in a Conservative Age.* New York: Routledge.

Apple, Michael W., and James A. Beane, eds. 1995. *Democratic Schools.* Alexandria, VA: Association for Supervision and Curriculum Development.

Arnstine, Donald. 1995. *Democracy and the Arts of Schooling.* Albany: State University of New York Press.

Beane, James A. 1997. *Curriculum Integration: Designing the Core of Democratic Education.* New York: Teachers College Press.

Beyer, Landon E., ed. 1996. *Creating Democratic Classrooms: The Struggle to Integrate Theory and Practice.* New York: Teachers College Press.

Bricker, David C. 1989. *Classroom Life as Civic Education: Individual Achievement and Student Cooperation in Schools.* New York: Teachers College Press.

Butchart, Ronald E., and Barbara McEwan, eds. 1998. *Classroom Discipline in American Schools: Problems and Possibilities for Democratic Education.* Albany: State University of New York Press.

Child Development Project. 1996. *Ways We Want Our Class to Be: Class Meetings that Build Commitment to Kindness and Learning.* Oakland, CA: Developmental Studies Center.

Dewey, John. [1916] 1966. *Democracy and Education.* New York: The Free Press.

Goodman, Jesse. 1992. *Elementary Schooling for Critical Democracy.* Albany: State University of New York Press.

Gutmann, Amy. 1987. *Democratic Education.* Princeton, NJ: Princeton University Press.

Kohn, Alfie. 1996. *Beyond Discipline: From Compliance to Community.* Alexandria, VA: Association for Supervision and Curriculum Development.

Levine, David, ed. 1995. *Rethinking Schools: An Agenda for Change.* New York: New Press.

Manke, Mary Phillips. 1997. *Classroom Power Relations: Understanding Student-Teacher Interaction.* Mahwah, NJ: Lawrence Erlbaum Associates.

McDermott, J. Cynthia, ed. 1999. *Beyond the Silence: Listening for Democracy.* Portsmouth, NH: Heinemann.

Nicholls, John G. 1989. *The Competitive Ethos and Democratic Education.* Cambridge: Harvard University Press.

Oldenquist, Andrew, ed. 1996. *Can Democracy Be Taught?* Bloomington, IN: Phi Delta Kappa Educational Foundation.

Oyler, Celia. 1996. *Making Room for Students: Sharing Teacher Authority in Room 106.* New York: Teachers College Press.

Soder, Roger, ed. 1996. *Democracy, Education and the Schools.* San Francisco: Jossey-Bass.

Wolk, Steven. 1998. *A Democratic Classroom.* Portsmouth, NH: Heinemann.

6

Performance and Power

Shifting Allegiances and Disappearing Oranges

In the intervening days between the decision to produce the class play and its implementation, the usual pastiche of classroom activities continued to swirl, and there was little time for play practice. The school carnival had come and gone, and literature study, math projects, Writers Guild, and Explorers Club presentations continued to put play rehearsals on the back burner. Although desire for play practice was expressed during class meetings, the meetings were dominated by conversations about other projects and problems. Students agreed to the schedules even when individuals bemoaned the absence of rehearsals, probably because classroom pursuits, particularly the writing, had not lost momentum. During Writers Guild, students were soliciting peer response more than ever before, and students vied for computer time to prepare for publications. The sex education unit, much of which involved combined fifth-grade classes, had begun, and this consumed a great deal of class time. Wednesday's visit of a doctor and his very pregnant patient was a highlight of this unit, as students were able to see an ultrasound image of the woman's embryo "live" on a TV monitor as, one by one, they were allowed to touch the woman's abdomen. Literature study was in full swing, and although four students—André, Billy, Anne, and Sally—had not kept up with their group's reading schedule, most students seemed to be probing their novels more deeply than ever before. Doug's inquiries about "3-D area" had turned into lively class explorations of volume, both during and outside of math time.

Although waves of rebellion no longer swept through the classroom, meanness occasionally disrupted the equilibrium. The worst incidents happened outside the classroom. Influential students from other classes were becoming even more bossy than Roberta's students, and recess conflicts between them proliferated. Conspiracies planned by students from Ms. Worthington's fifth-grade class, in which students arranged clandestine bathroom meetings to plan after-school intimidation sessions, occasionally involved students from Roberta's class. Gerald was the victim of a nasty recess incident in which a group of students from another class knocked him to the ground and threw dirt in his face. Students from our own class were less blatantly mean, but could be equally angry. When I arrived at school very early one morning, I saw Veronica standing alone on the playground, furiously hurling rocks at the school building. These incidents reminded me that some students had their own private rage that went beyond the confines of school.

Angry outbursts mostly occurred at recess and on the bus. There had been a number of recent fights on the playground involving other fifth-grade students, and one student had been suspended for being involved with a middle school group of marijuana users. During an interview, Mei-Ling told me that "popular" kids in other classes had been forcing the "little kids" to sit at the back of the bus. My questions about the complicity of her inaction, however, didn't seem to reach her; since she wasn't involved, she argued, she wasn't responsible.

Many problems were being solved by students who were volunteers on the Conflict Council. So far, Sally, Ben, and at least five other students had gone to the Conflict Council in recent weeks to settle personal disputes. They had returned to class satisfied, willing to work with each other again. Unfortunately, the strategies they had used to solve the conflicts did not become class meeting topics.

In Roberta's class, the gender intrigues had become more muted. Again, we heard about more incidents involving other fifth graders than we did about our own. Some of the parents from Roberta's classroom, however, had spoken with her about their children receiving an abundance of telephone calls concerning "dates," and Roberta mentioned this during informal conversations in the classroom. We continued to find telltale signs of students being pressured to "go with" or "break up with" a classmate of the opposite sex. After school one day, we found a crumpled paper on the floor with Doug's easily identifiable handwriting on it. Since Doug was usually a passive follower, he was the last student we'd have expected to be in charge of orchestrating romantic schemes. Yet here on this discarded paper was evidence of his social scheming. Under the heading "Accomplishments," Doug had written:

> Ted—get a kiss from Maureen
>
> Brian—get a date
>
> Doug—swipe a pink slip
>
> John—bring swimsuit
>
> Ben—ask Katherine out
>
> Charles—ask someone out
>
> Andrew—flirt with girl big time
>
> Must accomplish by the end of the year.

Other social intrigues continued. Sally and Veronica frequently orchestrated girls-only gossip sessions, and sometimes these talkathons interfered with work. When I noticed, for example, that a math group consisting of Katherine, Sally, and John was the only group not working on their math charts, I asked why not. Katherine, out of earshot of the other two, nodded at Sally and said, "Sally's too busy blabbering about fingernail polish." The topic of the girls' "blabbering," however, was usually André, Ben, or Brian, not fingernail polish. André continued to figure prominently in the dating schemes, and we heard from several students that his parents had been dropping him off at the mall for "dates."

André did not seem overly occupied with dating concerns at school, however, and his aggressive and inconsiderate actions were sometimes tempered by positive contributions. He had given encouraging feedback to other students several times during group meetings, and he and Bert had conducted an impressive presentation on Greek gods for Explorers Club. Since Roberta had detailed some behavioral problems in her narrative progress report in April, she and Dr. Lingle had been corresponding by e-mail to try to ensure that André keep up with his research projects and his reading. André had been staying after school every day to write in his journal and discuss his daily entry with Roberta, according to the arrangement his father had requested. Roberta, desperate for any straw that might help pull André out of his usual quagmire and rally his parents' support, had agreed to spend this time with André after school, and she often enjoyed her after-school conversations with him. One day, for example, Anne, who sometimes stayed after school when her mother worked late, joined Roberta and André in a discussion that Roberta described as "fantastic." During the conversation, André had expressed interest in both Roberta's and Anne's opinions, had asked many questions, and had paraphrased their comments in his own answers. These friendly overtures made her hopeful that he, like many other class members, had embarked upon a new, positive turn in which concern about others mediated selfish concerns.

As the weather became warmer, Roberta revived her morning walk tradition, recalling the friendly atmosphere during former spring strolls. When students arrived at school, they joined those of us who were already walking around the wooded periphery of the playing field. Since Ms. Wolf's fifth-grade class had also been walking with us, new popularity concerns arose. In past years, Roberta had found that groups would naturally shift and regroup according to their pace of walking, thus allowing students to mingle in a way that didn't always occur in class. This year, however, Roberta noticed that individuals were being snubbed, and told me that she wanted to address this during a class meeting sometime soon. As it turned out, a student raised the issue before she did.

Social concerns less directly related to gender issues became apparent that week when we asked students to list, in confidence, the names of several students they thought they could work well with and those they felt they couldn't work well with. Most students listed only their friends as potential working partners. We found it rather sad that Katherine, Gerald, and Anne, three of the kindest students in the class, were the only students who were not listed as desirable partners. André, Bert, Sally, Ben, and Veronica were the most sought-after partners. We were surprised that only three students wanted to work with Hope; her earlier popularity and tremendous influence upon the class had obviously waned in recent weeks. But perhaps the most revealing result of the questionnaire was the fact that most students listed more people they couldn't work with than people they could work with. Realizing that we had supplied the inlet for this toxic ooze, we wrote up a new questionnaire, as follows:

Thinking More Specifically About Workmates

When it comes to writing stories, I could really get good ideas from:

When I need help with editing and language conventions, I would seek help from:

When it comes to finding resources and doing research, some people who could help me are:

If I want to find the volume of my orange I could get help from:

I could get assistance making a really cool poster from:

Some people who could really help me focus and complete my work are:

If I'm looking for some people who value working with others and willingly accept ideas from others I would seek out:

If I want to read a good book and discuss it, I could seek out:

This questionnaire yielded a wider variety of names and helped us expand our perception of individual student strengths. It also precipitated an agreeable response to later groupings.

The balance of power between students, then, was a delicate one, easily shifting according to context. Interviews I had been conducting with each student revealed just how fickle the balance of power could be in social relationships. Many students felt extremely vulnerable to what some students called "pure" (rather than "peer") pressure, and some mentioned that Sally and several girls from other classes had threatened to beat up and spread vicious rumors about those who didn't comply with their demands. According to the students, unfounded rumors that Roberta had scolded or humiliated students during Bartlett Camp had proliferated during the crackdown. Apparently these rumors had died down, and students no longer brought up plans to "get even" with her as they had when rights and privileges were suspended.

During this same week, issues of trust came into play again when some of the oranges brought in for math /science activities disappeared. On Tuesday, the day before the first math activity involving oranges, Roberta had bought one orange for each child, and we had counted them twice. Yet four oranges were missing the next morning. We brought up the matter to the class, but no one confessed, either publicly or privately, any knowledge of the whereabouts of the missing oranges. Our disappointment that a student might have stolen the oranges lingered over the next few days, until the principal discreetly revealed to the teachers that custodians had found evidence that someone had been breaking into the school at night, probably to sleep there. Although the news was disquieting on one front, reason to believe that someone else, and not the children, had stolen the oranges was reassuring. Also comforting was the fact that, on their own, students decided to randomly determine who would not get an orange, since there were no longer enough to go around.

Once the math activities utilizing oranges were under way, disputes concerning who would keep the orange after the activity were quickly resolved. So many questions and hypotheses arose during the math session that many students kept working after the period was over and the observation sheets had been turned in. Susan was fascinated that her heavy ceramic mug was the same weight as her orange, and began to chart other objects for further weight comparisons. Crystal, surprised that the peel weighed so much, teamed up with others to compare peel weight ratios. Andrew's group, harking back to some of the water displacement activities from the beginning of the year, set up water displacement experiments. And Ben, continuing to discover new ways to study his orange, wanted his sheet back to add other observations. Later in the week, as the orange activities became more structured and the children began to share some of their findings, the learning continued to flourish.

Loose Ends

The school year was almost over, but various factions of the class were still at odds with each other. In spite of signs that the students were actively trying to create a better community, individuals were still snubbed, especially when popular students selectively pulled friends away from their work to plot a hallway gossip session or an after-school rendezvous at the mall. Ben and André continued to involve others in pranks, such as climbing into lockers or hiding someone's jacket. The question of who had used a permanent marker to write on Charles' baseball cap was never solved despite Roberta's attempts to persuade the responsible party to come forward. Unrestrained talking, though under control most of the time, occasionally disrupted otherwise fruitful discussions. At the beginning of the day on Wednesday, a class meeting about revision strategies was particularly ineffective. During the meeting, André, Jessica, and Sally talked with each other so intrusively that nearby students had to ask for comments to be repeated. Roberta again broke her resolve not to point out individual problems in front of the class.

"Is anyone else bothered," she asked the group, "when people have private conversations while others are speaking to the group?" Only five students raised their hands. Later that day, I interviewed students to determine why they weren't rectifying the situation. Again, they expressed fear that "popular" students would publicly ridicule them if they tried to stop interruptions or insulting remarks.

As students continued to kowtow to the prominent leaders, Roberta had to remind students several times that "sometimes things that people think are funny are hurtful." Sally, in particular, continued to make unflattering, and even slanderous, comments about others. On Wednesday, she spread rumors about Anne, implying that she'd had a sexual encounter with a boy from another class. The hurt look on Anne's face when someone asked her about it revealed the extent of her vulnerability when at the mercy of someone as powerful and ruthless as Sally. Anne happened to stay after school that day, and, when Julie's tutoring session finished, the two had a conversation with Roberta and me about what had happened. Julie, perhaps to make Anne feel better, mentioned that she too had been a victim of Sally's gossip.

"Sally kept going around and asking about André going out with me. I'm not saying she's a bad person, though; she's still my friend."

"Why does Sally have so much power?" asked Roberta.

"She threatens people," answered Anne. We asked more questions and learned that Sally would threaten a wide range of consequences for not obeying her, from public exposure of a personal matter to a beating after school.

"The popular people always get in trouble," noted Anne, "so I don't know why they're so popular."

On Thursday, May 22, Roberta and I inadvertently set ourselves apart from the community once again when we showed a video taken over two years earlier. In this video, the effective functioning of group meetings was clearly evident, and Roberta and I thought that it might help students re-evaluate the unruly nature of some of their recent group meetings. Roberta framed the discussion by wondering aloud how she might need to adjust her expectations in light of her past experiences with other groups. The students reacted in a hostile manner, accusing Roberta of favoring the class in the video and not giving their group a chance.

"That class, as you saw in the video, had a lot of latitude," she explained, "yet some of the disruption issues we've seen in here didn't come up. So should different classes be granted different latitudes? And sometimes you are much more responsible than at other times. So should different latitudes be applied at different times within one class?"

The defensive backlash continued. Students felt that they had been unfairly criticized and, ironically, weakened the legitimacy of their defense by all talking at once. "We're not so bad!" I heard above the din, along with another student's indignant claim that "we know how to be responsible just as much as they did!" When the furor died down, Roberta spoke.

"I apologize," she said, "for conveying the idea that I thought the class in the video was better than this class. That was not my intention. You have all done great things this year. I just thought the video would help us reflect on what builds success, particularly in class meetings."

"It seemed that way, though," hissed Hope, and several shouts of "yeah" immediately seconded her opinion.

Maureen helped turn the tide by using her prominent voice to speak up for the underdog.

"The problem is that some people aren't getting a voice in here," she asserted. "Everyone wants a voice."

"How do you develop voice?" asked Roberta.

A wave of opinions began to swell, as students began to analyze, this time in a turn-taking fashion, why some people had more voice than others. For the first time, popularity was openly addressed in a group meeting, and the interview conversations I'd had concerning this topic re-emerged in interesting forms. Dominant students, such as André, Ben, Brian, and Patrick, spoke at length about how the clothing you wear, the music you listen to, and the TV programs you watch help determine how accepted you are. Julie ventured her opinion that rap and violent TV shows aren't necessarily bad, and Elizabeth agreed, but added that "classical music and the Discovery channel aren't bad either." Several students then cited circumstances when they felt judged by other students because of their clothes or their taste in music and TV. Even Gerald spoke up, mentioning that he had felt judged when someone had put him down during the morning walk. Brian cynically lashed out, clutching his chest dramatically.

"Oh, Gerald," he moaned sarcastically, "I feel your pain!"

Reviled by Brian's contemptuous remark, Roberta and I poised to jump in, but we were not as quick on the draw as Elizabeth. As the tension peaked, Elizabeth plunged in and took a firm stand.

"It's not bad to be different!" she passionately declared. "And I have a story to tell." All eyes focused on Elizabeth.

"This morning, during the morning walk," she continued, "I was walking on my own, kind of fast. I suddenly noticed that I was almost caught up with Paul, from Ms. Wolf's class. Everybody thinks Paul's a geek, and I was suddenly afraid that people would talk about me. So I started walking fast, and as I passed Paul, he said, 'That's OK, you don't have to walk with me. Nobody wants to.' I felt really bad. I slowed down and started talking with him. And, you know, we had a really good conversation."

The force of Elizabeth's statement pulled the whole group forward in a silent current of reflection. The silence was broken by a crescendo of complimentary comments about Elizabeth's decision. At last someone had publicly defied popular opinion and rallied support for the fair and equal treatment of all individuals.

Lost Horizons: Reviving the Play

The next morning, Roberta and I called a class meeting to discuss the future of the class play. Roberta and I had decided that a commitment to producing the play hinged on one major condition: Every student would have to have a speaking part. Gerald was still not in the play, and Patrick, Sally, and several others had dropped out, creating yet more multiple roles in a play that already had a gigantic cast of characters. Furthermore, Roberta had talked with Gerald's mother and she felt strongly, as did we, that if there was a class play Gerald should have a part.

The students seemed to sense that a major announcement was imminent. There was absolute silence when Roberta spoke.

"I've talked with Mr. Koshewa," she began, "and we are both willing to devote as much class time as possible to help you produce the play and actually perform it." The class burst into applause.

"There is one condition we are expecting, however," she continued. "Everyone must have a speaking part in the play. So, for the moment, we need to know who does not have a speaking part."

Someone pointed out that Andrew had a major nonspeaking role as "the box" and should be exempted from the speaking requirement. Roberta agreed to the exemption and asked who else didn't have a speaking part. Five hands shot up.

"Are you willing," asked Roberta, addressing those five students, "to participate so that everyone will be included in the project?"

One by one, the students spoke, and the first four students quickly agreed to participate. Patrick was the last to speak.

"I don't want to be in the play," he said. "I dropped out because it wasn't going the way I thought it should."

"Do you mean," asked Roberta, "that you wouldn't be willing to say just a line or two in order to help achieve this group goal?"

"No," he emphatically answered, generating an immediate wave of whispers.

"In this case," said Roberta. "I don't think you'll have a choice."

Patrick was noticeably silent during the excited discussion that followed. There were many details to be worked out: how the script would be revised, how the parts would be reassigned, what committees needed to be formed to finalize props, costumes, sets, and other concerns. The entire morning and part of the afternoon were devoted to planning, and the students seemed to think of everything: scheduling the auditorium, lighting, crew assignments, staging, and many other aspects of the production. Roberta, having recently assisted in the production of a high school play, helped the students prioritize tasks. It seemed that nary a minute of the morning was wasted. Even Patrick joined in on the plans, although he remained unusually quiet.

Throughout, Ted and Brian solicited suggestions for revisions. I proposed that a narrator be added to introduce scenes and to help explain settings, characters, and cryptic references to those not familiar with *Star Wars.* The students responded enthusiastically. They brainstormed ideas about narration and suggested other changes. Ted and Brian agreed to finalize the revisions over the three-day holiday weekend.

In the afternoon, Roberta decided to test the waters. Partners were needed for the afternoon social studies activity, and she wanted to choose the pairs randomly by drawing numbered Popsicle sticks, which she had used throughout the year to arbitrarily select students. Roberta prefaced the random drawing with a challenge.

"I'm going to see if you can go the extra mile," she said, using a term she had brought up before in reference to high expectations. "I want to see what kind of signal you send to who you are picked to work with."

The students showed tremendous restraint in tempering expressions of relief or disappointment when their random partners were announced. Some partnerships were extraordinarily successful, and most were productive. The splashes of resistance, such as Jessica's comment to her partner, "Who do they think we are, fourth graders?" were quickly absorbed by the calm that pervaded the rest of the afternoon.

Student Sabotage, Parent Sabotage

After a three-day weekend, on Tuesday, May 27, Roberta and I, as well as most of the students in the class, were astonished to learn that Ted and Brian had not brought in the play revisions. Students were angry, but this time the anger was directed at Ted and Brian. Students immediately called a group meeting. Roberta started the meeting, honing in on the issue at hand.

"The first thing that I asked Ted when I saw him this morning was, 'How did the revision go?' and he said, 'Well, we didn't really get to it.' Ted, would you explain what happened?" The silence was pregnant as all eyes turned toward Ted.

"It was a busy weekend for me," said Ted, adopting the defensive tone that had become so common in recent months. "By the time I talked to Brian about doing the play, it was already Monday and we didn't have time to work on it. But maybe we could do it tonight, if you could give us one more day."

Roberta then turned to Brian.

"Brian, what do you want to say?"

"The reason I started to give up on it," said Brian, for the first time revealing a defeatist attitude toward the play, "is because during the play practices, if we would switch scenes, everyone was yelling and talking and stuff."

"It's in my learning logs," interjected Ted, who all along had been taking notes about the play practices.

"Yeah," agreed Brian. "People weren't on stage on time. We put four weeks into it and people still haven't got it through their heads."

"I want to say something in response to your statement," said Roberta calmly, "because I think that's what was really making people very frustrated this morning. Instead of saying, 'We just didn't get to it,' you sounded like you made a decision that was real different from the decision we agreed to on Friday. Mr. Koshewa and I said we would build in play practices if you and Ted could rewrite the play. And you said yes. So I don't think it's fair and I think that's what's disturbing everybody this morning. You made it sound like you made a decision to not do it because of the way practices were going."

"I was going to say no on that already, but everyone was just sitting there looking at me like 'You'd better do it' and stuff like that. And I'm thinking 'If I say no, then I'm going to get grief for my whole life.' "

Silently, at least ten hands shot into the air. Roberta broke the silence.

"I see a lot of hands up and it looks like people are really following the way we should talk in groups. But I don't want to waste our time, and it sounds like we need to come up with real constructive comments now. What's the problem we have to solve right now?"

Susan's response was simple and direct: "How we can get everybody to do this, to rewrite the play."

This became the primary mission of the day. By mid-afternoon, tentative revisions had been made and discussed. Roberta and I were pleasantly surprised at how much sense the play made once the narrator transitions had been added. The students also expressed satisfaction with the new suggestions. Ted and Brian agreed to incorporate the revisions into their computer file at home and bring in the new draft the next day.

At the end of the day, unexpected collaborations during social studies work showed that some students were already taking a proactive role in building a better classroom climate. Andrew and Susan, and at least five other pairs, were having excellent conversations about the information they'd found and were writing prolifically. Julie, once the most passive and unproductive member of the class, gently insisted that her partner help her with the writing activity. I overheard a rare compliment from Patrick, when he warmly told Billy, "Everybody likes your turtle painting." Even Sally was working peacefully with Gerald, despite the fact that Gerald was in an extremely hyperactive mode and kept asking Sally the same questions over and over, not listening to her answers.

Not all attempts to rectify past patterns of friction were successful, though. When John asked Brian, who was talking loudly about something totally unrelated to the assignment, "Brian, can you please lower your voice?" Brian shouted back a defiant "No!" Sally's collaboration with Gerald proved to be temporary, for soon she was distracting Elizabeth and John, regaling them with juicy accounts of who liked whom. And André, who had agreed to bring in some research notes from home, since he'd accomplished nothing during the previous social studies session, not only had come to this session empty-handed but did not write one word during the entire hour.

André did, however, write in his journal after school, and, as usual, his comments were much more pleasant than the sort of remarks he tended to make during class. Shortly after André began writing, he paused over his pencil, looked at Roberta and me, and said, "I wonder what my parents think about my journal." We asked him what he meant, because we assumed he had been discussing the entries with his parents. After all, his father had initiated the journal reflections as a way for them to keep track of André's progress, and both parents had planned to read the entries, as well as add to the responses that Roberta wrote on Post-Its every day.

"They don't say anything," he told us. "I show them what I write, but they don't say anything." André's tone of voice conveyed anger. We were reminded of two negative comments we'd recently overheard him make in class, one about his parents always "being on my case and yelling at me" and the other, overheard three separate times in recent months, about wanting to go to college after high school "to get away from my parents." We responded to the comment at hand by encouraging him to explicitly ask for feedback, which he did by writing a note to his parents in his journal, asking them to write down their reactions to his entries. The next morning the journal contained a note from Dr. Martine claiming that André had been forced to write things he didn't believe. Not only was the accusation absurd, but Roberta found it ludicrous that Dr. Martine was attacking her for the voluntary after-school tutoring her husband had requested. Talking to André, we learned that his mother had questioned his apologetic tone in his entry expressing regret about having mauled a dead rabbit on the playground. Roberta and I wondered why André's personal reaction to the rabbit incident had become an issue. And why was Dr. Martine questioning the journal? Was André playing parents against teacher, were his parents playing parent against parent, or were his parents playing child against teacher? We weren't sure why Dr. Martine had raised her hackles.

Closer to the Footlights

The next afternoon had been set aside for the long-awaited play rehearsal. In the morning, Roberta called a group meeting to obtain approval of the final script in time for it to be photocopied before the afternoon practice. Ted introduced the revised version, explaining the changes. The class's observations and suggestions concerning stage directions, narrator lines, and typos were thoroughly discussed. Roberta then brought up an issue that no one else had raised: the use of the term "acting like a sissy little girl" in one of the stage directions. The class unabashedly defended the use of the phrase. I told about my rejection of a good friend when I was a fifth grader, simply because he'd been labeled a "sissy," but my story failed to move them. Roberta mentioned that she could overrule the group decision, but thought it more important that the class see her point of view. Brian, feeling his ownership as coauthor threatened, revealed his ongoing desire for control by saying, "I don't want to do the play as much now because Ted and I don't have as much power anymore." Roberta responded by reminding him that producing the play was a group commitment that would entail personal sacrifice and shared power.

I then mentioned that stage directions are meant to describe what actors should *do,* and that instructing actors to "act like a sissy" not only reinforces stereotypes, but fails to focus on the action, like stage directions should. Several students agreed, perhaps just to end the dispute. But Veronica cut to the core of the issue before the rest of the class could be swayed.

"It's a *kid's* play," she protested. "We should be able to write it the way we want and writing 'like a sissy little girl' is no big deal."

"Insult terminology," insisted Roberta, "in stage directions *is* a big deal to me. Eliminating that phrase does not make the play *my* play; it's still a kid's play." She asked the class if this point really had to be deliberated, or if they would just scratch the phrase and move on. Enough grunts of agreement were conveyed to Ted for him to grab the Liquid Paper yet one more time. No one dwelled on the issue.

After lunch, with the new script complete and photocopied, casting became the most pressing need. Roberta and I volunteered to guide casting, and, while others studied the new script, we met in the hall with the writer/directors and the five students in need of speaking roles. Patrick, who had already publicly talked about "his" role as the narrator, again acted as if this casting was a given. I reminded him that the narrator role was important, and since someone else might be interested in it, there should be an audition for the role. Sally told the small group that there was a sixth student without a speaking role: Mei-Ling had a role, but no lines. So Mei-Ling was summoned to the hall.

Brian and Ted began the audition by asking who was interested in the smaller roles, and the four girls immediately chose four separate roles. They were asked to read a few lines of their chosen characters. After enthusiastic readings, the directors said the girls had done a good job and could have the parts they'd requested.

The moment of reckoning arrived. There was only one part left, that of the narrator, and Gerald and Patrick alone remained in the hall.

"Well," I said, "the logical move would be to divide the part in two. Are you both interested in being the narrator?"

As the two boys nodded, there was an agonized frown on Patrick's face. Agreeing to sharing the role was tantamount to forming an alliance with the class's most noticeable misfit. Not agreeing, however, would risk further loss of face, as he might be forced to compromise further or to give up the role completely.

"I guess we'll divide the role," said Patrick, casting a tentative glance at Gerald. Gerald looked incredulous that he might be able to get such an important role in the play.

"Hold on," interjected Brian. "You have to audition."

The intensity of the two readings was heightened by the nervous edge underlying them. Patrick delivered a pompous, self-conscious reading. Gerald's delivery, in contrast, lacked pretension but included several fits and starts, sounding choppy and uneven.

"Congratulations," said Ted, when Gerald had finished. "You both have the part."

The negotiations had just begun, however, since the next task was dividing the lines. Surprisingly, Patrick was willing to go along with the equitable decisions of others. Gerald and Patrick, distinctly dissimilar in personality yet both easily disregarded by others due to their social tactlessness, were now partners and forming the tenuous beginnings of a collaboration.

The next morning, another rehearsal took place. This rehearsal was characterized by a previously unsurpassed orderliness. Over half the class had their lines memorized. Impressed, Roberta asked the students to try to memorize their lines within two days, if they had not already done so. All but André successfully achieved this goal.

Play-Doh and Props

Throughout the week, play rehearsals continued to be marked by intense concentration and involvement. Formerly silent students frequently became involved in discussions concerning the acting, staging, or technical aspects of the play. Students previously on the fringe of classroom groups became active participants. Several class meetings were called to discuss preparations for practice in the auditorium.

Play rehearsals sometimes became arenas for contested control. Most students, aware that having a mere two weeks to produce a play would require a concerted effort, were eager to work together. Occasional power struggles emerged nevertheless. Brian had been frequently aligning himself with Billy, whose attention-seeking behavior often sidetracked group efforts.

Hope, whose stage experience made her an authority on play production, regained some of her former power to lead and influence the group, although her concerns were more self-centered than they had been earlier in the year. Patrick continued to vie for power by trying to devise ways to make his role as narrator even more prominent. Other power struggles ensued when a hitherto unassigned job, such as turning off the music during a scene, became a contest of wills. On the whole, however, the students were able to conduct rehearsals independently, with Roberta and I taking an active advisory role. When resolving conflicts, the students implemented a wider variety of problem-solving strategies than we had previously seen, and Roberta and I were often called upon for an opinion rather than to proclaim a final ruling.

Sometimes, of course, the teachers had to make proclamations because of property, safety, or educational issues. After the students had worked hard on making swords from rulers, for example, Roberta banned them as unsafe and, despite their disappointment, the students listened to and acknowledged her reasoning. In response, the props committee swooped in to design and construct cardboard swords as replacements.

Prop construction dominated the Invitations sessions that week. A basic precept of Invitations was that students could accept the invitations to explore the materials and activities displayed or refuse them by doing something else instead. This week, a number of students volunteered to set up Invitations that centered around creating props and sets for the play, with different categories of materials at different tables. The support for this move seemed unanimous, so Roberta and I were surprised when Gerald approached us and expressed disappointment that the props sessions would eliminate open-ended art using Play-Doh, an Invitations option that had repeatedly been Gerald's first choice. We asked him if he really wanted to play with Play-Doh rather than work on props, surprised that he was choosing social isolation even though other students were including him. His eager "yes" made us realize that, once again, commitment to the group cause was not as unanimous as we'd believed.

During Invitations, Gerald, hardly idle but in his own little world, happily squished Play-Doh into one shape after another while most of the other students focused on making props. Some of the engaged students, such as Maureen and Susan, worked hard but kept bossing others around. Mei-Ling proved to be a hard worker, and was thrilled when she managed to print *Star Wars* stills from the Internet. She subsequently set to work trying to make sure the set designs matched the pictures. Charles, Julie, Katherine, and many others were working fast and furiously on sets. Those not consumed by the play preparations included Henrietta, who was primping by the mirror in the reading corner. Andrew, after a vain attempt to find his prop list, was playing with an eraser. Sally and Veronica were conducting yet another of their frequent whispering sessions. When I asked them what they were working on, Veronica coquettishly replied, "Whatever André's working on." André, however, was still playing around with the swords he was supposed to be covering in foil. Hope, on the other hand, had taken on a queen bee role, actively spurring on her workers yet making it clear that props were her domain whenever someone else tried to organize them. Elizabeth was effectively helping coordinate set constructions, and was mediating disputes that had arisen. Networks of collaboration were rapidly spreading, even though six class members remained disconnected.

Community Self-Regulation

On Thursday afternoon, Dr. Schwartz, the anthropologist who had helped arrange the archaeology presentations and workshops earlier in the year, gave a presentation to the class. Realizing how concerned Roberta and I had been about community relations in recent weeks, Dr. Schwartz had chosen the question "How do different cultures regulate themselves?" as the theme of her talk.

At first, the rustling papers, murmured conversations, and shuffling through crate materials forebode another round of disrespect. Fortunately, the little disruptions abated quickly and, despite a rather academic introduction to the differences between a band, tribe, chiefdom, and state, students demonstrated complete absorption. When Dr. Schwartz began talking about conflict resolution in different societies, questions abounded. The students supplied examples of religion influencing belief, asked about supernatural resolutions that had been mentioned, and offered comments concerning the power of group opinion. Several students wanted to know more about reciprocity, and Kirsten even used the term "plea bargaining" at one point. Hope and Henrietta made plans to research Plato, since his philosophy was mentioned. The discussion brimmed with participation. The students were synthesizing what they'd learned from the trial inquiry and their independent research, and they also were reflecting on what they'd learned from experiencing the vicissitudes of a conflict-ridden community.

Later in the afternoon, every student accepted the invitation to write Dr. Schwartz thank-you notes. In their notes, many cited what they'd learned, and some wrote about personal connections. Some students had questions and included their addresses in the letter to ensure a reply, and Katherine even asked Dr. Schwartz advice about her relationship with her father. Many letters mentioned her field work experience and the artifacts she'd brought in. Julie included a web of ideas from the presentation in her letter. Patrick humbly wrote that he had never before thought about why some people have so much power. Veronica mentioned that the presentation made her think about "who has the power" and reflected that "I have authority over younger kids, and over people I can teach something to." Doug wrote that he "learned so much about how people regulate themselves." Billy, at the end of his letter, wrote that Dr. Schwartz always changed him whenever she came to class, as he always learned about new points of view. André's letter truly touched us because of its expression of empathy at the end. In his letter, he wrote about the presentation ideas he found most interesting, created a list of new words he'd learned, included two sketches related to the presentation, and added a personal P.S. expressing hope that Dr. Schwartz's voice would get better soon. Of all the students, he was the only one who remembered that Dr. Schwartz's hoarse voice was the result of a terrible sore throat.

Later that day, I ran into Patrick's mother in town. Thinking about how some of his recent comments had transcended his usual look-at-how-much-I-know mode, I mentioned how pleased I was about the genuine inquiries he had been putting forth recently.

"Yes," she said, "Patrick's *amazing*. I haven't even begun to plumb the depths of his mind." I couldn't help but think of the muckier aspects of the plumbing metaphor. Suddenly Ms. Bianco's tone of voice changed, and she became indignant.

"This hasn't been a good year for Patrick," she said. "I knew it wouldn't work from the beginning, and told Roberta that at the start of the year." I muttered something about feeling that I thought Patrick was at a crucial turning point of growth, both intellectually and socially. Ms. Bianco looked skeptical.

"He's just so *brilliant,* though," she intoned.

I began to wonder how many other parents, like Ms. Bianco, had hidden reservations about Roberta's competence. I also began to wonder about the undue measure of control that many of these students seemed to have over their parents. There was evidence that parents were involved in their children's social pursuits, providing them with designer clothing, transportation for movie dates, and money for flower deliveries. Some obtained many material gifts from their parents but spent little time with them. Recently, while talking with Ben, Billy, and other fifth graders about their skateboarding trips to the mall, I learned that much of their time out of school was unsupervised. I also learned that some students were very self-conscious about their limited wardrobe and felt that their "dorky" clothes excluded them from "cool" circles. One student told me about his experiences with guns. I realized that Roberta and I had remained ignorant of many students' experiences outside of school.

But there was little time to interview students about their home lives, as the school year was quickly waning and there was a lot left to accomplish. The last play rehearsal of the week was a short one, since a field trip to the local YMCA had been planned for the rest of the day. The limited time frame for the rehearsal was uppermost in the minds of many, and explained the quick resolution of problems such as Billy's attempts to sabotage an action scene and Brian's unwillingness to share directorial responsibilities.

The field trip went extremely well. High standards of courtesy came into play during the YMCA staff presentations, and students recruited those who didn't readily come forward to be on teams, including the students who were usually rejected. Katherine, Charles, and Sally were terribly out of shape, yet their difficulties during the obstacle course invoked no derision. During the swimming session, considered by all the students to be the highlight of the day, students shifted in and out of play groups, inviting others to join them. Throughout the entire day, no one was excluded from any groups. During the long walk back to school, a congenial spirit persisted. The students' self-regulation had attained new heights.

Mobilizing

The last full week of school had arrived, and two *Star Boars* performances had been scheduled: a dress rehearsal on Thursday, to be attended by Ms. Wolf's class, and the official performance on Friday afternoon, open to all classes. Monday would mark the first day of rehearsals in the auditorium, and energy levels were at an all-time high.

A class meeting was held as a prelude to the auditorium rehearsal. Now that time was of the essence, squeaky wheels were not given special attention. Veronica, for example, challenged Maureen's suggestion that "everybody not on stage should sit down and be quiet until your cue."

"I think I should be able to stand up if I want to," Veronica recriminated.

"We agreed that Maureen could help direct," said Kirsten, putting Veronica in her place. "So do what the director says."

"Arguing will waste time," piped up a voice at the back of the crowd. "Let's make our rehearsal run smooth." More and more, individuals were referring to group goals when resolving conflict. Even Billy, whose attempts to lengthen and restage action scenes had met some measure of approval the previous week, was told to think about others when he argued for "more chaos" in one of the fight scenes.

During the actual rehearsal, problems bubbled up, but a freer forum for problem solving allowed them to fizzle away one by one rather than build collective pressure. Rolling chairs were brought in to solve stage movement problems, positions were assigned to facilitate stage entrances, and individuals not on stage during given scenes were sent to the back of the auditorium to help make decisions about staging and voice projection.

Individual strengths were recognized and appreciated. Charles, playing an elderly woman, had projected such a wavery, modulated voice and such unstable, deliberate body movements that he earned a number of kudos. Hope, whose performance was widely lauded as well, was adept at recognizing when someone tried to steal a scene, and gently reminded offenders not to "take away from the actor." Several students had asked me to play the piano between scenes, and Kirsten brought in sheet music of the *Star Wars* theme for me to interpret as I saw fit. Patrick and Gerald had become a symbiotic pair, and I basked in Gerald's gusto when he rushed up to me, carrying a music stand, and exclaimed, "Look—Patrick got these stands for our scripts so we can look more professional!"

The artistry of individuals and the power of collaboration became more evident as inventive sets and props appeared. Andrew's costume, made at home with his parents' assistance, was an elaborate union of a rolling chair and a cardboard box, and was the source of constant amusement and delight. Paper stars, taped to the back curtains, provided a simple but effective backdrop. At first, the stars kept falling off the curtain and getting stepped on, but Susan and Elizabeth solved the problem by using their recess time to make sure the stars were permanently secured. Hope's plan for her character, Princess Liar (a parody of Princess Leia), to wear real honey buns showed what an original satiric spin *Star Boars* had. During an invasion scene, Princess Liar was supposed to break off pieces of the honey bun and give them to her attackers.

The honey bun hairpiece symbolized the importance of both teacher and peer guidance in helping students realize their goals. So that the scene would occur as planned, I brought in some honey buns and Roberta brought in some old earmuffs. When Hope attempted to fasten the buns to the muffs, they began falling off. She quickly gave up and began making paper simulations instead. It was only later, when her peers got very excited about using the real honey buns as adornment, that Hope invested time and energy into successfully affixing them to the earmuffs.

A dispute over the title of the play also showed how the influence of others can help individuals overcome apathy. The title was called into question during a group meeting, in which students were finalizing the *Star Boars* program before sending it out. As the students proofread the program, someone asked why the term "boars" had been used.

"It's because all the characters act selfish, like wild boars," answered Kirsten.

"No, that's not what I meant at all when I wrote it," Ted objected. Instead, he explained, he had intended to convey the "boring" quality of the continual wars, but had spelled the word wrong. The misunderstanding was probed further as many students offered their previous interpretations of the title. Ted took the position that the spelling didn't matter, and dismissed his classmates' reactions. Most of us felt strongly that the original intention needed to be conveyed through the correct spelling. Ted was not convinced. After more points of view were heard and the issue deliberated, the class decided to rename the play *Star Bores,* and fortunately it was not too late to correct the spelling on the program. Roberta and I, however, ended up taking the responsibility to ensure that the change was actually made, since Ted still seemed to be uncommitted to the group decision.

Collective group efforts were in evidence throughout the day, and even André was actively participating and helping others. Roberta had made fruit-juice Popsicles as an end-of-day surprise, and it seemed the perfect day for a Popsicle celebration. The treat induced a quiet spell and several polite thanks, and Roberta joked about giving out Popsicles every day. As students began to finish, André initiated the clean-up.

During the next few days, the students were focused and productive during play rehearsals. Billy and Brian were the two exceptions, as they frequently altered the script to accommodate their attention-seeking ad-libs. Some class members thought these alterations were funny at first, but it became increasingly apparent that they were confusing some of the actors and interfering with the effective execution of the play. Eventually, a group meeting unleashed such strong support for sticking to the script that the two boys had to accede.

Strong feelings were also aroused when it was suggested that the students use their mugs during the bar scene, the only scene besides the final one in which every student was on stage. Roberta questioned the logistics of this, but provisions for accommodating the placement of the mugs both on and off stage were quickly put forth. The mugs, as one student indicated, symbolized both their individuality and their "togetherness" as a class. So, as the final days of the school year approached, the importance of the "water mugs" loomed large as symbols of freedom, as they had done at the beginning of the year and at the height of the "crisis."

On Wednesday, a videotaped rehearsal led to the students' most insightful and incisive critique of their own work. Early on in the discussion of the videotaped performance, Roberta set the tone for gentle reminders, rather than harsh criticisms, by asking Ted, "Are you going to be in charge of the Mighty Duck cardboard?" instead of admonishing him for forgetting to change the scenery as planned. From then on, the discussion took on the form of observations and questions rather than the denouncements that had become the status quo in earlier months. Stage responsibilities, such as remembering cues and monitoring others, became even more clearly defined as students debated problems and diplomatically pointed out instances of inattention or carelessness. Remarkably, most of this critique was seriously considered and acted upon.

Billy and Brian were flies in the ointment, still attempting to ad-lib in a distracting manner. During a group meeting, their persistent clowning was denounced by the others as not contributing to group goals. Although both boys at first denied having been disruptive, they were humbled by the videotaped evidence. Brian mumbled something about "not meaning to cause problems," meek in the shadow of group censure. Again, peer approval ruled, but this time to maintain order, rather than disrupt it.

After school, the issue of individual versus group gain emerged yet again when Andrew's mother dropped by with Andrew to tell Roberta of her plans to take him to an amusement park on the day of the play. Roberta and I were taken aback, since Andrew appeared in many of the scenes and could not be easily replaced. We were again reminded that the overwhelming commitment to the play that kept revealing itself was not absolute by any means.

"If you're not here, Andrew," explained Roberta, "I think a lot of us are going to feel let down. I don't think your role can be replaced, and it's an important one."

Andrew's face expressed anguish, and his verbal fumbling conveyed that he "really wanted to go" to the amusement park. His mother suggested that, since they were taking two cars, one car could leave late.

Roberta and I, relieved at this conciliatory gesture, soon realized that Andrew was not willing to sacrifice a couple of hours at the amusement park. He squirmed, saying only, "Well . . ."

Ms. Stevens then said she wanted to see the play, and that they could stay a little later in the evening to compensate for starting late.

"OK," said Andrew, finally taking a stance. "I'll be in the play."

What other glitch, Roberta and I wondered, might arise between now and the final performance?

On Thursday morning, the day of the dress rehearsal, Roberta got a telephone call from Dr. Lingle just before school started. Dr. Lingle told Roberta that he had read André's Writers Guild piece and found the violent content objectionable. He asked Roberta if she'd seen it, and she said that no, she hadn't. He arrogantly claimed he couldn't believe that Roberta hadn't seen it and then said, as a consequence of its content, he wanted to keep André home all day. Roberta explained that, due to the performance, it was very important that André be at school in the morning, so Dr. Lingle reluctantly agreed to pick him up at noon, after the dress rehearsal.

By this time, students were already in the room and everyone was excitedly preparing for the performance. The classroom preparations for the dress rehearsal entailed some of the most focused hustling and bustling I'd ever seen. But again, the industrious classroom atmosphere was not all-inclusive. André, who had refused to wear his Tin Man costume until the final performance and therefore had no costume of his own to preoccupy him, was not helping those who needed assistance. When Charles wanted to consult Hope about his costume, I noticed she wasn't in the room. Going to the hall to search for her, I found her screaming with Sally, Ben, and Jessica, and the source of their screams and laughs turned out to be their "cuteness ratings" of other fifth-grade students. Even the exhilaration of preparing for the dress rehearsal had not transcended the popularity wars or led to universal participation.

The Dress Rehearsal

Ms. Wolf's class gave many signs of appreciation during the dress rehearsal, spontaneous laughter being the most salient. The performance, though largely successful, was somewhat sloppy. Many lines were spoken too rapidly or unclearly. Transitions were slow: a late entrance here, a clumsy scenery change there. During such moments, more than a few audience members yelled, clapped, shouted out students' names, and even booed. During the curtain call, as Ms. Wolf's students applauded, loud cries of "boo" echoed through the auditorium. Boos were even audible during the most vigorous applause, garnered by the popular students, particularly André and Ben.

As Roberta's students changed from their costumes and returned to the classroom, many indignant comments could be heard. I heard Susan say, "They actually *booed* us!"; André said he "thought they liked it, even though they were rude." When the last group of girls had entered the room, a class meeting was called.

"Don't you think it was really rude that people booed us?" asked Maureen, eager, as always, to lead the discussion.

"They didn't really mean it!" shouted a voice, followed by several assenting voices.

"We made some bad mistakes," said Ted, "but we didn't deserve those boos."

"Does whether they meant those boos as insults or not make a difference in this case?" asked Roberta. She had struck at the heart of the political correctness issue.

"No!" shouted one student. "It was rude even if they weren't trying to be mean."

There was no way for the students to avoid facing the fact that humor does not justify insensitivity. The students had tasted their own medicine and this experience was sensitizing them in a unique way. Individual calls for revenge, however, were rejected by other students. The group decided to forget about the booing, except for a few individuals who said they would mention it privately to their friends in the other class.

After the booing matter had been discussed, Roberta told the class she had obtained Andrew's permission to share a story. She then told the class about his decision to sacrifice part of a family trip in order to ensure that the play go on the next day. Kirsten's response echoed the sentiments of many.

"Doing this play, we've all helped each other more," she said, "and that's more important than anything we could have learned from social studies or math or any subject."

Climax and Anticlimax: Successes and Failures

On Friday, laughter broke the nervous edge of preperformance jitters when Hope's honey buns kept falling off her ears. André did not have his Tin Man costume and blamed his parents, claiming they had taken the costume out of his backpack before he left for school. A last-minute scramble to locate aluminum foil and construct a new costume consumed the energies of a small group of children. Several other costume concerns were still being finalized when it was time for the performance.

The anticipation we were all feeling was magnified by a glimpse of the full auditorium. Hundreds of children whispered and wiggled, and even Patrick, who normally tried to maintain bravado at any cost, admitted he was nervous. The cue to begin was given.

Unlike the dress rehearsal, this *Star Bores* performance shone and sparkled. As I watched from my position at the piano, I marvelled at the quiet, rapid scene change that preceded the bar scene. As the curtain opened and revealed the students, frozen in position, mugs in hand, waiting to spring into action, I marveled at the ability and aplomb that had led to this stunning staging. The audience broke into loud, spontaneous applause as soon as they saw the tableau, and the scene, as if timed to activate at that very moment, sprang into life. The vitality of that remarkable scene could be felt throughout the rest of the play, and the strong characterizations conveyed by many of the students surpassed those of any other performance to date.

The only blatant abandonment of restraint occurred in the final scene, in which an explosion kills the entire cast. Unwilling to follow the guidelines that had been so scrupulously carried out by the rest of the cast, Charles continued to "die" after the others had been rendered motionless. As the curtain closed, he convulsed and twitched his way to center stage and staggered in front of the closing curtain for a gasping last breath that would have embarrassed even Verdi.

The thunderous applause that followed transcended Charles' histrionics. Charles' scene-stealing did not provoke anger in the rest of the students, although I did notice two students holding onto his arms during the curtain call, and a few people later asked him why he went in front of the curtain. Their questions yielded only a shrug. The students, apparently, had overcome their tendency to jump on Charles for every false step.

Parent response to the play was effusive. Almost all the parents came, but when we looked for André's parents, we didn't see them. André affirmed that they had been unable to attend. Many parents visited the classroom after the students had changed from their costumes, and the atmosphere was one of exhilaration. Roberta's high spirits, however, were temporarily lowered when André's original foil costume was discovered behind his seat; his parents had not removed it from his backpack after all.

After props and costumes were boxed and bagged, we held a group meeting to debrief the play. Students gave ebullient feedback to others concerning aspects of their performance. There were no criticisms.

"Can we do it again?" was echoed several times, but the students knew that their efforts had culminated, and the play was over.

The school year was nearly over as well. That afternoon, we all received "What I Will Always Remember" booklets, compiled from comments we had written about each other. I was thrilled that, in my book, many students mentioned that I had spurred their learning in some way or another, and six specifically mentioned my "feedback" or "good response" to their writing. My constant notetaking was referenced frequently, and André alluded to my perfectionism by writing that I tried to make things perfect by critiquing them until they are just right. Another student wrote that I "could always expand on something," a euphemism, perhaps, for pontification. The students' emphasis on my help and feedback made me hope, as every teacher hopes, that somehow I had made a positive difference in their lives.

Many forms of reflection emerged that day. As the students cleaned, sorted, and set aside what needed to be brought home, many made nostalgic comments upon discovering a story written in the fall, a poster from a Focus Study presentation, or a forgotten note from another class member. When going through a jacket left in her locker, Hope found a sprig of lavender that she'd brought to school at the beginning of the year, and, summoning her charisma, immediately gained the attention of every class member.

"I put this in my pocket on the first day of the school year," she announced, "and now I'm finding it at the end of the year." She held it up to her nose for a dramatic sniff. "It still smells!"

André then shared a lovely story about traveling with his family in Europe the previous summer and coming across an immense field of lavender that stretched out in every direction. I marveled at the power of synchronicity, as I had just bought a good-bye card for Roberta with a photograph of a field of lavender on it. I pondered the amazing forces that had turned lavender and water mugs into powerful symbols of beginnings and endings.

Roberta and I felt a bittersweet exhaustion after the students left. Although we felt the afterglow of their positive exit, the selfish undercurrents that had pulled the class down during the year made it a Pyrrhic victory. We wondered if the successes were temporary, if the students had taken the recent community transformation to heart. We talked for several hours before going home, discussing every single student and our perceptions of their growth. Patrick had actually learned to contain his interruptions during group discussions, we noted, and recently had been willing to admit ignorance in the pursuit of knowledge. Kirsten's foray into the insult culture had been short-lived, her penchant for ensuring justice and fairness emerging strongly during the final week of class. Bert had retained his zest for learning and life and had emerged unscathed from the popularity wars, well-liked for his genuine, positive manner, even though other students didn't always seek him out. Anne, Julie, and Katherine had each undergone a metamorphosis, having previously been largely unsuccessful in school and now constantly exuding excitement about reading and research and other forms of learning. Gerald had experienced tremendous success. He seemed to emanate contentment these days, and had been achieving goals that before had seemed far out of reach. And despite being picked on during the year, he had gained a significant measure of acceptance and respect from his classmates, if not from other fifth graders.

Our exhilaration about positive transformations was tempered by our reflections on failures. Brian and Billy, though able to control their power-mongering during the play performances, still kept the welfare of others far from their locus of concern, and gossipmongers such as Sally and Jessica so infrequently conveyed compassion that we shuddered to think of how they might victimize others in the future. And André, our albatross, was a child consumed by disengagement and unhappiness. Like the others, however, his potential was never far from the surface, and he had at least temporarily transcended his failures during his recent attempts to express compassionate and aesthetic points of view.

We then began looking over the children's work. It was gratifying to compare September's efforts with recent ones—gains are so much more evident when they are not viewed from the snail's-eye view of daily progress. Students who could barely put two sentences together at the beginning of the year had written well-crafted essays and stories. There was an abundance of writing in their folders and portfolios, and the fits and starts of earlier drafts revealed the humble beginnings of polished pieces. Students who had been afraid and unskilled in math were able to solve complex problems and explain their solutions. Even the students' standardized test scores, blindly upheld by many as the benchmark of achievement, were higher than most fifth-grade classes in the town and compared favorably to scores from other classes within the school. Yet what we knew about the students' strengths and weaknesses in reading and writing, about their ways of articulating and solving math problems, about their varying abilities to initiate and sustain research, and, most of all, about their attitudes toward other people, made the test scores seem irrelevant. What concerned us most, as we talked, was whether the students had developed the compassion that would allow their academic progress to take root in the social soil of daily life. What good, we speculated, was understanding fractions if the students refused to share? What good were individual test scores if students were not willing to make the individual sacrifices that collaboration entails? Yes, the students had pooled resources and supported each other's growth to produce a successful play, but could the moral fiber of this growth withstand the parasitic competition that seemed to surround them?

We cannot give up hope, we concluded. Our hope, commented Roberta, would have to be supported, with next year's group, by an active solicitation of parent support and an even more intense focus upon the teacher's role as researcher. After all, she mused, if we had only realized the extent of the students' resistance earlier in the year. . . .

In short, our failure to consistently ensure a safe and supportive learning community until the very end of the school year made the many academic accomplishments pale. We were experienced teachers, we were committed to social betterment and social goals of learning, yet it took us all year to foster a level of collaboration that we were happy with. Had the academic gains and end-of-year collaboration compensated for the paralyzing effects of popularity and exclusion? Had we erred by not paying more attention to the social scheming that almost undermined some of the class projects? Or could social and academic concerns be separated in any practical sense at all?

Dr. Martine thought they not only could, but should, be separated. Although Roberta had sent a final e-mail message to Dr. Lingle reflecting upon

André's successes and failures, she never received a reply from him, but instead received a devastating e-mail letter from Dr. Martine. Dr. Martine's letter began with another criticism of the journal writing. She then launched into a series of accusations, claiming that Roberta had failed to communicate with her or her husband, that André had not learned much during the year, and that Roberta had focused on community while excluding any meaningful academic work from her curriculum. She implied that Roberta was a disorganized and irresponsible teacher, and delivered her final blow by writing that she planned to send a formal letter of complaint about Roberta's teaching to her principal and the district superintendent.

Roberta showed the message to the principal. Beth, having great faith in Roberta's teaching and knowing how Dr. Lingle and Dr. Martine had harassed André's previous teachers, dismissed Dr. Martine's message as inconsequential.

Saying "What You Want to Say"

Dr. Martine did not get the last word in, though, because flowers, cards, notes, and calls that Roberta received from other parents showed that at least a handful of parents were very appreciative of all she had given their children. My audiotapes of students talking in elated voices about their work throughout the year provided evidence of their learning, as did the videotaped Explorers Club presentations. And the "What I Will Always Remember" booklet the students had written for Roberta was an affirmation of their appreciation and respect for her.

The most common adjectives students used to describe Roberta in their notes were "fun," "cool," "nice," and "great." Many wrote that she was their "best" or "favorite" teacher. One student described her as "inventive," another as "unique." Several alluded to her teaching style; Maureen, for example, wrote that she had "different methods of learning." Another student wrote that her "way of teaching was fun," and yet another mentioned her "great ideas in teaching." Students referred to the "fun projects" they had worked on, and another wrote that she was "a great help to Star Bores." Her caring and helpfulness were mentioned by several students: "If I didn't understand something she would help me out"; "She cared about our health"; "She is nice, funny, smart, caring"; and "She trusts us." Sally's note was particularly moving: "I will always remember . . . how she cares a lot about her students. She doesn't act like a teacher. She acts like a mom." My most dominant impression of Roberta centered around caring also, as my own entry in the booklet reveals: "Whether you're analyzing students' work or relating an anecdote concerning what they've said or done, your care for them always shines through in a genuine glow."

In the notes that students wrote about each other, individual roles and participation in *Star Bores* came up over and over again. Students' frequent references to special individual traits and to topics they had researched made me realize how well they had gotten to know each other. John was admired for his loyalty ("He always stuck up for me"); Susan for her ideas and her concern about accuracy ("She is a good editor" and "She has good advice"); Hope for her honesty and audacity ("She doesn't hide anything" and "She actually wore buns on her ears"); Elizabeth for creativity in drawing ("She loves doodling"); and Mei-Ling for her persistence ("She was always determined about something and she always got it done"). A few students showed that they valued the opinions of the more silent students; one student, for example, wrote in Crystal's booklet that "when she voiced her opinen [opinion] it was great." In addition, new partnerships and acceptances were in evidence in many of the notes: Gerald mentioned Patrick's help as a fellow narrator in the play and wrote that Patrick also helped him with his work. Andrew was described as "helpful" and "a really good friend."

The students' voices continue to speak to me as I write. During the last week of class, I asked Mei-Ling, "What do you think is different or special about this class, compared to others you've had?" Her answer still resonates:

> We've had our feelings touched by each other. We show what is wrong. We have feelings when we think about the class and how it operates, how the community is. . . . There's a lot of work. But when you're supposed to work you can express how you feel. And if you say something kind of bad or something you feel, Ms. Taylor doesn't yell at you like other teachers and say, "Go to the principal!" She makes you responsible and say what you want to say.

Stepping Back: Compassionate Relationships

Roberta's students had touched each other's feelings in many ways, some good and some bad. But it appears that they all left with a sense of voice, a sense that they could "say what they want to say." Ultimately, it was Roberta's caring nature that gave students a sense of safety and support. Roberta tried to provide the conditions that Noddings (1992) finds essential to responsible communities: a sense of interpersonal stability, a sense of place, and a sense of belonging. Roberta's compliments, her gentle touches on the shoulder, and her celebrations of creative expression could be construed as "touchy-feely," a pejorative label frequently slapped on humanistic teaching approaches. Those who use this term seem to feel that teachers are not supposed to have personal connections or real relationships with their students, but instead need to completely separate intellectual concerns from social and emotional ones. Such a view is in direct contrast to Roberta's view of teaching as relationships.

On the other hand, student relationships with Roberta were not the only guiding force in the classroom. Peers still held tremendous sway over what was said and done in class, even though formerly silent students eventually began to speak up. Positive changes, such as Brian and Billy's concessions to group goals during final play rehearsals, were often the result of peer pressure. Although Roberta's friendliness and caring had a major impact on student behavior, so did the peer antipathy to open expressions of caring. Students consistently sought peer approval before taking a stance, and popularity retained much of its power even when students felt freer to behave compassionately. As peer pressure to resist being empathic and caring lessened at the end of the school year, the classroom climate became more positive.

Interpersonal knowing does not automatically lead to acceptance and empathy; familiarity can breed contempt as easily as it can breed caring. Therefore caring must be accompanied by an introspective look at how that caring is manifested. It is not enough to merely know about the interests and feelings of the students; students have to trust that their interests and feelings can make a difference in the classroom.

When empathy finally became prevalent in Roberta's class at the end of the year, it was facilitated by several strategies:

1. Roberta evoked narrative examples of empathy through active listening and through her own stories. She prioritized getting to know her students well, and utilized private conversations, questions, and stories to learn about the personal life of each student. She believed that interpersonal knowing is essential in community building. From the personal profile pieces during the first week of the year to the "What I Will Always Remember" booklets during the final week, she tried to learn about students' lives and convey the value of sharing personal experiences and ideas. Roberta frequently put notes in the students' classroom mailboxes to personalize her communication with students, and many students reciprocated. The value of these written exchanges did not go unnoticed by the students, many of whom cited the mailboxes as an important aspect of the classroom during interviews at the end of the school year.

Roberta sometimes used class meetings as a forum for reflecting on the importance of kindness and compassion. During the year, many kind and unkind interactions were examined by the class during group meetings.

Roberta would also tell stories to illustrate kindness, and she elicited stories from the students as well. Reflective discussions about how students treated each other forced the class to examine the role of empathy in the classroom community.

Roberta helped evoke narratives by modeling what Gordon (1989) calls active listening. The active listening model relies on the Rogerian approach of affirming the speaker by mirroring spoken perceptions and feelings through verbal acknowledgment and paraphrasing. Nordling (1992) calls this an "inner reality response." Using an adult's reaction to a child's comment that he doesn't want to go to school anymore as an example, she contrasts an outer-reality response—"But everyone has to go to school. . . . I have to go to work, even when I don't want to"—with an inner-reality response—"Gosh, what a tough day you must have had!" (203). Ishimine, McDermott, Haas, and Setoguchi (1999) refer to a similar stance of listening as "reflective listening," and recommend "shifting gears" when responses encounter resistance. Teachers who shift gears easily can "suspend, for the moment, getting a particular point across and instead [listen] reflectively to the other person's resistance" (90). There may be gender ramifications of listening. Although some researchers (Tannen 1994; Belenky, Bond, and Weinstock 1997) feel that empathic modes of listening are utilized more by women than by men in U.S. society, both men and women can effectively use active listening to elicit the personal stories that build relationships.

In order to develop empathy and help resolve conflict, active listening may entail confronting not only students' problems, but one's own as well. As Paley (1986) discovered, seeking the point of view of students sometimes means facing the "unwelcome disclosure of [one's] hidden attitudes" (124). Teachers sometimes must reveal assumptions or biases in order to build respect and share power. Conversely, the extent to which teachers earn respect and share power can determine whether active listening is merely a courtesy, or is a real avenue for open and honest communication. As both students and teachers share stories of struggle and moral conflict, they may be more equipped to empathize with each other and solve problems collaboratively.

2. Roberta constantly provided opportunities to reflect on moral choices. When Elizabeth confessed that talking with an unpopular boy was a worthwhile experience for her, she defied social norms and summoned the need for reflecting upon individual responsibility toward the exclusionary practices that often prevailed. Her confession that taking a moral stance was difficult but worthwhile was an extremely effective means of examining ethical components of empathy.

Noddings (1998) cautions against looking at moral development as an individual process and suggests that nurturing moral relations is more important than trying to develop individual moral agents. Character education, in contrast, focuses on individual moral reasoning and downplays the interpersonal negotiation of moral choices. Roberta realized that she couldn't make students feel empathy or make ethical choices, but she stressed the relationship between interpersonal knowing and moral development by creating empathic environments *with* students and providing opportunities to examine ethics.

3. Roberta saw herself as the students' friend without suspending her authority role as a teacher. Interpersonal knowing in a classroom will not lead to increased empathy unless the community members, including the teacher, learn to trust each other as friends. Students become distrustful of teachers who respond to students in an officious rather than a personal manner. Personal knowing in classrooms is often discouraged by a plethora of silent, individual seatwork, by the interrogation aspect of tests, and by a "self-protective split of personhood from practice encouraged by an academic culture that distrusts personal truth" (Palmer 1997, 19). Because of Roberta's belief in the social nature of curriculum, she tried to frame academic pursuits in authentic communication contexts. Roberta's synthesis of academic and social concerns doesn't mean that she constantly pursued idle chit-chat, revealed details of her personal life with students, or failed to establish her authority in the relationship. As Wolk (1998) explains,

> Many believe that if [teachers have] a "friendly" relationship with their students, the students won't respect them as an adult authority figure. But the fact is that I do consider myself my students' friend. I certainly don't see myself as their peer. That's a very different relationship. (189)

Roberta had no desire to win students' favor by appealing to their peer culture. Instead, Roberta acted as an ally and friend by frequently asking herself the question "How would I treat a friend?" to guide her responses to children.

4. Roberta constantly tried to elicit diverse opinions, viewpoints, and experiences. Although only at the end of the year did she ensure that all student voices were actively heard, she strived to elicit diverse ideas during class meetings and celebrated differences between students. Roberta's efforts to involve parents and community members, through projects such as Conjunctions and the law inquiry, also facilitated an appreciation of diversity. The Conjunctions sessions were particularly effective in expanding the concerns of the class, as they led to continued partnerships between the class and community members. Some of the students from the class, for example, visited

Dr. Schwartz at the Archaeology Museum throughout the school year, and a few continued to do so after leaving fifth grade.

Roberta continually raised important issues of gender, race, age, and other aspects of identity in class. She felt raising these issues was especially important in a school like hers, in which a majority of the students came from white, middle-class families. Many of her students rarely interacted with diverse groups of people and were likely to see members of these groups as "other." By encouraging discussion of differences to effect curricular and social change in the class, Roberta hoped to nurture empathy and respect for diversity.

Roberta also tried to help students understand and accept each other's differences. Sometimes this happened as a result of private conversations she had with students, and at other times as a result of her public efforts to include and value every student. The way that Gerald, Charles, Katherine, and other socially marginalized students were invited to participate in group activities during the YMCA field trip suggests that Roberta's ideals of inclusion and compassion were at last more fully understood by many of the students.

Without Roberta's willingness to entertain discussions of difference, Elizabeth might never have revealed her acceptance of Paul, a boy that other students considered "weird" and "different." Elizabeth's revelation conveyed the power of seeing someone else's point of view, learning about their interests, and hearing their stories. By talking with Paul, she was able to abandon the "geek" label that the group had given him. Students referred to Elizabeth's confession in subsequent group meetings, indicating that some of them had internalized her message of tolerance and understanding.

If curriculum is infused with different perspectives, and allows discussion of those differences to prosper, the environment may be more conducive to empathy and respect for diversity. Valuing differences affected academic growth too, as students presented different ways of solving math problems and shared Explorers Club presentations based on topics of personal interest. Empathy and respect for diversity, though, probably will become an inherent aspect of curriculum only if the teacher is committed to examining, discussing, and valuing differences.

5. Roberta consciously avoided comparing students with each other, and emphasized collaboration over competition. When she did inadvertently compare students by showing the video of a previous class, the dangers of comparison became evident. The students' hostile reaction to the video stemmed from their perception that they were perceived as inferior to the other group of students, and our airing of the video cast us as judges. As Gathercoal (1997) reminds us, "students simply want to be judged on their own merits and not be thrust into the shadows of others" (44). By showing the video, we had unwittingly introduced a competitive element into the community. We had meant to provide the students with an example of a nurturing democratic community, but the comparison aspect of our attempt overrode any potential the video might have had to serve as a positive demonstration.

The collaborative nature of Writers Guild, Explorers Club, Invitations, and Focus Study all allowed students to proceed at their own pace and build upon individual strengths within a collaborative milieu. Roberta did not feel the need to motivate students through the competition of grades or rewards. She utilized public and private reflections on projects, portfolios, and presentations to celebrate success.

6. Roberta, at the end of the year, provided ample deliberation time for problem solving during class meetings. Group resolutions of disputes concerning the play provided positive demonstrations of democratic practices. The effective use of voting in some of these circumstances shows that majority rule, even if not the crux of democratic communities, does have a place in democratic classrooms. Roberta's insistence that Patrick support the majority decision about universal participation in the play is a case in point. Roberta also supported other majority decisions when deliberation found them to be in everyone's best interests. When Ted and Brian almost sabotaged group goals by not revising the play, Roberta supported majority wishes. During class meetings at the end of the school year, students voted on decisions only after the voices of the minority had been heard. Roberta had to allow more deliberation time in order for this to happen, despite her reluctance to take time away from other teaching. This extensive deliberation, cited in student interviews as crucial to democratic processes, may in itself have promoted more receptivity and sympathy concerning other points of view, especially when personal stories were told to illustrate the principles being debated.

Deliberation is often given short shrift because outcomes have been the focus. Yet the outcomes of class meetings do not reveal how fair the decision-making process might have been. "If we would move our attention away from thinking only of outcomes and think of conditions," writes Goodlad (1999), "then we could start examining whether the conditions are democratic, whether the conditions are caring, whether the conditions provide equity" (17). Ample time for class meetings helps teachers examine these conditions and allows everyone in the classroom community to affect outcomes.

7. Roberta did not allow majority rule to support practices she felt were unsafe, unethical, or unkind. She realized that when and how majority rule is beneficial to all is difficult to ascertain, simply because individual and group conceptions of what is right can vary so tremendously. Kirsten, for example, was willing to forego her previous standards of courtesy when the majority began to value rudeness and derision. In cases like this, Roberta explicitly exposed the parameters of her tolerance. In other circumstances, she used her veto power to overrule majority decisions that would put individuals at a significant disadvantage. When she did this, she usually explained her rationale and gauged student support before proceeding. During the crackdown, when she failed to either explain or solicit support for overriding group wishes, the positive effects of countering the majority for the benefit of all were overshadowed by student resistance.

During the final weeks of the school year, students began to question the power of popular opinion. The booing incident during the dress rehearsal brought this issue to the forefront. Roberta called a class meeting after the incident to discuss the individual's role in challenging negative group norms. This was one of many instances in which she questioned majority rule, using her authority as a teacher to highlight what she felt was right and fair. Students had previously ignored the hurtful effect of insulting jokes. But the booing incident helped some of them realize that what has been agreed upon by the majority does not necessarily represent a vision of the common good. Roberta continually critiqued mob mentality, and the students finally became more committed to challenging majority rule that didn't serve the interests of all.

8. Roberta sought positive one-on-one conversations with students from the first day of school, before problems occurred. Even during the orientation session before classes started, she actively attempted to learn about and remember students' interests and experiences. She incorporated what she had learned into private conversations whenever possible, striving to follow up on events in students' lives outside of school.

When problems did occur, she tried to discuss them privately whenever possible, and focused on getting each student's perspective of the problem. As Levy (1996) points out, balancing grace and justice is not easy, since a second chance may build a student's confidence and respect but send a message to others that violations need not have consequences. Students do not want to be publicly shamed, but teachers do not want to leave the impression that serious violations are ignored. Gathercoal (1997) emphasizes redemptive restitution, an opportunity to balance a destructive deed with an act of goodness, as the key to conflict resolution. He recommends that the first mention of behavior problems be in the form of a question—but not "why" questions, which tend to elicit defensive reactions. Asking questions that get at facts "avoids accusatory statements and lectures" (115) and immediately gives students the power to speak. It also assumes that the student acted on the basis of a perceived need.

9. Roberta consistently tried to remain calm when students were angry. She usually tried to defuse angry students by having private conversations. During these conversations, she would maintain eye contact, stand close to the students, and sometimes touch them in a gentle manner, sending a message that she was there to help them. Like several discipline theorists (Gathercoal 1997; Curwin and Mendler 1997; Axelrod and Holtje 1997), she believes that demeaning others, delivering lectures, demanding respect, becoming defensive, acting sarcastic, using intimidation, and displaying power in other ways are ineffective ways of dealing with anger. Roberta used touch as a calming strategy, and gave a number of students hugs throughout the year. Such affection is inhibited by the current climate in which teachers, particularly male teachers, are easy prey to false accusations of inappropriate touch. Roberta, however, believed strongly in the power of a supportive arm around the shoulder or a reassuring hug, despite the potential liability of touching a child during a private conversation.

Many of Roberta's problems during the year, such as the victimization of Gerald and Charles, the destruction of the toy horse, and the conspiracy plans induced by the withdrawal of classroom rights, were the result of anger. The roots of such anger are not easily unearthed, but their visible outgrowths must be kept in check to avoid the violent expression of anger within a classroom. Both students and teachers need to restrain the expression of anger, even though there may be times when anger must be expressed. Allowing anger to smolder is an unhealthy repression, whereas allowing it to explode is an unhealthy lack of restraint. Restraining anger involves shifting perspectives and letting go in a way that repressing anger does not. Just as anger can inhibit empathy and good interpersonal relationships, empathy and good interpersonal relationships can facilitate the transcendence of anger.

Roberta consciously tried not to express anger or to judge students when she felt angry with them. Popular belief holds that the spontaneous expression of anger is healthy, yet Tavris (1989) is one of several researchers who convincingly argue that the expression of anger is frequently both mentally and physically unhealthy. She recommends transcending anger by practicing relaxation strategies, depersonalizing conflicts, overcoming the tendency to think and speak inflammatory labels, seeking more information about problem situations, and working through conflict by writing about and/or talking through the issues with a third party. Weeks (1992) takes a more moderate position, claiming that anger does need to be expressed but can be expressed constructively through sharing responsibility for the anger, depersonalizing the anger by focusing on the behavior and not the person or group, and reserving anger for occasions in which the depth of the conflict needs to be communicated. Canada (1995) recommends peace education, teacher advocacy for students who are victims of family violence, and critical discussions about media violence and gun laws as ways to minimize violence in the classroom.

Of course, strategies for defusing anger and violence must be accompanied by empathy and compassion. As Tenzin Gyatso (1991), the fourteenth Dalai Lama, writes, "True compassion is not just an emotional response but a firm commitment founded on reason. Therefore, a truly compassionate attitude towards others does not change even if they behave negatively" (9). Teachers who readily yell, humiliate students, or lose self-control in other angry ways exhibit a lack of compassion and communicate that these are acceptable modes of dealing with anger within the classroom community. When teachers respond calmly and respectfully even when angry, they demonstrate self-discipline and self-restraint.

10. Roberta was not afraid to discuss her own failures. She believes that we learn from mistakes, and would talk about her own mistakes during group meetings. When something in class wasn't working, she took on part of the responsibility and invited critique concerning what she could do differently. When she felt that she had been rash or unfair, she would always apologize. All of these practices helped students understand and sympathize with her position, which may ultimately have led to more caring in the classroom. As Curwin and Mendler (1997) write, "genuine remorse [is] essential to the development of conscience and empathy" (52).

Roberta felt that she had failed to establish a good relationship with André's parents, and periodically discussed this with me. She realized that she had made herself vulnerable by telling them about her frustration with André and admitting that strategies she tried hadn't always worked. In her past experience, however, such honesty had engendered empathy rather than antipathy. At the end of the year, Roberta told me that she was distressed by the feeling that not only had she failed to reach André's parents, she had failed to reach André. Roberta had shared many of Dr. Lingle's and Dr. Martine's concerns about André's lack of engagement, motivation, and persistence. She had often fretted that she had been either too lenient or too harsh with André. At the end of the school year, it occurred to Roberta that some of André's problems could have had a biochemical basis, and she regretted that she hadn't thought of this earlier. She also wished she had confronted Dr. Martine's antagonism more directly. Roberta's frank discussion of these failures made her more sympathetic to the plight of Dr. Lingle and Dr. Martine, and also spurred her to prioritize parent communication at the beginning of the subsequent school year.

11. While acknowledging failure, Roberta also realized that caring means not feeling solely responsible for others' problems. That she was not solely responsible for the communication problems with André's parents hit home with Roberta at the end of the year, when she shared her feelings about Dr. Lingle and Dr. Martine with Laura, a third-grade teacher who had taught André. When Roberta told her about her problems with André's parents, Laura immediately wept and said that Dr. Lingle and Dr. Martine had made her feel incompetent and humiliated. Laura's confession helped Roberta take the antagonism less personally. Although Roberta had felt guilty about not communicating more often and more directly with Dr. Martine, she also knew that she was protecting herself, since her communication attempts had incited anger and abusive accusations. Dr. Martine, unlike her husband, had not taken up Roberta's invitation to visit the class, but seemed to prefer the impersonal shield of e-mail. Roberta wished she had been able to take Dr. Martine's attacks less personally from the beginning, and having more compassion toward Dr. Martine's desperation might have helped. But empathy and compassion are not easily acquired commodities, and there is a fine line between caring and taking excessive responsibility for the problems of others.

12. Roberta frequently confronted disagreements in a direct yet negotiable manner. Her sense of shared responsibility for problems usually allowed her to find mutually satisfactory compromises with difficult students and difficult parents. Although Roberta may have sidestepped confrontations with André's parents, she successfully patched the differences she had had with Ms. Katz. From the beginning, she invited Ms. Katz to voice her concerns but clearly pointed out when she breached important conditions of trust in the teacher's ability to make good professional decisions. When I talked with Roberta in April 1998 about why she was able to deal with Ms. Katz so directly yet felt intimidated by Dr. Lingle and Dr. Martine, she didn't have a ready answer. Like André's parents, Ms. Katz could be abrasive with teachers, she had written some negative correspondence to Roberta, and her son had had a history of problems at school. But unlike André's parents, she seemed to do everything she could to help her son and always followed through when she and Roberta came up with a joint plan. And, as Roberta pointed out, both Mr. and Ms. Katz always asked questions, and when they didn't like Roberta's answers, they would discuss the issues. At any rate, Roberta felt strongly that she and Ms. Katz had listened to each other and gotten to know each other well, and, as a result, had learned to empathize with each other despite their conflicts early in the school year.

13. Roberta neglected to prioritize service learning, an important means of developing empathy. Her students had few opportunities outside of the classroom to help those needier than themselves, despite the fact that such opportunities can often redirect the negative energy of angry students. Curwin and Mendler (1997) take the position that violent students need to be "reawakened to empathy" by being put in positions that require helping people, or even pets, in need of special care. They caution that students who have committed violent acts may "need to be supervised [in service learning situations] because students lacking empathy have often been emotionally wounded and abused" (53). They cite success with delinquent youth who have been mentors for severely disabled students, cared for babies at nursery schools, and participated in performances for children and senior citizens. In situations like these, students who do not feel empowered can utilize their strengths and develop self-esteem, social conscience, and empathic relationships.

By the end of the year, Roberta's classroom was characterized by less anger and more empathy, and the unanimous collaboration that made the play a success allowed the students to get to know each other better. Nevertheless, their social world of popularity wrangling certainly hadn't dissipated, and perhaps no amount of collaboration could eliminate the students' driving need to be accepted by the "cool" people. If the students had been in the position of helping others in severe need from the beginning of the year, however, their service might have spurred the interpersonal knowing that can nurture empathy, decrease violence, and build communities that value each individual.

Listening to Students: Trust and Fear

During interviews at the end of the year, students strongly contended that having opportunities to interact socially made them feel trusted and facilitated their academic achievement. Many students mentioned that they knew each other well, and implied that this interpersonal knowledge allowed them to draw upon each others' strengths as learners. Both high-achieving and low-achieving students valued the opportunity to help others. All of the students felt that more demands to "stay on task" would not have made them work any harder. Several students saw the ability to pursue social conversation when working in groups as an opportunity to become more responsible, and the word *responsible* came up over and over in the context of student discussions about their Focus Study and Explorers Club research.

About half of the students claimed that Roberta allowed for more open communication and friendship than any previous teacher. Kirsten, for example, felt that Roberta's flexible allocation of work time helped them all know each other better than ever before:

AK: Do you feel there's a strong sense of community in this classroom, and why or why not?

K: Yes, I do, because everyone seems to care about each other and when they do tease they don't tease just to be mean. They tease just in fun.

AK: So you don't think there's any meanness in the class?

K: There *is* some, but it's better than most classes.

AK: Does the way the class is set up contribute to that?

K: Sort of, because we get to know each other better as we have more free time. We get to meet each other and talk to each other more than in other classrooms . . . and we care about what we're doing.

Patrick, during much of the year, was frequently unreceptive to other points of view. Yet an interview with him at the end of year revealed a genuine enthusiasm about the interpersonal aspects of the curriculum:

AK: I would like you to say a little about inclusion and exclusion issues.

P: You mean, like people excluding people because maybe they're not as smart or kind or big?

AK: Yeah, they don't want to work with them for one reason or another, they don't want to play with them for one reason or another. How has that affected community this year? Do you think it's changed throughout the year?

P: I guess it *has* changed, because people have learned more about people. Either they've learned more that they don't like or more that they do like.

AK: Do you think that happens, for example, when people are choosing books according to what books interest them and then they end up working with whatever group chose that book? Is that a way for that to happen?

P: Yeah! . . . You can just start up a discussion group or something about the things you're interested in and then people will come who are interested in the same thing, and you might find some new friends, girlfriends, whatever.

AK: Does What's on My Mind? serve that purpose sometimes?

P: Yeah! Because you're talking about something you're concerned or interested in. And people who are interested or concerned in it can speak up and you can just start talking about it. And you might find another friend.

Patrick indeed was at last finding friends, now that he was beginning to listen to others and learning to empathize.

Other students spontaneously mentioned interpersonal knowing as an important aspect of the school year. Katherine, in an end-of-year interview, mentioned "knowing people well" as a way to develop understanding and tolerance. She told me that she had been "almost afraid of boys," and that knowing boys in the class had helped dispel her fear.

Several students felt that they had helped each other more in Roberta's class than in previous classes. Brian felt that "helping each other" was as important as group rules in "making a community together":

> If everyone's nice to each other and respecting and helpful and non-rude, then you can probably get a community out of that. . . . Probably rules and such will uphold it a little better, but I think if we all just decide to cooperate, there's no need for rules.

Brian's emphasis on helpfulness as a way to build community was particularly interesting in light of Susan's earlier interview, conducted shortly after the crackdown, in which she revealed that a number of students had decided to deliberately "refuse to help the teacher."

The students tended to feel that they were socially responsible despite the evidence of social practices that most adults would find irresponsible. Many students were aware that their treatment of each other was greatly affected by the need to be accepted by the most powerful members of the group, and that this led to some unkind actions. A great majority of the students nevertheless perceived the social climate of previous years to be much worse. Even Charles, Gerald, Julie, Katherine, Anne, and Patrick, the students who were most consistently ignored or left out of groups, experienced a greater sense of belonging and acceptance in Roberta's fifth-grade class than in previous classes.

Peer pressure to conform, however, lurked beneath the umbrella of trust and even made the children fearful of each other. Six students implied, during interviews, that they were afraid to expose their thoughts and opinions. Even though the students in Roberta's class had spent a whole year together, they sometimes didn't know what their peers really thought because of the taboo against challenging group norms. Adequate class time for deliberation, according to some students, was a way to draw out voices, but the chicken and egg relationship between empathy and hearing minority voices is a complex one.

When interviewed, students periodically referred to narrative—conveyed through reading literature, storytelling, autobiographical writing, and class meeting anecdotes—as a powerful conduit for overcoming distrust and understanding different points of view. Even sharing approaches to solving math problems, according to Ben, provided a channel for sharing personal stories. Ben claimed that explanations of problem solving often led to personal narratives about the process that students enjoyed hearing. Sally pointed to the importance of narrative when, during the last week of school, she mentioned that hearing others' stories helped her think twice about being unkind. She said that, after hearing stories about other people's personal problems, "you put yourself in the other person's shoes and see how they feel. . . . It makes you think."

Students also mentioned each other's writing as a vehicle for understanding and accepting each other. Exchanging mailbox notes, comparing journal entries, sharing poetry, and reading each other's compositions during Writers Guild were perceived as important ways to learn about each other's ideas in the classroom. On the other hand, as Susan pointed out when discussing Writers Guild, some students really weren't interested in others' points of view:

S: I love to write. In other classrooms, they didn't let you just write. They said, "Well write a story about a rock." But they wouldn't just give you freedom to write. And I really like to just have the freedom to write. In this classroom, I've gotten to just write and I really like doing that. And also, when I've gone back over, it's helped me because I've learned what kind of stories people like, what kind of stories I like, and how you need to write them.

AK: And do you feel like you've changed them a lot during the writing?

S: It depends. On some, I got responses like "Oh it all stinks. Rewrite it." And so I just ignored that. But there are other ones who said, "Well I think you should change this part" and that I did do. But some people weren't really serious about giving help and it was kind of hard.

AK: So you think an indicator of the seriousness of a response is how specific it is about what might need to be changed?

S: Yes. If you ask them to read and they read it and it's five pages long and then I say, "Well which part do you think I should change?" and they say, "the fifth page," and you ask what on the fifth page and they say, "just work on that page," then you get the feeling that they don't really care. They're just telling you to do something because that's what they're supposed to do. They're not really saying, "Well I don't think you should have that in it but I do think you should have that."

AK: So, in other words, if people really give reasons that make it clear—

S: Then they're paying attention. And I don't always agree with all their suggestions, but I do take some of them, some much more than others.

Sharing writing in response groups as a way to prepare for publishing was cited by several other students as an important way of getting to know each other. Publishing was also mentioned as a way for students to read and appreciate each other's work. But Susan's response provides a cautionary note that genuine interest in and effective response to written work are not automatic, but must be demonstrated, facilitated, and nurtured.

Some students also seemed disinterested in developing empathic relationships. A conversation between Roberta and Hope exemplified the reactive stance that commonly prevented empathic ways of responding to others:

H: Sometimes my little brother is so annoying. He'll be eating an apple or something and he'll be chewing it, like, right over my shoulder while I'm doing something. It's so gross. And I'll say "Stop it!" and I'll get really mad.

R: I'll share an experience like that I had with my own husband. I've had times when I thought, "Why is he breathing like that?" You wouldn't think a wife would feel that way about her husband but I realized that the only time I feel that way is when I'm angry with myself. . . .

Students readily assumed that the behavior of others was ill intentioned. The ease with which they adopted an accusatory or angry mode shows how their distrust prevented them from being respectful and empathic. Students who were convinced that others were out to "get them" were not open to listening to others and responding compassionately.

Fortunately, the distrust and disrespect that infected the classroom during the year did not permanently deter positive community growth. By the end of the year, students were relying upon each other more than ever, and the collaboration that flourished during the play production helped students respect each other's abilities and points of view. Acceptance, rather than rejection, pervaded the classroom, and the culminating experience of the play performance was a vibrant example of a collective community spirit. As the students themselves indicated in interviews, they felt accepted in Roberta's class, had many opportunities to know each other well, and had chances to make collective decisions. All of these experiences contributed to trust and respect within the classroom community. When I asked Maureen what was most important about the classroom community, she said:

> I think one of the main things you need is just respect. It's probably the most important thing you need, because if you respect other people—other people's right to speak, other people's right to have an idea and stuff like that—then you might learn something that you never knew before.

Maureen, like many of the other students, understood that respect and empathy are important foundations of learning.

Lingering Questions

What characterizes a caring teacher?

What are the limits of teacher responsibility for student achievement?

How should teachers deal with parent harassment?

What is the relationship between trust and vigilance, both of which can prevent behavior problems?

How can teachers demonstrate caring while at the same time foster independence?

How can we better understand the relationship between freedom and social responsibility?

Further Reading

Countering Violence in Schools

Brosnan, Michael. 1997. *Against the Current: How One School Struggled and Succeeded with At-risk Teens.* Portsmouth, NH: Heinemann.

Canada, Geoffrey. 1995. *Fist Stick Knife Gun.* Boston: Beacon Press.

Charney, Ruth S. 1992. *Teaching Children to Care: Management in the Responsive Classroom.* Greenfield, MA: Northeast Foundation for Children.

Curwin, Richard L., and Allen M. Mendler. 1997. *As Tough as Necessary: Countering Violence, Aggression, and Hostility in Our Schools.* Alexandria, VA: Association for Supervision and Curriculum Development.

Dennison, George. 1969. *The Lives of Children: The Story of the First Street School.* Reading, MA: Addison-Wesley.

Girard, Kathryn, and Susan J. Koch. 1996. *Conflict Resolution in the Schools: A Manual for Educators.* San Francisco: Jossey-Bass Publishers.

Goleman, Daniel. 1995. *Emotional Intelligence.* New York: Bantam Books.

Haberman, Martin. 1995. *Star Teachers of Children in Poverty.* West Lafayette, IN: Kappa Delta Pi.

Levin, Diane E. 1994. *Teaching Young Children in Violent Times: Building a Peaceable Classroom.* Philadelphia: New Society Publishers.

Tavris, Carol. 1989. *Anger: The Misunderstood Emotion.* Revised ed. New York: Simon & Schuster.

Weeks, Dudley. 1992. *The Eight Essential Steps to Conflict Resolution: Preserving Relationships at Work, at Home, and in the Community.* New York: G. P. Putnam's Sons.

Building Caring Communities

Bridges, Lois. 1995. *Creating Your Classroom Community.* York, ME: Stenhouse Publishers.

Dalton, Joan, and Marilyn Watson. 1997. *Among Friends: Classrooms Where Caring and Learning Prevail.* Oakland, CA: Developmental Studies Center.

Fried, Robert L. 1995. *The Passionate Teacher: A Practical Guide.* Boston: Beacon Press.

Gibbs, Jeanne. 1995. *Tribes: A New Way of Learning and Being Together.* Sausalito, CA: Center Source Systems.

Glasser, William. 1998. *Choice Theory.* New York: HarperCollins.

Noddings, Nell. 1992. *The Challenge to Care in Schools: An Alternative Approach to Education.* New York: Teachers College Press.

Paley, Vivian G. 1999. *The Kindness of Children.* Cambridge: Harvard University Press.

Discipline Approaches

Butchart, Ronald E., and Barbara McEwan, eds. 1998. *Classroom Discipline in American Schools: Problems and Possibilities for Democratic Education.* Albany: State University of New York Press.

Fay, Jim, and David Funk. 1995. *Teaching with Love and Logic: Taking Control of the Classroom.* Golden, CO: The Love and Logic Press.

Gathercoal, Forrest. 1997. *Judicious Discipline.* 4th ed. San Francisco: Caddo Gap Press.

Ginott, Haim. 1972. *Teacher and Child: A Book for Parents and Teachers.* New York: Avon Books.

Gordon, Thomas. 1989. *Teaching Children Self-Discipline at Home and at School.* New York: Times Books.

Jones, Vernon F., and Louise S. Jones. 1998. *Comprehensive Classroom Management: Creating Communities of Support and Solving Problems.* 5th ed. Needham Heights, MA: Allyn & Bacon.

Nelsen, Jane, Roslyn Duffy, Linda Escobar, Kate Ortolano, and Debbie Owen-Sohocki. 1996. *Positive Discipline: A Teacher's A-Z Guide.* Rocklin, CA: Prima Publishing.

Nelsen, Jane, Lynn Lott, and H. Stephen Glenn. 1993. *Positive Discipline in the Classroom.* Rocklin, CA: Prima.

7

Freedom and Control

Thinking on Your Feet

After three years of observing Roberta's fifth-grade classes, I was convinced that she was a superior teacher. Her classroom had been a thriving community of learners, and discipline, apart from isolated problems with difficult students, was rarely an issue. Her democratic approach had earned the students' trust, facilitated remarkable academic growth, and garnered a large measure of respect from colleagues, administrators, and members of the community. As a result of my observations, I expected the 1996–97 school year to be equally harmonious. When it turned out to be a year of jarring dissonance, I had to reconceptualize both my idealization of community and my notion that Roberta, or any other teacher, could attain a permanent plateau of excellence. A teacher can become more adept or seasoned or astute, but even a "master teacher" can struggle and fail.

The errors that all teachers inevitably make can often have far-reaching consequences. Not monitoring a rambunctious student carefully can lead to a serious injury. A hasty head count during a field trip can result in a lost child. And, as Roberta and I learned, group punishment for individual offenses can lead to weeks of resentment and distrust. One can never iron out all the problems that crop up in teaching, particularly when strong leaders in the class are belligerent.

On the other hand, the far-reaching consequences of poor teacher decisions may not be irreversible. Roberta faced belligerence during the 1996–97 school year, and her ensuing struggles revealed the wrinkles inherent in the fabric of teaching. But she eventually was able to craft a sense of community in her classroom, in spite of failures that almost soured the sweetness of success. After observing how Roberta's defiant students managed to sabotage her techniques and talents, I was reminded that even superior teachers can falter and fail when faced with the unexpected resistance of selfish, unkind students. Yet I was also reminded that superior teachers do not give up easily, but continue to find new ways to enact their convictions in the face of adversity.

Although Roberta's students may have been self-centered and unkind, or even hellish, they really weren't the kids from hell. Some teachers reading this story probably have been thinking: "If Roberta was frustrated by this group, she should see the kids *I* have to face every day." The students were difficult, but not impossible, and Roberta's strong guidance compensated for her lapses of control. During much of the year, harmonious collaboration was dominant in Roberta's classroom, and order could usually be summoned whenever necessary. The undercurrent of discord that rippled, and eventually raced, through the classroom was the result of a selfishness that can threaten all communities, even democratic ones. Roberta's principal, Beth Waters, described the students during a 1998 interview:

AK: There seemed to be a real strong social climate amongst last year's group. I mean, I saw some things happening with the kids in the other classes that were happening in Roberta's, so I often wondered how much of it was the relationships within her class and how much of it was that peer culture of the flowers and the mall trips and the skateboard incidents—

B: And that is still there this year.

AK: With that group?

B: Not just your group—the whole fifth grade, who are now sixth graders . . . those kinds of behaviors were showing up in all of the fifth grade. It was a fairly unusual group; it's an unusual group in the sixth grade this year.

AK: How are they faring this year?

B: Well—I don't know. They're all right. They're not delinquents; they're not like a few kids we had in the sixth grade last year.

AK: Yeah, I remember.

B: So they're not like that, for which I'm eternally grateful. [Laughs] Those are the ones that just create havoc in your school, those kinds of behavior disorders. But probably the thing that is most evident is that they are not kind to each other.

AK: That's what struck us.

B: It's the least kind group of kids. Fortunately, there are lots of them who are; there are tons of kids who are just wonderful kids, but they are so

> overshadowed by this group of about twenty, from all groups, from each of your classrooms. So it wasn't any one teacher who somehow created a group of uncaring kids. But they are so unkind to each other. And they are really self-centered; it's like they think the world revolves around them. I don't know how they got that way, but they sure are unkind.

As Beth indicated, there were many wonderful, caring students in Roberta's 1996–97 group. But it was discouraging to hear that the leaders were still acting unkind in the sixth grade.

Roberta usually managed to draw out the best in her students. Even when their abuse of democratic practices was at its worst, her students were not immune to her influence. Despite Roberta's concern over the state of the class during the crackdown, she retained a sense that, somehow, things could be "put right."

Teachers are in the business of "putting things right," for instilling respect, self-discipline, and a love of learning, but how this is done can only be analyzed within the context of a particular group of students. The same teacher may take drastically different approaches to discipline with different groups. I have taught groups of students for an entire year without getting angry at any of them, and I have had groups that tested my patience on a daily basis and prompted me to constantly examine issues of fairness in the classroom. Yet the principled perspectives that guide decisions about freedom and control are virtually the same with any group of students. All teachers need to balance trust and vigilance, latitude and constraint. How much freedom we allow children, and how and when we intervene to address the abuse of that freedom, constitute the essence of classroom management. Teachers make crucial decisions by thinking on their feet, by assessing the complex implications of the moment. Even with the best of guidance, a given group of students may make poor judgments. This is why democratic approaches to discipline can never be "mastered."

Establishing Versus Exerting Control

Teachers cannot foster democratic communities overnight; democratic modes of thinking take time to develop. The ease and extent to which students control their thoughts and actions are not merely the result of school experiences. The complex mesh of parent, peer, community, and genetic influences also creates a wide range of dispositions to learning. This is why different classes may call for different approaches to teaching. If most children in a classroom have little adult supervision outside of school and are used to making decisions without considering others, how and why individual and group goals should be balanced must be explicitly demonstrated with examples. Students used to authoritarian home environments must learn that polite requests can be just as powerful as shouted commands. If students are constantly exposed to violence, they need to see alternatives to violent responses. Students who are accustomed to getting attention in disruptive ways need to be given attention for positive actions, no matter how incidental. While gauging the social needs of students within the school context, teachers who offer democratic choices must constantly decide what kinds of learning experiences establish, rather than exert, control.

An important aspect of establishing control is creating conditions that prevent social problems. For example, building rapport with individual students through private conversations before problems occur paves the way for effective problem solving. Even relatively small problems such as not following class job guidelines can be more easily resolved if a climate of responsibility, rather than a system of compliance, has been established.

Problems will crop up in the most democratic of systems, even if preventive conditions are in place, and teachers should be prepared for the unexpected. At the same time, anticipating problems does not necessarily entail predetermined solutions. Some teachers start out the year in a strict manner, establishing many rules and consequences and acting as vigilant as possible to ensure that small abuses of rights and privileges are nipped in the bud. Other teachers address problems as they crop up, distinguishing between minor and major disruptions at the beginning of the year as they do later on. But even if teachers anticipate problems, the manner in which control is established and exerted must constantly be re-examined in terms of how, when, and why students make responsible choices.

Establishing control involves a greater degree of trust than exerting control. According to a recent article on the enforcement of no-smoking laws in California, trusting smokers to follow the law didn't work, whereas undercover policing has fuelled hostility, resistance, and fear (Perry 1999). Police sergeant Sam Campbell is quoted as saying, "If paranoia gets compliance, I can live with it" (A21). Yet the problem—getting smokers to respect the rights of nonsmokers in a civil manner—has not really been addressed. The paranoia of undercover arrests might increase compliance, but it highlights legal, rather than social, responsibility. Most teachers tend to stress social responsibility, knowing that constantly invoking rules builds hostility and resistance, which in turn inhibit learning. Fear of punishment is not likely to nurture self-control and a sense of responsibility toward the classroom community. On the other hand, self-control and a sense of community responsibility are not likely to develop unless teachers provide choices, demonstrate responsible actions, and carefully monitor student decisions. Democratic classroom environments must be supported by a balance of trust and vigilance, and such a balance is difficult to attain. Furthermore, democratic classrooms are not a panacea; they cannot overcome the problems of severely needy students who respond to neither authoritarian nor democratic approaches.

Rules and consistent procedures may help maintain order, but democratic decision making and autonomous self-regulation also require conditions that are more global than regulations and routines. As I reflect on the ramifications of Roberta's 1996–97 school year, I will highlight six important conditions for facilitating a democratic learning environment: a teacher-researcher stance, social components of curriculum, aesthetic experiences, a commitment to justice and equality, class meetings, and interpersonal caring.

Developing a Teacher-Researcher Stance

Teachers who think about the research aspect of teaching know that just when they feel comfortable that their practices correspond to their beliefs and theories, a wrench can be thrown into the works. Suddenly, the relationship between the teacher's ideas and the realities of the classroom must be reconsidered. Roberta's ongoing assessment of what was and wasn't working helped her address problems and prevented the students' rebellion in early May from becoming a complete disaster. Her attempts to articulate her theories and adjust practice accordingly led to judicious and effective decisions during the last weeks of school. These decisions fostered the strong commitment to democratic practices that the final class meetings represented. On the other hand, she sometimes miscalculated her students' needs, and an honest appraisal of her failures spurred her to make changes in her teaching.

One change that Roberta implemented was more regular communication with individual students and parents. Along with a renewed commitment to finding out about students and their interests, she implemented subtle changes in the way she collaborated with students and parents. Roberta tried to avoid the communication problems of the previous year by holding individual conferences with students and parents at the beginning of the year, and she sought student feedback on classroom decisions more than ever before. Roberta felt that the collaborative research she and I had conducted during the previous year helped her ask authentic questions and hear student voices more astutely than ever before. She implemented more checkpoints to help children keep up with and assess their work. With parents, she held more conferences and stayed in closer touch. She described some of these changes in an e-mail message, sent to me during the final term of her 1997–98 school year:

> [This year] I have folders that I send home with student work—sometimes in progress—that parents have to sign and return. It's interesting when you put the effort into a system like that how frustrating it can be. I thought it was extremely clear—I explained it at Open House—how I wanted this to go home at night and come back the next day. If they hadn't had time to look at things the students could bring it home again. Well, as you can imagine, folders [were] left at home, emptied at home, etc. I don't think it's a bad idea [but] I don't feel the need for it as much now. Parents seem very happy.
>
> [This year] I had a conference with every family within the first three weeks of school. That's the best change. However, I don't have any parents like André's this year (and never had before either). Then I had a conference in early November and another one the end of February. I know you always said you conferenced a lot. It's a wonderful feeling. . . .
>
> Would last year have been any better if we had had three scheduled conferences with André's parents? Essentially we did—but we didn't call them. Would they have responded to the "work" folder? I don't think so. Their stance was to evaluate the work we were doing. Nothing seemed valuable to them—except perhaps the poetry unit.

Roberta realized that any "system" she implemented in order to facilitate order and discipline was, in the long run, less important than the relationships she established. She no longer felt guilty about the disjunctions between herself and André's parents, having accepted the fact that her view of teaching as ongoing assessment was in basic conflict with their view of teaching as evaluation. By continuing to try to understand and document students' learning within the context of their conversations, actions, and written work, Roberta encouraged the personal and political expression of voice in the classroom.

After the turbulent 1996–97 school year, Roberta was more conscious about inviting her students to take on a teacher-researcher role. Students had already taken on this role by presenting Explorers Club and Focus Study research, by running class meetings, and by making decisions about curriculum. With her subsequent classes, however, Roberta closely examined student leadership to help students become better researchers and presenters.

Addressing Social Components of Curriculum

Students who face humiliation at home, peer bullying, and other social issues may not be predisposed to participating in a math lesson or independently pursuing a social studies project. Individual self-worth and collaborative social support are both essential for academic growth. Social concerns always involve the relationship between individuals and the community, and discussion about those concerns cannot always occur within the confines of content-area instruction. Students need explicit demonstrations of and discussion about how to get along with each other and how to balance majority and minority concerns.

Although Roberta's students found it difficult to develop social networks that supported democratic decisions, their emphasis upon social responsibility during the play production was instrumental in creating a more democratic climate. An earlier focus upon social issues might have enhanced responsibility and led to a more inclusive, democratic community, but from the beginning the students sensed the curricular importance of addressing how they wanted to be in the classroom. Student interviews, however, implied that deliberation about social issues was often curtailed. Preoccupation with subject matter frequently prevented more in-depth discussion of social problems unrelated to classroom studies, despite Roberta's attempts to incorporate social and academic concerns. Her willingness to let student interests guide inquiries, such as the extensive inquiry on court proceedings, allowed the academic aspects of social concerns to flourish, showing that social issues can sometimes be addressed within academic contexts. Later, she realized that social issues not directly related to content area concerns perhaps should have been addressed more extensively during class time.

Bartlett Camp and the Conjunctions workshops established ties between Roberta's class and the greater community. Bartlett Camp allowed curriculum to extend beyond the confines of the classroom. Conjunctions brought parents and community members into the classroom. The two experiences led to many ongoing relationships, and also allowed interests, rather than popularity, to propel new groupings. Both Bartlett Camp and Conjunctions demonstrated the power of a socially constructed curriculum to spur intellectual effort by stressing collaborative participation rather than performance.

The value judgments that Roberta and I made about the students' preoccupations with social concerns during the 1996–97 school year may have prevented us from giving those preoccupations the attention they were due. "The students were wasting more time today," I once remarked, "talking about who likes somebody from another classroom." I hadn't stopped to think that perhaps this conversation raised important issues of friendship and gender relations that needed to be discussed as a group. Throughout the year Roberta, likewise, criticized the students' preoccupation with designer clothing, "going steady," and trying to top each other's insults. By judging the children's status-seeking too harshly, we may have stultified more open dialogue regarding its effects on peer acceptance and conflict resolution. Only at the end of the year, when universal participation in the play became a class goal, did the social concerns that were driving so much of the students' behavior become a focal point of the curriculum. And it was only at that point that students took more responsibility toward ensuring that individual behavior served group needs.

Roberta's reflections on the social concerns of her 1996–97 class led her to make several changes in subsequent years. When planning the 1997–98 curriculum, for example, she and the other fifth-grade teachers at Robinson scheduled the Bartlett Woods trip for the fall instead of the spring. This, she felt, helped classroom relationships gel early in the year. In addition, follow-up activities could occur for many months. Another change concerned parent contact: As she strived to understand the social world of the students, she sought more parent input concerning the students' peer relationships, and devised ways for students to explicitly address how they interacted and regulated themselves as a group. After witnessing the breakdown of democracy during the previous year, Roberta felt a pressing need to confront the differences between the students' values and her own—especially values concerning popularity and other power issues. How the students treated each other was no longer a discipline matter to be resolved and forgotten, but a central aspect of curriculum. Without understanding the social dynamics of a community and addressing social problems, she realized, the fairness of democratic processes cannot be effectively assessed.

Providing Aesthetic Experiences

Aesthetic experiences facilitate awareness, creativity, and communication. Their importance in nurturing individual voice, building school success, and supporting all academic disciplines has been largely ignored in public schools. Fortunately, Roberta realized the learning value of alternate sign systems and gave her students many opportunities to explore art, drama, and other communication systems. Students relished these creative options, often citing Invitations sessions as a favorite element of Roberta's class. They loved using paints, clay, Legos, musical instruments, geometric shapes, and other materials in order to freely create. Heartened by the positive feedback during group meetings, many students worked on these creations over time, in effect revising, editing, and publishing them in one form or another. A similar process orientation to writing spurred the public discussion of each other's poems, stories, and plays. Even unpopular students received positive feedback on their achievements in art, songwriting, poetry, and drama. This, in turn, boosted self-esteem and self-discipline as the students endeavored to refine their creative work.

Roberta sometimes has had to convince skeptical parents of the value of spending class time on artistic endeavors. In March 1998, she described her conference with some parents who had dismissed the role of picture books in her classroom:

> Since I had been talking with [Alan's mother] all year I kind of continued my conversation with her. Alan had done really superficial research on Hawaii. I had asked him to look for the picture book *The Last Princess*, which he never did. His mother finally got it for him, but after the [presentation]. At the conference I thanked her for that and the father kind of humphed and said, "I thought we were done with picture books in second or third grade." I asked if he had seen it, that picture books were full of information for adults too.

Roberta had realized, sadly, that convincing Alan's father of the benefit of the aesthetic aspects of the picture book was a major battle, and chose instead to justify the picture book on the basis of its informational import. The father's dismissal was, however, a typical example of the low value placed on art as a sign system.

The positive effect that *Star Bores* had on democratic processes in the class spurred Roberta to once more produce a class play the following year. Again, she found that theater experience provided many opportunities for democratic deliberation. The children perceived play preparation as "fun," yet the nitty gritty of memorizing lines, constructing sets, and other time-consuming tasks involved determination and sustained engagement. As before, producing a play led to a tremendous pooling of resources and social bonding that may not have been possible through other means. As it did the previous year, producing a play developed students' self-discipline, conflict resolution strategies, and aesthetic appreciation. Two years later, in spring 1999, some of Roberta's 1996–97 students were still writing and producing original plays in the seventh grade.

Maintaining a Commitment to Justice and Equality

Although the injustices of school systems, and society in general, can drag down students and teachers alike, a belief that justice and equality are worth striving for can provide hope and inspiration. While many downtrodden students trudge along, others awaken to learning and discover that exciting possibilities await them. As they become more interested in others and the world around them, students who are empowered by teacher commitment to fair practices create a positive ripple that gives teachers the sense that, yes, the struggle of teaching is worthwhile after all.

Yet teacher commitment alone may not be able to promote social democracy. Democratic practices are learned experiences, and living in a political democracy does not automatically confer understanding of how to be fair and inclusive. Roberta was committed to democratic practices and provided opportunities to experience them, yet there were many instances of injustice and inequality in her classroom. Many students were victimized by their classmates' abuse of power. Some of these victims perpetuated the problems, and some became advocates for the underdog. Patrick, for example, was often denied participation but frequently denied the equal participation of others, while Katherine, often the recipient of unkind remarks due to her weight and her hesitancy to follow the crowd, became more and more committed to kindness as the year transpired. When the students experienced the injustice of being booed after the *Star Bores* dress rehearsal, they were at last able to critically examine their ongoing justification of insulting remarks. Roberta, because of her democratic beliefs, tried to ensure that such incidents became opportunities for rectification rather than retaliation.

From the first few months of the school year, when an interest in legal proceedings burgeoned, students were interested in issues of equality and justice. But it wasn't until the end of the year that many of those concerns became internalized through personal experiences. When the students began to actively examine the relationship between individual and group rights, students became more inclusive despite the overwhelming forces of popularity that supported exclusionary practices.

Sharing personal narratives also helped demonstrate a commitment to concerns of justice and equality. When students brought stories of being mistreated or excluded to group meetings, particularly at the end of the year, undemocratic practices were scrutinized in a way that otherwise might not have been possible. Elizabeth's poignant narrative about taking the risk of socializing with Paul, the "geek," was the most salient example; her story seemed to touch the entire group. Before this disclosure, few students were willing to risk group censure by going against popular norms, but afterward a more inclusive community began to form.

Roberta's avoidance of rewards and punishments, temporarily abandoned during the crackdown, was consistent with her commitment to fairness and equality. An approach to discipline that utilizes exclusion as punishment, she feels, often fuels unjust practices and resentment of authority. Such an approach was implemented by sixth-grade teachers at Robinson, particularly during the 1997–98 school year. Sixth graders who misbehaved were given detention during weekly afternoon activities. Roberta, in spring 1998, reported that André was often in trouble:

> I've seen André in the office—once he was in a fistfight. Another day he had "three strikes" so he missed the Friday afternoon sixth grade treat. I wonder

> how many of those he misses. I knew about the three strikes, but thought that that was a program they just implemented at the end of the year when they were having control problems. Now it seems to be a once-a-week thing. I wonder if it's because of this particular class or because there's a different combination of teachers. Don't you wonder if they can justify it—if they reflect on whether it really changes the behavior of the kids that need to make changes?

The ineffectiveness of a rewards and punishment mode of teaching was most apparent to us during our crackdown in early May. Although some students I interviewed indicated that the crackdown made them more aware of the importance of their rights and privileges, most felt that the anger and resentment of authority that it engendered made the class even more resistant to democratic ideals.

After witnessing the frequent exclusion of individuals during the 1996–97 school year, Roberta vowed to find ways to prevent this during the following year. One approach that she found useful was having the students sit with different classmates every day at the beginning of the year. Random groupings ensured that students worked with many class members within a short period of time, and Roberta feels that this practice helped prevent the kind of exclusion that she had witnessed during the previous year. She has relied more on the Conflict Council as well, and has gotten more involved in facilitating it. She has tried to ensure that democratic decisions are based on ample deliberation, so that all student voices can affect classroom community decisions. At the same time, she has been more aware of when she needs to use veto power to ensure justice and fairness. Fortunately, as Beth Waters affirmed in March 1998, she needed it less frequently with her subsequent class:

> Roberta runs a genuinely democratic class . . . with veto power, though, which she probably had to use more times last year than she's had to use this year, because of the group. But I think she is [democratic] in terms of choices or community meetings, talking about things and coming to conclusions with the group or a small group, either on academic issues or social issues.

Conducting Class Meetings

When students discuss and debate issues, they are learning important lessons about negotiating difference in a social democracy. Even when class meetings are used for the critique or appreciation of student artwork, the value of individual voice is being nurtured. When class meetings go beyond social sharing to become mechanisms for student decision making concerning their self-regulation, they become vital instruments of democracy.

Roberta's students used class meetings as a forum for discussing issues, making curriculum decisions, critiquing and celebrating creative achievements, solving problems, and following up on prior solutions. Students increasingly gained confidence and voice during class meetings, particularly when they brought their writing or artwork to share or discuss. Because of the power of a popular few, however, it was not until the end of the year that the viewpoints of unpopular students were seriously debated.

Class meetings were often sites of conflict, but, as DeStigter (1998) reminds us, "truly democratic communities must not only allow for dissent, but [also] in fact depend on it" (36). The students' social attachments, their competition for popularity, and their strong investment in consensual opinion all led to undercurrents of disharmony. Even before we realized the depth of those undercurrents, we should have been prepared to accept the anger, conflict, and disorder that investing the students with power might entail. To conceive of a flourishing community as either perpetually harmonious or continually rife with strife is erroneous. It is the ebb and flow between agreement and disagreement, between harmony and discord, between support and critique, that helps unleash the democratic potential of a classroom community.

As students pointed out in interviews, it was only at the end of the year that class meetings were consistently characterized by thorough deliberation. Before that time, they were often dysfunctional due to an abuse of power and the resulting unequal participation. Roberta gave the students a great deal of control over their own learning, but the students pursued a "hidden curriculum" by replicating societal hierarchies in which powerful people wield undue influence over others. Some students viewed the opportunity to share power democratically as a way to usurp power from the teacher. The group goal of producing the play, which transcended the manipulations of a power-hungry few, and Roberta's persistent efforts to solicit minority views helped the students run truly democratic class meetings. This did not happen, however, without conflict and extensive deliberation. At the end of the year, students were able to solve problems as a community in which Roberta was an important member, but not the sole arbitrator. Even though it had taken the entire school year for the students to take ownership over the meetings in a fair and equitable manner, it was worth the wait. When students learned to deal with conflict in a calm, accepting way, they were better equipped to see democratic problem solving as an opportunity for growth and learning.

Facilitating Caring, Interpersonal Relationships

Only those teachers who view relationships as fundamental to teaching will establish the pursuit of liberty and happiness as the goal of classroom democracy. Teachers who focus on the worth and potential growth of each student nurture concern for individual rights. Helping students appreciate the potential strength of a supportive community is a major challenge, because many students have not experienced caring environments and have legitimate reasons for distrusting others. But the more that teachers trust and respect students, the more students will seek experiences that build individual and collective success. Even more important, students who feel respected will learn to trust in the resilience of the human spirit.

Roberta's emphasis on her relationships with students helped her put confrontations and conflicts into a broader perspective. After Kirsten, for example, rudely criticized her voice during a class meeting, Roberta made a special effort to initiate private conversations with her whenever possible. Nearly a year after the rude remark, Roberta sought her out in order to learn about her perspective of the incident. Kirsten not only remembered it, but said she had thought about it many times since and felt terrible about it. Roberta then apologized for not having expressed her disapproval privately. Kirsten seemed surprised, exclaiming that Roberta had "every right" to criticize her publicly. Roberta agreed, but maintained that refraining from public censure might have been a better way to handle the problem. They ended the conversation with a hug.

Throughout the year, Roberta often thought through problem situations with students by thinking how she would react as a friend. During the crackdown, she was no longer asking that question as she normally did, and students, as a consequence of her authoritarian stance, were even less willing than before to be democratic. When she abandoned her authoritarian stance, once more thinking through her role as a friend and advocate, resistance waned. Supported by a universal commitment to producing *Star Bores,* the students at last began to demonstrate that they cared about each classroom community member.

At the end of the year, there were several examples of this interpersonal growth. During group meetings, students began to applaud inclusionary practices. During final preparations for the play, supportive collaborations thrived. And during the YMCA field trip, students actively attempted to include everyone in the sports activities. In each of these circumstances, empathy played a major role in rebuilding the damaged class climate that the students' rebellion and the resultant crackdown had brought about. During the last two weeks of class, we were able to trust each other again, and there were no visible remnants of the animosity that had prevailed in early May.

The trusting relationships that usually characterize Roberta's classroom communities can be long lasting. Former students frequently linger in her class after school, and middle school and even high school students come back to talk with her. Roberta, however, has told me that there are always some students she feels close to in class who later "walk by expressionless" once they've moved on to sixth grade. In the spring of 1998, I asked her what kinds of interactions she had encountered with her 1996–97 group. She e-mailed me that some former students

> started the year somewhat aloof but [that's] not so now. Elizabeth just stopped in to share a poem she had written. Veronica was very helpful and friendly when we were on bus duty together. Sally always speaks. Hope (not surprisingly) is always in my room before school starts. Susan has just started coming in and looking around (asked to borrow a bean bag chair for the sixth grade read-a-thon). Patrick is very friendly (so is his mother), André speaks as he walks by . . .

Roberta later recounted other stories about the students. André came to her room one day and carried on small talk before at last revealing an ulterior motive for the visit: He wanted Roberta to get him a Coke from the teachers' lounge. She told him that she wouldn't go against school policy by doing that. A short while later, she saw him bolt from the lounge, his attempt to get a Coke aborted by an approaching teacher. Roberta also told me about her encounter with Sally at a grocery store. Sally had greeted her like a long-lost friend and, after a leisurely talk, was reluctant to end the conversation. Jessica was the only student who ignored Roberta for most of her sixth-grade year. She would not make eye contact, even when Roberta said hello to her. In April 1998, however, Jessica approached Roberta at the science fair. They ended up having an extensive discussion about Jessica's science fair project on liquid nitrogen.

Even the most defiant students from the 1996–97 class, as subsequent interactions revealed, developed respect for Roberta. Interviews with students affirmed this, and several individuals indicated that feeling accepted helped them understand the importance of a caring community. As Maureen suggested in an interview, the link between respect and learning is vital. The social dimension of learning is dependent upon respect for other people; without it, we cannot cooperate with and learn from others. In a social democracy, regulations and procedures can facilitate the smooth functioning of a community, but ultimately it is a climate of interpersonal respect that allows discipline to become a framework for principled perspective, rather than a system of control.

Discipline and Democracy

Freedom and control in the classroom cannot be guided by rules alone. Those who rally around rules might feel that student parameters in Roberta's class were not clear, and that this loose structure allowed students to easily abuse democratic means to serve their own ends. Yet defiance is a power issue whether rules are explicit or not. And clearly defined rules and consequences are always subject to exceptions and interpretations. When Roberta unquestioningly accepted the students' assurance that they "knew the school rules" at the beginning of the year, she may have missed an opportunity to make her expectations more explicit. On the other hand, she *did* articulate her expectations as she chose how and when to address behavior on an ongoing basis.

Those who stress procedural clarity as a device for discipline might also question the loose rein of talk and movement in Roberta's classroom. Yet students usually met, and sometimes exceeded, expectations. Roberta established goals, made plans, and solved problems in tandem with students. She supported their curricular and behavioral choices and wielded her authority only when their choices violated the rights of others. The flexibility of her approach vitalized the curriculum and allowed teachable moments to flourish.

It is possible for teachers to encounter less conflict by establishing firm rules and consequences and by implementing predictable procedures. Yet more control may not create the best environment for learning. A certain measure of disorder may be inherent to the greater range of choice that is part of democracy. Furthermore, conflict may stimulate creative problem solving and promote inquiry. Too much order restricts social choices and responsibilities, and sometimes confronting conflict in a constructive way creates alternatives and fosters respect within a community.

Teachers garner respect by creating conditions for caring democratic communities. A teacher-researcher stance and a social curriculum help teachers understand and empathize with students' life experiences. Aesthetic opportunities allow those experiences to be expressed in a multitude of ways. Teacher commitment to democratic principles and the demonstration of those principles in class meetings help place individual experiences in community contexts. Demonstrations of caring make those community contexts safe and supportive. These conditions are not magic keys to success, but they do build respect within a classroom community. And, as Roberta's experiences reveal, academic success is contingent upon the interpersonal respect that supports self-discipline and democratic practices.

Discipline involves respecting the limitations of liberty. If we believe in discipline, we expect individuals to understand the parameters of civility, which can best be understood if community members constantly attempt to balance individual and group rights. As Roberta demonstrated, a democratic approach to discipline unleashes the potential of liberty by empowering individuals through choices that consider consequences. If we believe in democracy, we have to provide choices unfettered by undue political influence. In a democratic classroom, teachers build *self*-discipline, and students learn that freedom is contingent upon respecting the rights of others. Whether or not Roberta's students consistently internalized the relationship between freedom and respect for civil rights, their exposure to democratic practices gave them exceptional choices. And those who have tasted freedom are more likely to develop self-discipline and democratic dispositions.

Lingering Questions

Can democratic learning environments be established in any given classroom?

How can teachers better accept conflict as an essential part of democratic processes?

What are the best ways to prevent discipline problems and still provide a wide range of choice?

How can school experiences help students internalize democratic dispositions?

What is the relationship between discipline and democracy?

What kind of political advocacy facilitates social conditions that promote discipline and democracy?

References

Anderson, Terry. 1998. "Democratic Classrooms: Addressing the Needs of Children at Risk." *Primary Voices, K–6* 7 (2): 13–19.

Angell, Ann V. 1991. "Democratic Climates in Elementary Classrooms: A Review of Theory and Research. *Theory and Research in Social Education* 19 (3): 241–66.

Arnove, Robert F. 1980. Introduction. In *Philanthropy and Cultural Imperialism: The Foundations at Home and Abroad,* edited by Robert F. Arnove, 1–24. Boston: G. K. Hall.

Axelrod, Alan, and Jim Holtje. 1997. *Two Hundred and One Ways to Deal with Difficult People.* New York: McGraw-Hill.

Beane, James A. 1998. "Reclaiming a Democratic Purpose for Education." *Educational Leadership* 56 (2): 8–11.

Beane, James A. 1997. *Curriculum Integration: Designing the Core of Democratic Education.* New York: Teachers College Press.

Beane, James A., and Michael W. Apple. 1995. "The Case for Democratic Schools." In *Democratic Schools,* edited by Michael W. Apple and James A. Beane, 1–25. Alexandria, VA: Association for Supervision and Curriculum Development.

Belenky, Mary F., Lynne A. Bond, and Jacqueline S. Weinstock. 1997. *A Tradition That Has No Name.* New York: Basic Books.

Best, Judy. 1995. Personal communication with author.

Blackburn, Lois. 1998. *Whole Music: A Whole Language Approach to Teaching Music.* Portsmouth, NH: Heinemann.

Butchart, Ronald E. 1998. Introduction. In *Classroom Discipline in American Schools: Problems and Possibilities for Democratic Education,* edited by Ronald E. Butchart and Barbara McEwan, 1–16. Albany: State University of New York Press.

Canada, Geoffrey. 1995. *Fist Stick Knife Gun.* Boston: Beacon Press.

Canter, Lee, and Marlene Canter. 1992. *Lee Canter's Assertive Discipline: Positive Behavior Management for Today's Classroom.* Santa Monica, CA: Lee Canter & Associates.

Chernow, Carol, and Fred B. Chernow. 1989. *Classroom Discipline Survival Guide for Middle School/Junior High Teachers.* West Nyack, NY: The Center for Applied Research in Education.

Christensen, Linda. 1994. "Building Community from Chaos." *Rethinking Schools* 1: 1, 14–17, 19.

Curwin, Richard L., and Allen M. Mendler. 1997. *As Tough as Necessary: Countering Violence, Aggression, and Hostility in Our Schools.* Alexandria, VA: Association for Supervision and Curriculum Development.

Dahl, Roald. 1988. *Matilda.* New York: Viking Penguin.

Darling-Hammond, Linda, and Jacqueline Ancess. 1996. "Democracy and Access to Education." In *Democracy, Education and the Schools,* edited by Roger Soder, 151–81. San Francisco: Jossey-Bass.

Darling-Hammond, Linda, and Jon Snyder. 1992. "Curriculum Studies and the Traditions of Inquiry: The Scientific Tradition." In *Handbook of Research on Curriculum,* edited by Philip Jackson, 41–78. New York: American Educational Research Association.

De Bernardi, Bianca. 1996. "How Teachers Construe Pupils' Intelligence." In *The Construction of Group Realities,* edited by Devorah Kalekin-Fishman and Beverly M. Walker. Malabar, FL: Krieger Publishing Company.

DeStigter, Todd. 1998. "The Tesoros Literacy Project: An Experiment in Democratic Communities." *Research in the Teaching of English* 32 (1): 10–42.

Dewey, John. [1915] 1971. *The School and Society.* Chicago: University of Chicago Press.

Dewey, John. 1925. *Experience and Nature.* Chicago: Open Court.

Dewey, John. 1938. *Experience and Education.* New York: Collier Macmillan Publishers.

Doyle, Walter. 1985. "Classroom Organization and Management." In *Handbook of Research on Teaching,* 3d ed., edited by Merlin C. Wittock, 392–431. New York: Macmillan.

Elshtain, Jean Bethke. 1995. *Democracy on Trial.* New York: Basic Books.

Erickson, Frederick. 1982. "Taught Cognitive Learning in Its Immediate Environments: A Neglected Topic in the Anthropology of Education." *Anthropology and Education Quarterly* 8 (2): 149–81.

Finkelstein, Barbara. 1989. *Governing the Young: Teacher Behavior in Popular Primary Schools in 19th Century United States.* New York: Falmer Press.

Fleischman, Paul. 1988. *Rondo in C.* New York: HarperCollins.

Fox, Paula. 1991. *Slave Dancer.* New York: Dell Publishing Company.

Freire, Paulo. 1998. *Teachers as Cultural Workers: Letters to Those Who Dare Teach.* Translated by Daniel Macedo, Dale Koike, and Alexandre Oliveira. Boulder, CO: Westview Press.

Fried, Robert L. 1995. *The Passionate Teacher: A Practical Guide.* Boston: Beacon Press.

Gathercoal, Forrest. 1997. *Judicious Discipline.* 4th ed. San Francisco: Caddo Gap Press.

Geertz, Clifford. 1988. *Works and Lives: The Anthropologist as Author.* Stanford, CA: Stanford University Press.

Glass, Doug. 1998. "Researchers Find Vitamin A Suspect in Frog Deformities." *The Oregonian,* 17 March, A6.

Goldberg, Lazer. 1970/1997. *Teaching Science to Children.* Mineola, NY: Dover Publications.

Goodlad, John. 1999. "Renewing the Profession of Teaching: A Conversation with John Goodlad." *Educational Leadership* 56 (8): 14–19.

Goodlad, John. 1997. *In Praise of Education.* New York: Teachers College Press.

Goodman, Jesse. 1992. *Elementary Schooling for Critical Democracy.* Albany: State University of New York Press.

Gordon, Thomas. 1989. *Teaching Children Self-Discipline at Home and at School.* New York: Times Books.

Graves, Donald H. 1999. *Bring Life into Learning: Create a Lasting Literacy.* Portsmouth, NH: Heinemann.

Gutmann, Amy. 1987. *Democratic Education.* Princeton, NJ: Princeton University Press.

Gyatso, Tenzin. 1991. *Compassion and the Individual.* Boston: Wisdom Publications.

Haberman, Martin. 1995. *Star Teachers of Children in Poverty.* West Lafayette, IN: Kappa Delta Pi.

Harste, Jerome C. 1994. "Literacy as Curricular Conversations About Knowledge, Inquiry, and Morality." In *Theoretical Models and Processes of Reading,* 4th ed., edited by Martha R. Ruddell, Robert B. Ruddell, and Harry Singer, 1220–42. Newark, DE: International Reading Association.

Ishimine, JoAnne, J. Cynthia McDermott, Jeff Haas, and Sharon Setoguchi. 1999. "Emotions, Conflict, and Their Importance in Educating the Whole Person." In *Beyond the Silence: Listening for Democracy,* edited by J. Cynthia McDermott, 83–91. Portsmouth, NH: Heinemann.

Jackson, Michael. 1995. *At Home in the World.* Durham, NC: Duke University Press.

Keller, Helen. 1955. *Teacher: Annie Sullivan Macy.* New York: Doubleday & Company.

Kohn, Alfie. 1999. "Offering Challenges, Creating Cognitive Dissonance." In *Beyond the Silence: Listening for Democracy,* edited by J. Cynthia McDermott, 6–15. Portsmouth, NH: Heinemann.

Kohn, Alfie. 1998. "Adventures in Ethics Versus Behavior Control: A Reply to My Critics." *Phi Delta Kappan* 79 (6): 455–60.

Kohn, Alfie. 1993. *Punished by Rewards: The Trouble with Gold Stars, Incentive Plans, As, Praise, and Other Bribes.* Boston: Houghton Mifflin.

Kucer, Stephen. 1998. "Engagement, Conflict, and Avoidance in a Whole Language Classroom." *Language Arts* 75 (2): 90–96.

Levin, Diane E. 1994. *Teaching Young Children in Violent Times: Building a Peaceable Classroom.* Philadelphia: New Society Publishers.

Levy, Steven. 1996. *Starting from Scratch: One Classroom Builds Its Own Curriculum.* Portsmouth, NH: Heinemann.

Lyotard, Jean-François. 1988. *Peregrinations: Law, Form, Event.* New York: Columbia University Press.

Manke, Mary Phillips. 1997. *Classroom Power Relations: Understanding Student-Teacher Interaction.* Mahwah, NJ: Lawrence Erlbaum Associates.

Martin, Bill, Jr. 1987. *Knots on a Counting Rope.* New York: Henry Holt & Company.

McCarthy, Lucille. 1998. "Qualitative Research in a Deweyan Classroom." In *John Dewey and the Challenge of Classroom Practice,* edited by Stephen M. Fishman and Lucille McCarthy, 113–31. New York: Teachers College Press.

McEwan, Barbara. 1998. "Contradiction, Paradox, and Irony: The World of Classroom Management." In *Classroom Discipline in American Schools: Problems and Possibilities for Democratic Education,* edited by Ronald E. Butchart and Barbara McEwan, 135–55. Albany: State University of New York Press.

Meier, Deborah. 1995. *The Power of Their Ideas: Lessons for America from a Small School in Harlem.* Boston: Beacon Press.

Murphy, Sharon, with Patrick Shannon, Peter Johnston, and Jane Hansen. 1998. *Fragile Evidence: A Critique of Reading Assessment.* Mahwah, NJ: Lawrence Erlbaum Associates.

Nicholls, John G. 1989. *The Competitive Ethos and Democratic Education.* Cambridge: Harvard University Press.

Noddings, Nell. 1998. "Care and Moral Education." In *Critical Social Issues in American Education,* 2d ed., edited by H. Svi Shapiro and David E. Purpel, 309–20. Mahwah, NJ: Lawrence Erlbaum Associates.

Noddings, Nell. 1992. *The Challenge to Care in Schools: An Alternative Approach to Education.* New York: Teachers College Press.

Nordling, JoAnne. 1992. *Taking Charge: A Parent and Teacher Guide to Loving Discipline.* Saratoga, CA: R & E Publishers.

Ohanian, Susan. 1999. *One Size Fits Few: The Folly of Educational Standards.* Portsmouth, NH: Heinemann.

Ohanian, Susan. 1994. *Who's In Charge? A Teacher Speaks Her Mind.* Portsmouth, NH: Heinemann.

Osborne, Jonathan. 1995. "Science from a Child's Perspective." In *Science with Reason,* edited by Sue Atkinson and Marilyn Fleer, 15–25. Portsmouth, NH: Heinemann.

Oyler, Celia. 1996. *Making Room for Students: Sharing Teacher Authority in Room 106.* New York: Teachers College Press.

Paley, Vivian. 1992. *You Can't Say You Can't Play.* Cambridge: Harvard University Press.

Paley, Vivian. 1986. "On Listening to What the Children Say." *Harvard Educational Review* 56 (2): 122–32.

Palmer, Parker J. 1997. "The Heart of a Teacher: Identity and Integrity in Teaching." *Change* 29 (6): 15–21.

Paulsen, Gary. 1995. *The Rifle.* San Diego, CA: Harcourt Brace & Company.

Peacock, James L. 1986. *The Anthropological Lens: Harsh Light, Soft Focus.* Cambridge, England: Cambridge University Press.

Perry, Tony. 1999. "San Diego Police Say Smokers Fight for Rights in Bars." *The Sunday Oregonian,* 28 February, A21.

Rich, Adrienne. 1993. *What Is Found There: Notebooks on Poetry and Politics.* New York: W. W. Norton & Company.

Schellenberg, James A. 1996. *Conflict Resolution: Theory, Research, and Practice.* Albany: State University of New York Press.

Scieszka, Jon. 1989. *The True Story of the Three Little Pigs.* New York: Scholastic.

Seeman, Howard. 1994. *Preventing Classroom Discipline Problems: A Guide for Educators.* Lancaster, PA: Technomic Publishing Company.

Short, Kathy G., Jerome Harste, and Carolyn Burke. 1996. *Creating Classrooms for Authors and Inquirers.* 2d ed. Portsmouth, NH: Heinemann.

Sizer, Ted. 1984. *Horace's Compromise: The Dilemma of the American High School.* Boston: Houghton Mifflin.

Smith, Frank. 1995. *Between Hope and Havoc: Essays into Human Learning and Education.* Portsmouth, NH: Heinemann.

Spinelli, Jerry. 1991. *Fourth Grade Rats.* New York: Scholastic.

Spolin, Viola. 1983. *Improvisation for the Theater: A Handbook of Teaching and Directing Techniques.* Evanston, IL: Northwestern University Press.

Stanley, Sharon A. 1998. "Empathic Caring in Classroom Management and Discipline." In *Classroom Discipline in American Schools: Problems and Possibilities for Democratic Education,* edited by Ronald E. Butchart and Barbara McEwan, 237–68. Albany: State University of New York Press.

Tannen, Deborah. 1994. *Gender and Discourse.* New York: Oxford University Press.

Tavris, Carol. 1989. *Anger: The Misunderstood Emotion.* Revised ed. New York: Simon & Schuster.

Weeks, Dudley. 1992. *The Eight Essential Steps to Conflict Resolution: Preserving Relationships at Work, at Home, and in the Community.* New York: G. P. Putnam's Sons.

Wolk, Steven. 1998. *A Democratic Classroom.* Portsmouth, NH: Heinemann.